THE POSSIBLE FORM OF
AN INTERLOCUTION

NAHUM DIMITRI CHANDLER

THE POSSIBLE FORM OF AN INTERLOCUTION

....

W. E. B. Du Bois and Max Weber

in Correspondence

DUKE UNIVERSITY PRESS *Durham & London* 2025

Project Editor: Livia Tenzer
Cover designed by A. Mattson Gallagher
Typeset in Garamond Premier Pro and Trade Gothic
by Westchester Publishing Services

Library of Congress Cataloging-in-Publication Data
Names: Chandler, Nahum Dimitri, author. | Du Bois, W. E. B.
(William Edward Burghardt), 1868–1963. Correspondence. Selections. |
Weber, Max, 1864–1920. Correspondence. Selections.
Title: The possible form of an interlocution : W. E. B. Du Bois and Max
Weber in correspondence / Nahum Dimitri Chandler.
Other titles: W. E. B. Du Bois and Max Weber in correspondence
Description: Durham : Duke University Press, 2025. | Includes
bibliographical references and index.
Identifiers: LCCN 2025009450 (print)
LCCN 2025009451 (ebook)
ISBN 9781478032489 (paperback)
ISBN 9781478029144 (hardcover)
ISBN 9781478061366 (ebook)
ISBN 9781478094517 (ebook/other)
Subjects: LCSH: Du Bois, W. E. B. (William Edward Burghardt), 1868–
1963—Correspondence. | Weber, Max, 1864–1920—Correspondence. |
African Americans—Social conditions—To 1964. | United States—Race
relations. | LCGFT: Personal correspondence.
Classification: LCC PS3507.U147 A4 2025 (print) |
LCC PS3507.U147 (ebook)
LC record available at https://lccn.loc.gov/2025009450
LC ebook record available at https://lccn.loc.gov/2025009451

Cover art: W. E. B. Du Bois, 1907. W. E. B. Du Bois Papers,
Robert S. Cox Special Collections and University Archives Research Center, UMass Amherst Libraries.

This book is freely available in an open access edition thanks to
the generous support of the University of California Libraries.

Duke University Press gratefully acknowledges the Humanities Commons of the School of Humanities at the University of
California, Irvine, which provided funds toward the publication of this book.

for

Eugene Lunn

am memoriam

and

Joseph Fracchia

for living well

I am quite sure to come back to your country as soon as possible and especially to the South, because I am absolutely convinced that the "color-line" problem will be the paramount problem of the time to come, here and everywhere in the world.

—MAX WEBER to W. E. B. Du Bois (1904)

And above all consider one thing: the day of the colored races dawns. It is insanity to delay this development; it is wisdom to promote what it promises us in light and hope for the future.

—W. E. B. DU BOIS, "Die Negerfrage in den Vereinigten Staaten" (1906)

CONTENTS

....

NOTE ON CITATIONS

....

FOR WORKS BY W. E. B. DU BOIS

1

The essay "Die Negerfrage in den Vereinigten Staaten" ("The Negro Question in the United States") by W. E. B. Du Bois, our primary concern in this study, is usually cited herein by abbreviated title as reference to the English translation by Joseph Fracchia from the 1906 German-language publication of the text. That translation of the text is included as an appendix in this study, as noted on the contents page. That translation is also included in *The Problem of the Color Line at the Turn of the Twentieth Century: The Essential Early Essays*, published in 2015 (Du Bois 2015f), for the appendix is a republication of the version in that volume. That collection is now widely available online as part of the American Council of Learned Societies (ACLS) Humanities Ebook Collection, at https://hdl.handle.net/2027/heb.33779. The paragraph enumeration given in the translation included in the collection of essays just cited is determined according to and follows (as precisely as possible) the original publication in German (Du Bois 1906a). Hence, readers with the 2015 English-language collection or the 1906 German text at hand should easily find any section- or paragraph-level citation to that essay, "Die Negerfrage," that is given in this study. The texts included in the 2015 collection are complete versions of the essays as originally published or as extant in Du Bois's unpublished papers, edited and annotated, according to contemporary scholarship.

2

While I have taken scholastic reference to the original publication or to the unpublished manuscript of texts by W. E. B. Du Bois in every case of his writings engaged in this study, with citations noted within the text where possible or appropriate, I have also, without exception, also consulted the versions of all published texts included in the thirty-seven volumes of the Complete Published Works of W. E. B. Du Bois, published from 1973 to 1986 by the Kraus-Thomson Organization and edited and introduced by Herbert Aptheker, as well as the six volumes of Du Bois's texts published from 1973 to 1985 by the University of Massachusetts Press, also edited and introduced by Aptheker, which include three volumes of selected correspondence and three of selections of other texts, including previously unpublished texts and documents. The bibliographical details of those texts edited by Aptheker, if cited here, are listed in the references section at the end of this volume.

3

The Souls of Black Folk: Essays and Sketches is cited here from the first edition of its original publication (Du Bois 1903f). A full-text version of the second edition, with no major changes from the first edition, is available online through open access from the University of North Carolina's Documenting the American South project (Du Bois 1903g; see https://docsouth.unc.edu/church/duboissouls/dubois.html). I consider that presentation of the book, in its second edition from June 1903, an accurate and reliable work of scholarship. The pagination is the same in the first and second editions. In-text citations are given later in parentheses with the relevant page number(s), the chapter number, and the paragraph number(s) within the chapter. For example, the in-text cite Du Bois 1903f, 213, chap. 11, para. 13 indicates page 213, chapter 11, paragraph 13, based on the first and second editions of the book, each issued in 1903.

4

When quoting from or referencing *The Philadelphia Negro: A Social Study* (1899), published under the authorship of Du Bois with an additional text by Isabel Eaton (the report of a study on African American women domestic workers), I cite the first published edition (Du Bois and Eaton 1899). It is the first edition that is the decisive basis of my references, because subsequent editions of *The Philadelphia Negro* may be abridged and thus not yield a reliable match with that first published edition. Several of those later editions notably also leave aside Du Bois's own original and important preface.

5

When referencing *Dusk of Dawn: An Essay Toward an Autobiography of a Race Concept*, originally published in 1940, I cite the version published as part of the Complete Published Works of W. E. B. Du Bois series (Du Bois 1975b). While the 1975 edition is not a facsimile of the 1940 edition, the pagination follows exactly that of the first edition. Thus, the reader should easily be able to determine the in-text context of my citation according to the first edition of Du Bois's original published text as a whole.

6

I occasionally refer to material found only among the W. E. B. Du Bois Papers (MS 312 as part of series 3, subseries C) at the Special Collections and University Archives, University of Massachusetts, Amherst, Libraries, housed in the W. E. B. Du Bois Library or in the microfilmed version of those papers (Du Bois 1980f). These papers have been digitized and are open access material in the libraries' online repository Credo (https://credo.library.umass.edu/view/collection/mums312). Additional bibliographic detail for specific notable citations from among these papers is found in the endnotes or in the reference section at the end of this volume. The original papers were compiled and edited by Herbert Aptheker, whereas the microfilm edition was supervised by Robert C. McDonnell.

FOR WORKS BY MAX WEBER

For the principal work by Max Weber engaged in this study, "Die Protestantische Ethik und der 'Geist' des Kapitalismus," I refer to the two-part essay in which Weber first presented his idea (Weber 1905a, 1905b). I have consulted the English-language translation of those essays issued in 2002 in *The Protestant Ethic and the "Spirit" of Capitalism and Other Writings*, edited and translated by Peter Baehr and Gordon C. Wells (Weber 2002d). Likewise, I have taken reference to the relatively recent publication of those original essays as part of *Die Protestantische Ethik und der Geist des Kapitalismus/Die Protestantischen Sekten und der Geist des Kapitalismus: Schriften 1904–1920*, edited by Wolfgang Schluchter, with assistance from Ursula Bube, as part of the *Max Weber–Gesamtausgabe* (Complete works of Max Weber), volume 1/18, first released in 2016; notably, it is cited here as issued in a *Studienausgabe* (study edition) in 2021 as volume 1/18, supplemented with texts from volume 1/9 of the *Max Weber–Gesamtausgabe* (Weber 2021). As can be noted throughout the text and the reference list, I have consulted and cited as relevant other texts from the collected works by Max Weber as they have been issued as part of the *Max Weber–Gesamtausgabe*, edited by multiple scholars over the decades, and published since 1984 by J. C. B. Mohr (Paul Siebeck) in Tübingen, Germany (Weber 1984a).

ACKNOWLEDGMENTS

....

Eugene Lunn (1941–1990), a scholar of intellectual history, was a pivotal teacher for me, and for many, many others at the University of California (UC), Davis, during my undergraduate study there. Lunn's yearlong course in European intellectual history was famous among some two decades of students at UC Davis as the trial by fire through which one had to pass if one were to be taken seriously. Only in this course, as we began by reading Kant, Goethe, Hegel, and Marx, then moved on to Nietzsche and Freud, did I suddenly feel that, finally, here in college was an address that broached questions as seriously and profoundly as the discussion that had long come to me through my father's teaching in our daily family morning devotions and as the pastor of our church. Professor Lunn also would no doubt appreciate that my father was, and remained, the first example of a teacher for me. From there, it was only a matter of time before I would connect the curve of my trajectory that was marked out in the year of courses with Professor Lunn back to an orientation that had its incipit somewhere near the very beginning: the one announced by the figure of W. E. B. Du Bois. Years later, long after I had left UC Davis as a student— and, indeed, had left the academy—Professor Lunn would play a key role in supporting my efforts to return to the university context for doctoral study.

In 2002, I was privileged to serve for a term as a visiting professor in the comparative literature program at my alma mater. (The invitation had come with no knowledge on their part that I was an alumnus.) Donna Reed, Professor Lunn's widow and companion of the heart during those years, was my office neighbor—a quiet, unexpected, profound gift. I acknowledge and thank Harriett Murav, then the chair of UC Davis's comparative literature program; the late Marc Blanchard and Gail Finney, faculty in the program; and David Luis Brown, my co-visitor. I also thank several doctoral students in my seminar, especially Mary Christine Evans, Yvonne Cardenas, and Proshot Kalami, for their collective and individual hospitality and, especially, for their careful, considered, rich interlocution in seminar.

Then there was Joseph Fracchia, now a beloved professor emeritus at the University of Oregon, where more than two generations of students at Clark Honors College had the benefit of his remarkable intellect and generosity. He was almost as famous as Professor Lunn had been on the UC Davis campus those three generations ago and had, in fact, served as the quintessential doctoral assistant in Lunn's European intellectual history course. Professor Fracchia's scrupulous approach to teaching meant that UC Davis students got almost two for the price of one—except that he was in Europe during the year I took the course. By chance, through mutual friends connected to that course, we were later introduced and became lifelong friends. While he certainly remains, for me, the most outstanding example of Professor Lunn's many superb students, he is on his own terms truly one of the most gifted, dedicated, and accomplished teachers I have come to know. Perhaps my endless address to him in the form of *the question* has been an effort to make up for his missing presence during my year in the course at UC Davis. It was Professor Fracchia's initiative that led to the translation of Du Bois's "Die Negerfrage in den Vereinigten Staaten" that would provide the spark for this study. As I can now hold his monumental two-volume study on historicity and human corporeal organization (Fracchia 2022) in my hands, I am sometimes led to imagine that his engagement in translating "Die Negerfrage," itself an early expression of an indefatigable scholar's lifelong commitment to the recognition within the discourses of knowledge of the world-historical importance in the modern era of the labor of "Black folk" (to maintain Du Bois's turn-of-the-twentieth-century metaphor), helped sustain Professor Fracchia in the realization of his master work.

And here I must turn and recall, also, what only a scholar would care to remember: a moment when William W. Hagen, perhaps Professor Lunn's closest colleague, to whom I had been referred for guidance on a bibliography pertaining to Eastern Europe, sat down and thoughtfully typed out references as they came to his mind while pulling softly on his pipe. He doubtless would not recall this moment. This apparently small gesture—normal for him, I am sure—remains emblematic for me of how a scholar can also be a teacher. As can be seen from this volume's reference list, Professor Hagen's own work proved an essential reference and guidance in my eventual development of this study (see Hagen 1980, 2002, 2012, 2018).

Finally, Professor Lunn's first major scholarly work was on the intellectual history of the early Weimar period in Germany. It should be remarked that, although the figure on whom he focused, Gustav Landauer, took an approach to that moment that was very different from that of Max Weber, Professor Lunn placed two quotations from Weber at the head of his study of Landauer (Lunn 1973). He had a deep paradoxical respect and persisting fascination with Weber. But perhaps especially, he would have followed keenly the possibility of seeing the figure of Du Bois brought into a different, and perhaps new, kind of intellectual relief by the articulation of his figure in this intellectual topography that Professor Lunn knew so well. I also imagine that had a certain Du Bois been rendered legible for his generation, Professor Lunn would have found his deep experience of the arts and, above all, music a passion in common (Lunn 1982). As a simple mark of my deep and abiding respect and affection for his work as a teacher and a scholar, and for his sense of appreciation for his wife as a companion, as well as his way in music—and then, too, that his family ancestry was Jewish on both sides from Kiev, Ukraine, and Poland, respectively—this text is dedicated to the memory of Eugene Lunn.

And for the gift of a lifetime's worth of friendship, this text is also dedicated to Joseph Fracchia, the Babo.

During the summer of 1997, through the kind suggestion of Leslie Allen Adelson, I was privileged to participate in a seminar on the future of German studies funded by the Deutscher Akademischer Austauschdienst (German Academic Exchange Service), hosted by the Institute for German Cultural Studies at Cornell University, and led by Peter Uwe Hohendahl. While my relation to the humanities was an initial basis for my participation, it was the question of the relation of German studies and African American studies that became definitive in my experience of the sessions. While it is appearing here in book form two-and-a-half decades after that summer, this study remains the most legible public trace of that indelible experience. I thank both Professor Hohendahl and Professor Adelson for their interest and generosity, which made that experience possible.

In the autumn of 2006, I served as a visiting professor at the Institute for Research in African American Studies at Columbia University while completing the principal work on this study. I thank, first and especially, Nuri Richards for her untiring hospitality, without which this work could not have been sustained during my time there. I also thank Sharon Harris and Shawn Mendoza for their consideration, and the students of my seminars for their generous and ongoing engagement. Most especially I am grateful to the late Manning Marable. He and the late Leith Mullings, his wife and the companion of his heart, provided me with a most considerate welcome and an office, along with the invitation to lecture for the

Center for Contemporary Black History in October 2007. This became a signal occasion for me. And more, they shared with me an evening repast at the time of my lecture, even as Professor Marable was in the midst of a sabbatical year.

Over the course of all the stages of my work on this study, the thoughtful consideration of Danielle Kovacs, then lead curator of the W. E. B. Du Bois Collection in the Special Collections Department at the W. E. B Du Bois Library, University of Massachusetts, Amherst—and now head curator of all collections—proved indispensable. I salute her careful and precise assistance.

At Duke University Press: I am thankful that the text was brought to final form under the exact yet generous care and guidance of Livia Tenzer, with support from Susan Deeks and Stephanie Attia; likewise I am thankful for the bold, careful line given in the design work of A. Mattson Gallagher. Yet, most especially it is always such a high-level pleasure to work with Ryan Kendall, for which I remain simply grateful, and so too for this volume. Then it must be said: It was Ken Wissoker as editor who just over a dozen years ago affirmed the integrity of the statement now proposed in this book and has stood firm to see it realized. The pleasure has been all mine.

AN OPENING OCCASION

....

In late October or early November 1904, just after concluding a whirlwind train tour of the eastern half of the United States—a circuit that included, on the outgoing leg from New York City, stops in Buffalo, Chicago, St. Louis, and New Orleans, as well as excursions to Niagara Falls, to a community of the Cherokee in Oklahoma, and to the Tuskegee Institute in Alabama, and a visit to relatives in the Blue Ridge Mountains of western North Carolina and, on the return leg, a hurried passage through the East Coast cities of Washington, DC, Baltimore, Philadelphia, and Boston, before landing back in New York City—Max Weber, traveling with his wife, Marianne, wrote in his own hand on stationery from the Holland House in Manhattan (located at Fifth Avenue and 30th Street) to W. E. B. Du Bois, in Atlanta. At that time, Du Bois lived in Georgia (his home already for more than seven years) and worked as a professor at Atlanta University, residing on its campus situated among the slight red hills overlooking the center of the city of Atlanta from the southwest.

The letter contained an apology and a request.

An account of the provenance of that letter and the correspondence that followed it may, in turn, make it possible to begin to render legible the terms of address that organized an interlocution between W. E. B. Du Bois and Max Weber in late 1904 and early 1905. Likewise, such an account may well provide initial lexical and discursive references such that we can begin to elaborate some of the epistemological and theoretical terms of such an interlocution—the terms of a historical condition that was at once social and theoretical, epistemological, and actual (if you will) and virtual—of a certain form of commonness, as problems of understanding with regard to matters of difference among human groups. The force and implications of this preceded the epistolary conversation of these two figures and may persist in its virtual sense, not only beyond their time. It is a problematization of social life across the centuries of the modern era and throughout the world—in general and, as such, throughout the planet as a whole—that may not only persist as the questions at stake for them then but also remain so for us now, in our present. So, too, perhaps, this fundamental problematization—a matter of our epistemological conditions and our theoretical commitments for our understanding of matters of supposed categorical difference among human groups—this question, such as it was at stake then and is decisive for us now, may well remain intractable for critical social thought well beyond our own time.

In affirmative response to an invitation from Weber, Du Bois prepared an essay in English on matters of the so-called Negro question in America. The essay was first published in a German translation under the title "Die Negerfrage in den Vereinigten Staaten," translated as "The Negro Question in the United States" (Du Bois 1906a, 2006).

It was published in the January 1906 issue of the *Archiv für Sozialwissenschaft und Sozialpolitik* (Journal of social science and social policy), edited in Heidelberg by Max Weber, Edgar Jaffé, and Werner Sombart. The *Archiv*, which Weber and Jaffé, his former student, took over when Jaffé purchased it in 1903, existed under that name from 1904 to 1933. It became one of the most influential scholarly journals published in Europe during the first half of the twentieth century (Factor 1988).

It was that essay by Du Bois—the text as published in German in 1906, a certain kind of archival document—that set in motion my considerations in this study.

The text of an English-language essay was sent by Du Bois from Atlanta to Weber (and his associates) in Heidelberg in the early spring of 1905. The essay was drawn, in part, from previously written and published texts by Du Bois. Emendations and revisions of those earlier writings were combined with newly drafted text and assembled into a freestanding essay of some fifty pages. Du Bois's English version of the essay as a whole apparently is no longer extant. (I briefly annotate this question later.) And although it was translated and published in German through the initiative of the editors of the *Archiv*, who carried out the translation remains uncertain. As I also annotate later, the main work of translation into German was likely done by Else von Richthofen, based on at least one epistolary reference in the 1905 correspondence between Atlanta and Heidelberg, with some editorial participation by Weber (as the key editor of the *Archiv* for the issue in question) and, perhaps, with some participation by Jaffé (who was also an editor—and the owner—of the *Archiv*, as well as von Richthofen's husband).

The essay as published in German in 1906 was first *published in English translation* as a whole, freestanding essay in 2006 in the journal

CR: The New Centennial Review under the title "Die Negerfrage in den Vereinigten Staaten (The Negro Question in the United States)." It was translated from the published German text of 1906 by Joseph Fracchia, a long-standing scholar of modern European intellectual history. Fracchia's translation was republished in 2015 without any modification or deletion of the translation of text written by Du Bois (for the 1906 German publication) as the closing essay of a newly compiled and edited collection of Du Bois's early essays, including several texts previously unpublished or not easily available in complete or unabridged form. That edited collection was issued under the title *The Problem of the Color Line at the Turn of the Twentieth Century: The Essential Early Essays* (Du Bois 2015f). That 2015 fully annotated version of the English translation of the 1906 publication of the essay in German is included in this book as an appendix. I consider it both an integral reference for this book as a whole and the core reference for my thetic discourse in this study. The 2015 republication of the essay's English translation does, however, include additions to the work—namely, my scholastic annotations presented as endnotes, most notably annotations pertaining to other writings by Du Bois from which he drew in the spring of 1905 to produce the freestanding essay published in German in 1906 under the title "Die Negerfrage in den Vereinigten Staaten." As in 2015, in the appendix my editorial annotations to the English translation of Du Bois's essay are presented as endnotes. So it must be highlighted that Du Bois gave only one note for the text published by the *Archiv* in 1906: He appended to the closing paragraph of his 1906 text a set of citations—mainly to his own texts, authored or edited, but also to some works by others—pertaining to matters African American. The bibliographic notations given by Du Bois followed from a specific solicitation to him from Weber in their correspondence, an interest that Weber also noted in his headnote to the *Archiv*'s publication of Du Bois's essay (see the appendix). The full bibliographic information for Du Bois's citations is provided in the volume's reference section.

This book thus has two main parts, a closing coda as a third part, and the appendix. The commentary given as part I of this study addresses, respectively, the correspondence and the essay itself. In the latter case, I also offer a brief outline of the concerns of the essay, along with the question of its place in the thought of Du Bois. All known extant letters from the correspondence between Weber and Du Bois, are given in their entirety, as transcribed from the Du Bois papers. They provide the essential archival reference for my approach in this study, a reconsideration of the relation of the thought and practice of Du Bois and Weber. This correspondence made legible a direct interlocution of these two thinkers. To account for this interlocution in the sense of its general theoretical and epistemological possibility became the study's guiding problematic. My effort here, thus, is simply an extended annotation of *one aspect* of the terms of emergence of Du Bois's essay as a certain kind of discourse, a work of scholarship and learning on the terms of its solicitation from, and interest for, a major contemporary scholar of his own time.

For a brief account of "Die Negerfrage in den Vereinigten Staaten" itself, one can proceed directly to the second section of this opening part of the study.

In the work at hand, the thetic commitments and interpretive accomplishments of Du Bois's "Die Negerfrage," as well as the basis of those contributions in scholarship and as an understanding of matters of historiography, are not subject to a sustained critical engagement as a distinct line of inquiry. The essay, in fact, gathers references from across the whole of Du Bois's early itinerary (intellectual and political and, certainly, academic) from late 1894 to early 1905. In a proper sense, such an engagement is the work of an additional study. It would most certainly require a careful critical understanding, at once archival and theoretical, of the actual writing and the whole horizon of references to his own work that Du Bois makes in the essay. Such a horizon is indicated in the annotations included in the 2015 publication of the essay (see Du Bois 2015d) and in the presentation of that same annotated version of the English translation included as the appendix. Such engagement would also certainly entail a consideration of "Die Negerfrage" (Du Bois 1906a), most specifically and especially in relation to the work that is gathered in *The Souls of Black Folk: Essays and Sketches* (Du Bois 1903f, 1903g), some indications of which are also given in the annotations for the appendix. Likewise, reference to Du Bois's own scholastic practice that was committed to the cultivation of a certain understanding of matters African American, which he thought of as a new science of human practice that, by the mid-1890s, he had already begun to call "sociology," is only adumbrated in this study; my brief indication is given in the later sections of part I, leaving a more complete annotation for a separate study devoted to a full reconsideration Du Bois's projection in the human sciences as a whole—that is, social thought in general. In part I, my privileged concern is to provide essential references for understanding the itinerary of Du Bois in relation to his correspondence with Weber in late 1904 and early 1905.

Part II proposes certain terms of thought for our understanding of the possible interlocution of Du Bois and Weber. It opens by questioning a deeply problematic supposition about Du Bois's thought and scholarly practice in relation to the work and itinerary of Weber. It then formulates and outlines the terms of another approach that we might take in understanding the relation of the itineraries in thought and practice of these thinkers.

Certain archival references found among Du Bois's papers, in particular, provide historical and textual footing for the scholastic questioning of a perspective that emerged proximate to the time of World War II; that subsequently became conventional; and that then remained presumptive in discourse about Du Bois, even though, by all appearances, it also often remained obscure to general scholastic discourse. It was an easy, yet profoundly erroneous, understanding that has judged Du Bois's thought on the basis of reductive terms supposedly derived from the itinerary of Weber. This approach not only persisted through the second half of the twentieth century, as Weber's intellectual standing rose, but has remained afoot in the third decade of the twenty-first century.

In addition to published texts by both Weber and Du Bois, there are unpublished texts, documents in general, among Du Bois's papers that allow us to propose a premise for understanding the relation of these two thinkers that both is grounded in scholarship and indexes a horizon of epistemological and political problematization on a world-historical scale of reference that inscribed them in common. This was so even if the precise inhabitation of this problematization remained respective to each thinker. That commonality was how to think about the future of relations among different groups that had come into new forms of relation—group to group—but were strongly marked by supposed hierarchical differences within a worldwide horizon. This entails, of course, direct differences of power and authority. Yet, with regard to an understanding of such forms of difference as expressions of supposed more fundamental difference of kind within or among groups of humans, it also pertains within a new global scenario or worldwide level of reference.

This perspective is to suggest that the respective itineraries and thought of Du Bois and Weber must yet—also—be thought together and in relation.

That is to say, still working on the basis of archival and scholastic references such as those in part I, part II, in both its aspects (critical or questioning and affirmative or propositional), is elaborated on the basis of further reference to archival resource. On the basis of those scholastic references, in the latter sections of part II, I propose an exemplary theoretical elaboration of a different, somewhat new approach to understanding the relation of the thought and practice of Du Bois and Weber.

The signal proposition of this book is a theoretical elaboration of the bearing of Du Bois's thought on "the problem of the color line" for our understanding of the possible interlocution of Du Bois and Weber in 1904 and 1905 and for contemporary considerations of the thought of Weber. (I initially proposed this line of thought in a two-part journal essay [see Chandler 2006, 2007]; this book emplaces the two parts as a coherent whole and thus allows greater access to the through line that marks out the distinctive contribution of this study.) In likewise manner, this elaboration offers a deep-seated understanding of Du Bois's thought by reinscribing and proposing the value of a contemporary critical theoretical elaboration of his formulation of "the problem of the color line." This phrase may be considered a term of art for Du Bois. This new approach is offered instead of the previous and widely dispersed (even if, at times, rather obscure) conventional accounts that considered this relation as essentially that of a theoretical benefactor (Weber) to a beneficiary (Du Bois), occasionally understood and presented under the guise of a broadly patronizing reference or consideration. The perspective offered here is a reconsideration that not only challenges contemporary scholarship directly about Weber's itinerary and thought but that should also challenge such scholarship to come to a more profound understanding of Du Bois's thought. It likewise thereby also implicates much social thought in general that is contemporary to our time.

For most of the past two decades, the scholarship on the matter of the *relation* of the thought and itinerary of Du Bois and that of Weber has remained remarkably limited in its partiality. At best, the discourse of scholars principally concerned with Du Bois has remained uncertain and imprecise, both in general as to Du Bois's thought and when conceptualizing the relation of his practice (in thought and in social and political itinerary) to the practice of Weber (in a parallel sense of itinerary). At the same time, in a similar yet different manner, the scholarship concerned with Weber has retained profoundly presumptuous and long-outdated premises about his relation to matters of Du Bois and thus has remained misleading in this domain or, worse, has persisted without explicit reflection or consideration of matters that were put directly at stake in their correspondence—their interlocution—of 1904 and 1905. At play in discourses on Weber are presumptions that I addressed directly in the second part of my previous two-part essay (see Chandler 2007), a questioning that I propose again in part II of this book. I had hoped that the annotations on "Die Negerfrage in den Vereinigten Staaten" I had proposed in the two-part essay would enable a more collaborative and complete engagement with a common horizon of problematization that was at stake for these two profound thinkers. In my judgment, contemporary critical engagement with this common problematization that is commensurate with the questions at stake for our time is yet to come in scholarship and theoretical discourse.

In the coda, I provide brief remarks on the scholarship of the past decade and a half and more.

I present this study and annotated translation in book form here as an expression of my hope that future scholarship and theoretical discourse in social thought will find it a sober and informative reference for future efforts in the pursuit of radical and fundamental understanding in self-reflexive, or critical, social thought. Perhaps we can recognize anew our own inscription within the centuries-long problematization at stake in the question that inscribed the practices of Du Bois and Weber.

What they shared in common, as a historical and epistemological problematization of social life on a world-historical scale of reference, inscribed their thinking and their theoretical projection differently. Indeed, this form of a common problematic, this very commonness, was such that it would articulate and devolve for each of them as, respectively, their situation and practice—as if the social and historical production of differences between them could be an expression of a supposed categorical truth or essence for their thought—as well as for their supposed social and historical forms of being.

What matters for thought today is that, across the century and more since their time, this general historical problematization remains at stake in our time. That is, it remains also our problematization, for it is also of our time—this twenty-first century. It is my proposition that we, even if differentially and respectively among ourselves, hold this fundamental historical problematization in common with them. So it may also remain in future historical-epistemological horizons for some generations to come—that is, within our own time yet also, perhaps, beyond our time (e.g., in this century) to which we may be understood to belong in our present.

August 31, 2024

PART I

The Letters and the Essay

1. THE CORRESPONDENCE BETWEEN W. E. B. DU BOIS AND MAX WEBER, 1904–1905

A. THE IMPOSSIBLE PRESENT OF THE PAST: W. E. B. DU BOIS AND MAX WEBER IN CORRESPONDENCE

Only part of the original letter from Max Weber in November 1904—its first two pages—has come down to us. Three different hand scripts show on the first page. One is presumably Weber's, for the body of the letter is in this hand. Another is perhaps that of W. E. B. Du Bois: A date—"Nov. 8th"—is inscribed in the place where he (or his secretary) habitually marked the occasion of his reply in these early years; this, therefore, is when he most likely responded to Weber's initial letter, an assumption in which we are more or less confirmed by Weber's signed 17 November reply to a letter by Du Bois of that earlier date. A third style of handwriting at the top of the right-hand corner of the page, with brackets around the phrase "1904? Max Weber; fragment," is likely that of the late Herbert Aptheker, Du Bois's literary executor and the curator of his unpublished writings and correspondence. Or it might be an inscription made by his wife, Fay Aptheker, who often assisted him. Our first text, then, on stationery issued from the Holland House hotel in New York City, reads:

Holland House
Fifth Avenue and Thirtieth Street, NY
H. M. Kinsley and Baumann
Cable Address "Kinsley New York"
167 Madison Avenue, New York

Dear Sir:

(until 18th Nov., Heidelberg, Germany)
Nov. 8.

I learned from you at St. Louis that you hoped to be back at Atlanta after the 20th of October.[1] Unfortunately my wife could not stand the climate of the South and so I failed to see your University and to make your acquaintance,— the few minutes at St. Louis not counting in this respect. I hope to be allowed to do so another time.

To-day I beg you to take into consideration a request I have to make as editor (together with Prof. Sombart of the Archiv für Sozialwissenschaft und Sozialpolitik).[2] Until now, I failed in finding in the American (and of course any other) litterature [*sic*] an investigation about the relations between the (so called) "race-problem" and the (so called) "class-problem" in your country, although it is impossible to have any conversation with white people of the South without feeling the connection. We have to meet to-day in Germany not only the dilettantic litterature [*sic*] à la H. St. Chamberlain & Com.,[3] but a "scientific" race-theory, built up on purely anthropological fundaments, too,—and so we have to accentuate[4] especially those connections and the influence of social-economic conditions upon the relations of races to each other. I saw that you spoke some weeks ago about this very question and I should be very glad if you would find yourself in a position to give us, for our periodical, an essay about that object.[5] So, I beg you to write me, whether you should be willing to do so, and at what time?

The extant manuscript of this letter ends at this point. There is no signature page. The writer inscribes in his own hand another address in Manhattan, different from that of the Holland House, to which a reply might be sent, as well as his permanent address in Heidelberg, Germany. Given similar indications in the signed correspondence between Du Bois and Weber that occurred subsequent to this letter from early November, in addition to its content and the author's self-reference as an editor of the *Archiv für Sozialwissenschaft und Sozialpolitik* (Journal of social science and social policy), it is reasonable to conclude that the author of the initial letter was indeed Max Weber.[6]

In all, we have more or less direct evidence, from the extant correspondence, that at least nine letters were exchanged between Du Bois and Weber from November 1904 to May 1905.[7] Six of those letters have survived, in whole, in part, or perhaps in draft form. We know of five from Weber, all of which have been maintained among the papers of Du Bois, and so far, we have only one incomplete letter from Du Bois, also among his papers. Judging from its hurried form—for example, there are several slips where an obviously implied word is absent from the text as inscribed—the Du Bois letter is most likely a draft for the letter that was actually sent.[8] It seems quite possible, based on a consideration of the content of the extant letters, that Du Bois sent one additional letter to Weber in late March or early April 1905. However, this point of fact remains indeterminate because, with the exception of the text that is apparently a draft letter, we do not have Du Bois's side of the correspondence.

In the next letter that we have, dated 17 November, Weber writes again from New York to Atlanta in reply to intervening correspondence from Du Bois. The letter is inscribed on plain white paper, not on stationery. There is no letterhead. Given that the first letter was on the stationery of the Holland House—considered a premier hotel when it was completed in 1891 and standing next to the impressive buildings of the Reformed Protestant Dutch Church of New York City (known today as the Marble Collegiate Church), dating from the 1850s—this change suggests that Weber and his wife, Marianne, moved from those lodgings to rooms at the handwritten address inscribed on the initial letter, 167 Madison Avenue, just a few blocks away. Furthermore, by 17 November there would have been little need for a return address in New York, as the Webers would shortly depart for Germany.

New York 17.XI.04

Dear Sir—

I received your kind letter dated November 8th and am indeed very glad, that you are disposed to give us the essay I asked for. I will with pleasure read the studies about the race problem you kindly promised to send me, and hope to be allowed to ask you also for a report and schedule of the lectures of the Atlanta University, showing if possible the text books now in the social-science-lectures, *if* I could see them.

I am quite sure to come back to your country as soon as possible and especially to the South, because I am absolutely convinced that the "color-line" problem will be the paramount problem of the time to come, here and everywhere in the world.

My German address is simply: Prof. M. W., Heidelberg. I am going there this Saturday, and am

Yours very respectfully, Max Weber

From this letter, we can reasonably conclude that Du Bois wrote on 8 November in reply to Weber's initial solicitation—thus, the notation of that date in script that is most likely Du Bois's (or that of his secretary) on the initial undated fragment of the first correspondence from Weber that is among the Du Bois papers. If so, then it is probable that Weber had written to Du Bois sometime during the last days of October or the first day or so of November, at the latest. This time frame coincides more or less with what we know about the likely date of the Webers' arrival in New York after their tour, which lasted slightly longer than one and a half months.[9]

Since we do not have Du Bois's letter of 8 November 1904 in hand, we can only surmise some of its likely content from Weber's response to it and from other moments in the correspondence. From Weber's letter of 17 November, we learn that Du Bois accepted the invitation. Given that Weber had requested in his initial letter that Du Bois propose a date for the delivery of his essay and the statement of expectation in a letter from Weber several months later, on 30 March 1905, we can surmise that Du Bois had promised to send his essay by the late winter or the early spring of 1905. In addition, Du Bois apparently promised in his 8 November letter to send Weber some of the most recent studies on the so-called race problem in America. Doubtless these would have been understood by Du Bois to include some of his own work and publications from the Atlanta University conferences in general. Yet it should be specifically noted that in his 17 November letter, Weber directly requested information from Du Bois on the Atlanta University project on the study of the Negro. And finally, while one cannot be certain, and even though it could have come from another source, it would not be too much to hypothesize that Du Bois mentioned something of his thought about the problem of the color line, for Weber directly engages this formulation in his reply.

From the end of November 1904 until sometime in March of the following year the correspondence is silent. We know for sure that in March it resumed. It is Weber himself who, at the head of his next communication, will note and thus record for us that Du Bois sent a letter to him that had arrived sometime in March. The next extant text of the correspondence is a reply by Weber to that apparently now lost letter from Du Bois. It is the only letter of this correspondence that has previously been published in its entirety. It was included by Aptheker in the first of the three volumes of selections from Du Bois's correspondence that he published (Du Bois 1973a, 106–7; 1997, 106–7).[10] It is dated 30 March 1905.

Heidelberg

30/III 05[11]

Dear Sir,

I was glad to receive your kind letter. When at the 15th, your article was not yet in hand, I supposed you might perhaps be prevented of writing the same now, and so we had to dispose about the space of the next number of the "Archiv." So, your article will be published at the head of the number to be edited *November 1st* of this year—it would be hardly possible at any earlier time.

Your splendid work: "The Souls of Black Folk" ought *to be translated in German*. I do not know whether anybody has already undertaken to make a translation. *If not* I am authorized to beg you for your authorization to Mrs. Elizabeth *Jaffé*-von Richthofen here, a scholar and friend of mine, late factory inspector of Karlsruhe, now wife of my fellow-teacher and fellow-editor, Dr. [Edgar] Jaffé.[12] I should like to write a short introduction about [the] [*sic*] Negro question and literature and should be much obliged to you for some information about your life, viz: age, birthplace, descent, positions held by you—of course only *if you give* your authorization.

I think Mrs. Jaffé would be a very able translator, which will be of some importance, your vocabulary and style being very peculiar: it reminds me sometimes of Gladstone's idioms although the spirit is a different one.[13]

I should like to give in one of the numbers of the "Archiv" a short review of the recent publications about the race problem in America. Beside your own work and the "Character-building" of Mr. Booker Washington, I got only the book of Mr. Page ("The Negro, the Southern[er's] [*sic*] Problem"—very superficial me thinks) the Occasional Papers of your academy and the article of Mr. Wilcox in the Yale Review.[14] If there is anything else to be reviewed, I should be much obliged to you for any information (of course I saw the article of Viereck in the official publication).—[15]

Please excuse my bad English—I seldom here had the opportunity to speak it and realize a language in speaking and writing it is very different.

Yours very respectfully, Professor Max Weber[16]

In all, we have evidence, direct or circumstantial, of six letters that were exchanged between these two figures during this time, from the middle of March to the beginning of May. The circumstantial evidence is of the sort of mention that Weber gives in this letter dated 30 March of his receipt of a prior letter from Du Bois.

In his now apparently lost March 1905 letter to Weber, Du Bois most likely offered an apology for his delay in sending along the promised essay. And even though Weber may have purchased a copy of *The Souls of Black Folk: Essays and Sketches* while in the United States, it is not improbable that Du Bois's March correspondence included a copy the book. In his reply on 30 March, Weber mentions this text for the first time in this correspondence. He also indicates that he has now read the text and found it compelling. The book, of course, had already become something of a bestseller by the time the Webers arrived in the United States in the autumn of 1904. It was already in its fourth edition. Given this fact, along with other circumstances, it is perhaps reasonable to assume that if Weber had read the text at any time earlier than the end of November 1904, he would have mentioned it by name in one of his letters to Du Bois during that month. Specifically, it would have been the most likely terms of his address to Du Bois in his initial letter from Manhattan. Or if Weber's statement in his 17 November 1904 letter that "I am absolutely convinced that the 'color-line' problem will be the paramount problem of the time to come, here and everywhere in the world" bespeaks a hearing of Du Bois's line from the "Forethought" of that text ("This meaning is not without interest to you, Gentle Reader; for the problem of the Twentieth Century is the problem of the color-line"), it is doubtful that it echoes a hearing of the discourse of the book as whole. It is more probable that Weber first read the text of *The Souls of Black Folk: Essays and Sketches* sometime after his return to Germany, perhaps over the course of the winter months; he most assuredly had done so by late March 1905, possibly when he received Du Bois's correspondence.[17] Given the character of the text that Du Bois would eventually send to Weber, which would include substantial verbatim excerpts from chapter 9 of the book, it would not be untoward to imagine that Du Bois had proposed in his March correspondence that he would be sending a text that addressed the question at issue along these lines. Perhaps the text of the *Souls of Black Folk: Essays and Sketches* could have been included in Du Bois's March correspondence to Weber in part to give depth to the meaning of such a proposition.

Of the remaining three letters that we have, the next one, a reply from Weber to another correspondence from Du Bois that is no longer extant, is the briefest in the entire group.

Heidelberg

17.4.05

Dear Sir—

Your manuscript came to my hand today. We shall provide for the translation as soon as possible, as it will be published in the number of November 1st of this year. I hope you have received my letter on behalf of Frau Dr. Jaffé.

I thank you very much for your very useful article and am

Yours very respectfully,

Prof. Max Weber

The letter from Du Bois, with the manuscript enclosed, to which Weber refers seems likely to have been mailed sometime near 1 April, judging from the posting and reply dates of the extant letters in this cycle. That letter would have then been posted at roughly the same time as Weber's letter to Du Bois of 30 March.

Du Bois's response to Weber's 30 March letter, or a draft of it (and the probability that it is a draft is high, as it is the only one of Du Bois's letters to Weber that has remained among his papers), is dated 18 March, again proximate to Weber's posting to Du Bois on 17 April.

4/18

My Dear Prof. Weber:

It is very kind for you to offer Madame Jaffa[*sic*]-von Richthofen's services in the translation of my book and if the necessary business arrangements can be made I shall be delighted to accept her services. I have written my publishers Messrs. A. C. McClurg & Co., in whose name my book is copyrighted and told them of your offer. They reply that they are negotiating for a French translation with their Paris representation, M. Terquem[,] and that thru him they will take up your proposition and see if they can interest some German publishers.

Meantime may I ask if you know of any German publisher who would probably be willing to undertake the publishing of a German translation. If you do kindly let me know. I [*sic*] write you on the matter again as soon as I hear further.

I trust that my manuscript is by this time in your hand. It is a rather hurried piece of work and if it is not just what you want do not hesitate to cut it down or reject it.

As to literature on the Negro problems the recent publications include:

> Sinclair: Aftermath of Slavery (Small Maynard & Co.)
> Johnson: Light Ahead for the Negro (Grafton Press)
> Collins: Domestic Slave Trade (Broadway Pub. Co.)[18]

The extant letter ends at this point. Just as it is likely that it is a draft, it is also a fragment. There is no signature page. It is the only tangible example of Du Bois's interlocution with Weber that has come to us in his own hand. If Du Bois received Weber's 30 March letter on the 11 April, perhaps the delay in his reply was due to the fact that he appears to have corresponded in the interim with the publisher of *The Souls of Black Folk: Essays and Sketches*, A. C. McClurg and Company of Chicago, regarding Weber's proposition for a translation of the text into German. Two extant letters dated 14 and 16 April 1905 from Francis Fisher Browne of McClurg to Du Bois confirm this supposition (Du Bois 1980f, reel 2, frames 433–518). From Weber's reply on 1 May, it would appear that Du Bois included with this letter copies of several reports from the Atlanta University Conferences on the Study of the Negro Problems that had been published up to April 1905. It is also possible that such communication was sent on 11 April—perhaps in the form of a simple enclosure of the Atlanta University texts, and perhaps of other documents, and if so, most likely a brief cover letter. If the latter occurred, this would constitute a correspondence other than that for which we have at least indirect documentary indication, and the number of letters directly exchanged between Weber and Du Bois would number at least ten. As the annual Atlanta conference was imminent—it would take place within five weeks of Weber's query—and as its theme for 1905 was precisely the matter of the "bibliography" of the discourses of the Negro, Du Bois's recommendations may well have been more on point than usual, and it should be noted that he was a superbly attentive bibliographer who indeed stands as a pioneer in this aspect of African American studies.[19] In this sense, the published report of the conference from May 1905 might well be taken as filling out the remainder of the now lost list of texts that Du Bois sent to Weber in April (Du Bois 1905).[20]

On 1 May, Weber wrote the last direct communication between these two thinkers for which there is present documentation.

> Heidelberg
> 1.V.05

My Dear Colleague!

I thank you very much for your kind letter. *We have engaged* a publisher—Dr. P. Siebeck (firm: F. C. B. Mohr) Tübingen, the publisher of the "Archiv für Sozialpolitik"—*of course* with reservation of your previous consent to the making of the translation. I beg you to inform your publishers and hope there will be no difficulties.—

The library of our University will certainly, be very glad to have your University publications. I thank you very much for your useful informations [*sic*].

Will you not have your "Sabbath-year" one of the next years? I hope you will come to Germany then, [illegible], and visit us. And so then,[21] I shall come to the United States, I think, 1907 or 8.

> Yours very respectfully
> Prof. Max Weber
>
> Address of the before-mentioned publisher:
> Herrn F. C. B. Mohr's Verlag Herrn Dr. Paul Siebeck
> Tübingen (Württemberg)[22]

The direct conversation as we know it ends here. Weber never returned to the United States. And Du Bois did not return to Germany until six years after Weber's death, in 1926. For all appearances, there is no further communication between these two figures over the next fifteen years of Weber's life. And even though they were both in attendance at the Versailles Peace Conference in Paris in 1919, it is unclear whether they met on that occasion; there is certainly no record of a substantive interlocution at that time.[23] And as noted later, they would most likely have approached the postwar situation from fundamentally opposing positions.

On this occasion—the approximate time at which Du Bois had apparently indicated that he would try to deliver his text for the *Archiv* and, more or less, the deadline for the issue that would appear in print over the course of the summer of 1905—the most promising possibility of the terms of this interlocution are rendered legible. That is to say, there has developed in this correspondence a modicum of common problematic: an intersection of two different inquiries about the possibilities of modern social forms, specifically as an organization of *relations among groups of humans understood according to some order of reference as somehow fundamentally different in kind*, each of which took as a grounding premise a fundamental engagement with the empirical order of situation and the example. In this case, in the terms of this interlocution, they were both addressing this question according to the titular guide of the situation and the example of the Negro in America, even as both, in their own respective ways, understood such exemplarity in the configured and relative norms of a comparative and worldwide horizon.

For both these figures, this would become a most remarkable moment. In *the sense of the future form of the immediate* instance, both thinkers were at pivotal junctures in their respective itineraries. For each thinker, the activity of these months would become definitive for his own lived sense of his life. The same is true for our contemporary sense of their legacies. For each thinker, in a distinct manner, the activity of these months would take shape as a nodal turning point in the configuration of the terms of his future.

At the end of the previous year, from December 1904, Du Bois, along with others, had begun to organize a group that would seek to provide new leadership, at once intellectual and political, for African Americans in the United States that would be different from, and beyond the direction of, that being promulgated by Booker T. Washington. Sometime during the first months of 1905, Du Bois prepared and sent by post a confidential letter that would serve as the definitive solicitation for the organization of the project that would come to be known as the Niagara Movement. In March 1905, the first historic meeting was just three months away. This activity would eventually lead Du Bois to leave the academy. This would occur in June 1910.[24] He eventually reorganized his institutional intellectual project into the position of editor of a journal for the new organization that grew from this movement: *The Crisis*: *A Record of the Darker Races*, the monthly magazine of the National Association for the Advancement of Colored People. Du Bois would hold this position for the next twenty-three years.[25] What must be understood is that, from the early autumn of 1896 to the early autumn of 1906, and during the time of this interlocution, Du Bois was in the midst of what he considered at that time, as well as later, his "real life work" (Du Bois 1920; 1975a, 20). It would be half a decade before he would realize that the terms of his intellectual project could not be sustained in the organization of the American academy as it existed in the American South, at Atlanta University, at that time. During his life course from thirty-five to forty-two, Du Bois would gradually come to find himself derailed from the scholastic track of his practice by the very conditions that he was engaged to study. The so-called Negro question was not just an object of inquiry. It was also a constitutive aspect of the organization of the conditions, simultaneously political and epistemological, by which it could be studied. The movement into the arena of a public intellectual, something that discomfited Du Bois for the rest of his life, would become decisive. It is indeed this public legacy that has thus far remained the most legible one for contemporary generations that would engage his practice.

In the months just before and just after his visit to the United States, Weber wrote the text that would become his most famous and would come to stand indisputably as one of the most recognized statements of the twentieth century: the two-part essay on "the Protestant ethic and the spirit of capitalism" (Weber 1905a, 1905b). It is likely that he had just completed the preparation of the second part or was still engaged in its writing when Du Bois's March communication arrived.[26] The problematic announced in Weber's 1905 essay would devolve in its eventuality and come to name the most fundamental character of his thought: first, for him, as a question of political economy that had become a general sociological one about a transformation in the essential dimensions of social life in the modern West, in which the development of capitalism would be understood as fundamental and irreversible; then second, by 1909, as a general question about the status of the ostensible *historical* singularity of the projection of a certain rationalism in Europe, the latter of which, however variegated and multifaceted in and of itself, took on a distinctive profile for him when understood in historically comparative terms. In this latter form it can be understood to have been gathered up and served as the horizon of problematic for all of Weber's work after 1905 as it evolved into an exceedingly rich and far-flung comparative global inquiry over the remaining fifteen years of his life.[27]

By way of the scholastic project of the *Archiv* that began in 1904, but especially from 1906 to 1907 (when Weber received an inheritance that allowed him to withdraw from obligations arising from his university affiliation), Weber and the other two editors were able to propose a whole approach to the study of the social: to elaborate not just the problem of science in relation to social reform, which remained the bread and butter of the journal, but to make thematic in conjunction with that concern the philosophical and general theoretical problems of historical social-science study. In one order of epistemological sense, and in general terms, it was a sustained attempt to formulate the conceptual and theoretical dimension of late nineteenth-century German liberal historicism on a more fundamental basis than had yet been attempted. On another level—that of the epistemic in general—it was an attempt to think historicity as such as a problem of knowledge. Once Weber had officially withdrawn from teaching due to continuing problems with his health and enabled by his modest inheritance, the journal, edited at Heidelberg, was the principal means by which he could announce his work and engage in intellectual debate. Over the first third of the twentieth century, some of the major social thinkers of Germany and Central Europe would publish and debate there: Georg Simmel, Robert Michels, Werner Sombart, Ernst Troeltsch, Alfred Tonnies, Emil Lederer, Ludwig von Mises, Joseph Schumpeter, and Alfred Weber, among others. W. E. B. Du Bois must also be included here. Perhaps it can be said that its rival in this pioneering domain was *L'Année Sociologique*, founded in Paris in 1895 by Émile Durkheim, which lasted in its initial form until 1925.[28] The years 1904–1905 then marked the first articulations of the staging that would provide the most consistent platform for the constitution of Weber's work during his lifetime and for the record and maintenance of his intellectual legacy afterward.

C. A PASSAGE OF THE POSSIBLE: THE UNSPEAKABLE REMAINDER OF A QUESTION

As the firm salute of the correspondence of Du Bois and Weber suddenly goes dormant ("My Dear Prof. Weber" and "My Dear Colleague!"), another scene of this possible interlocution appears.

A letter addressed to Du Bois in November 1905 from Else Jaffé-von Richthofen, whom Weber had proposed as the translator of *The Souls of*

Black Folk: Essays and Sketches into German, remains among Du Bois's papers. While quite factual and real in its statements, it has, in the context of the fragmented archive that we have recalled here, an almost apparitional quality, for in the background of this text, in its barely audible lower registers, is a bit of the noise of the everyday in the intellectual life of Heidelberg at the time. Reading the letter, perhaps in the imaginary memory of the mind's eye, the scene of a house to which one might have been invited on a cool Autumn early evening comes into view. And viewing from afar a play of light across the curtains of an open window, one remembers, or imagines, that perhaps just inside was a place—a sitting room, a parlor, a warm kitchen, a spacious and well-organized home office—from which one might begin to hear the rising and falling tones of voices engaged in respectful conversation that could last long into an evening.[29] Who was invited there to be a part of such conversation, one wonders, and on what terms? Across the question about the practical matters of the occasion moves another one among the soft shadows: What was the depth and breadth of such sharing? What made it possible?

It is apparent from its opening statement that Jaffé's letter is a reply to one sent by Du Bois on 9 October. The original text is in German.[30]

Archiv für Soziale Gesetzgebung und [S]tatistik [31]
Edited by Heidelberg, 10.
November 1905
Werner Sombart, Max Weber,
Rohnbacherstrasse 21
[Uferstrasse and Edgar Jaffé 8A]
Mr. Professor Du Bois Atlanta University

Very honored Mr. Professor:

Please allow me to respond directly to your last communication of October 9 in regard to the translation of your book "The Souls of Black Folk." Since nothing stands in the way on the part of your publisher, I intend to follow the suggestion of Mr. Professor Weber and attempt the translation of your book. I say 'attempt' because I have several other responsibilities and I cannot always depend on my health. Above all, it will become clear in the course of my attempt whether I am able to do justice to your work. It will not be at all easy to give to the German reader even a slight impression of the plasticity and simultaneously the charming simplicity[32] of your language. I will keep you apprised of the progress of my work [on the translation].

I also want to say, at my husband's behest, that in the next several days you will receive the proofs of the translation of your article on the Negro question in the United States along with the original manuscript. The manuscript of the translation comes [back] to us. There are also two pages with your original tables that are lacking in the manuscript which has been sent back to you.

Because however we will compare once again the corrector [i.e.,] the corrected manuscript] with the manuscript of the translation, that doesn't mean anything [i.e., that is not a problem]. Because our journal suffers from a chronic lack of space, Mr. Professor Weber undertook to make some minor cuts which he begs you to excuse.

As far as I remember, you twice used the expression "turpentine farm" in your essay. We could not figure out what is meant by this expression. Perhaps you will be so good as to clarify this for the German reader with a short footnote.

Respectfully, Elisabeth Jaffé

From Jaffé's letter alone we could suppose that Du Bois had written in October to indicate that McClurg and Company had finally cleared the legal terrain that would allow for this proposed translation. However, an extant letter among Du Bois's papers dated 12 October 1905 from Francis Fisher Browne, Du Bois's editor at McClurg, and addressed to Du Bois, along with Du Bois's handwritten draft of a reply, indicates that there was prior correspondence among F. C. B. Mohr, the publishers of the *Archiv*, and the Paris representatives of McClurg (Du Bois 1980f, reel 2, frames 433–518). No doubt, Du Bois wrote to Weber, and hence to Else Jaffé-von Richthofen, on the basis of the conclusion of these discussions. Further, Jaffé-von Richthofen's letter gives us information on the provenance of the text at hand, Du Bois's essay for the *Archiv*, "Die Negerfrage in den Vereinigten Staaten." Along with Weber's notation in the letter of 17 April included earlier in the chapter, she indicates that the final text is a translation and that it is one that Du Bois reviewed; also, we now know that Weber proposed some editorial reductions, apparently minor, that Du Bois also accepted (which he had indicated was his prior disposition in his letter of 18 April, the draft of which is included earlier). It is not unreasonable to suppose that it was Jaffé who undertook the primary work of rendering Du Bois's text into German, as she indicates in her letter that she had in fact read it and at that moment was wondering about the meaning of a particular reference.

Among Du Bois's papers, we also have what appears to be a draft of Du Bois's reply to Jaffé-von Richthofen, dated two weeks later. It is in Du Bois's hand script, on two sheets. It has no signature page.

11/24

Frau Elizabeth Jaffé 8A Uferstrasse
Heidelberg German[y][33]

My Dear Madame:

   Your kind letter of the 10th is at hand and I wish I dared trust my German in reply[.] But I do not. I thank you very heartily for your bravery in attempting to translate my little book, and I shall do all I can to help you. You will of course not hesitate to call on me. The proofs of my article have not arrived yet but I will correct them as soon as possible when they come.

   A "Turpentine Farm" is not a farm at all[,] but a *Fichtenhain*"[34] or grove of yellow pine trees (turpentine-*baüme*) which are regularly tapped for the pitch by gangs of workmen. I trust to hear from you at your leisure.

And with this passage as its closure, a draft letter with no signature, the correspondence ceases for all appearances.

One pauses here to wonder what would have been the life course of a translation of Du Bois's book of "the *strivings* of the souls of Black folk" (the fifth chapter of which offers a trenchant riposte to the uncritical participation by Negro Americans in American "commercialism") if it had in fact been rendered into German so soon after its original publication, and if it had been delivered to its readership by way of an introduction from the scholar who was just proposing the thesis of "the Protestant ethic and the spirit of capitalism." One might assume, for example, that Du Bois's "little book" did indeed move among a few hands in Heidelberg in the spring and summer or fall of 1905. According to the moment, a translation into German might have delivered it to such circles in Berlin, Munich, or Vienna, and perhaps even to Budapest, Prague, and Krakow or Warsaw.[35]

Doubtless, the idea for a translation of his book into German was of unusual interest for Du Bois. His relation to German discourses and attention to German cultural history had arisen early in his life and was of a truly profound character, deepened especially during his two years of doctoral study in Berlin. It would remain fundamental for him throughout his career. His relation to matters German was not just one among others.[36] And the incipient dialogue with another profound scholar working in the nascent discipline of "sociology" would also have had special appeal for Du Bois. Thus, even though he was caught up in the second wave of his initial activity, launching what we now know as the Niagara Movement, it seems reasonable to conclude that the translation project's lack of completion was not due to any absence of attention on his part. And here it must also be recalled that the entire archival record of this passage of events—or, at least, our nodal awareness of it—comes by way of his act of maintenance. Thus, if a further initiative had come from Heidelberg, it is more than likely that Du Bois would have responded with alacrity.

Yet the translation was not completed.[37]

Briefly put, we know that Weber himself became deeply entranced with the unfolding of the first Russian revolution of the twentieth century. Indeed, his interest was such that by the end of the summer of 1905, just after the cessation of the correspondence concerning Du Bois's contribution to the *Archiv*, Weber undertook an intensive three-month study of the Russian language to read and follow events and debates in Russia. This interest yielded an ensemble of essays by Weber over the next several years (Weber 1995). While these essays have begun to attract sustained attention from scholars in the English-speaking context, they may be of even greater importance than has yet been recognized. They issue from a constitutive dimension of Weber's intellectual work. These revolutions entailed two fundamental aspects of modern history, both of which pertained to Weber's formative intellectual concerns of the early 1890s—both scholastic and political—and were directly linked to the terms of his interest in the question he addressed to Du Bois. In one sense, Russia's revolutions were fundamentally about the status of historical forms of "landlordism" in relation to the status of a peasantry or a proletarian class of workers. An engagement with this question was decisive in Weber's itinerary; its pertinence should become more legible later. In another aspect, Weber's concern with the Russian problematic, as Wolfgang Mommsen indicated some sixty years ago, entailed what has (too) often been called across diverse contexts the "minority question": How can different ethnic and cultural identifications and their relation to the organization of basic political and economic processes be resolved in the situation of a *new* state (Mommsen 1984, 57–58)? (Further, the implication of this revolution for the sovereignty of German Prussia and the German Reich as a whole formed the titular heading of his concern—that is, as I show in part

II, in the terms of Weber's own formulation.) In this sense, the question that solicited Weber's attention in the American scene, which led him to propose a dialogue with Du Bois, would be reapproached in his concern with the Russian situation. Perhaps this new scene so entailed Weber's attention that, as an intellectual force, it dissipated his capacity for developing the direct conversation with Du Bois. In part II, I show that both of these contexts were transpositions of a question by which Weber had already been solicited on the level of the German nation-state.

One also notes that there is a slight delay, compared with the letters between Du Bois and Weber in the spring of 1905, in the reply to Du Bois's 9 October letter. Also, the reply came not from Weber but from Jaffé-von Richthofen. However, we cannot assume therefore that Du Bois's letter was addressed directly to her. The opening sentence of her letter suggests otherwise: that the letter had been addressed to Weber, but that it was she who responded. As the proposed translator of *The Souls of Black Folk: Essays and Sketches*, she could be understood as its ultimate addressee. Of the additional responsibilities to which Jaffé-von Richthofen alludes, it must be noted that she had given birth to her first child earlier that year. In addition, along with Marianne Weber and both their husbands, she was a major player in the very active social and intellectual life of Heidelberg. The circle around the Webers during these years has remained famous into our own time. However, perhaps other matters in Jaffé-von Richthofen's life, above and beyond social demands and her health, took her away from the task of translating Du Bois's book.[38] So one might ask: Was there no further correspondence from Du Bois to Weber, or from Du Bois to Jaffé-von Richthofen, concerning either the essay or the translation? Was there no further correspondence from Weber or Jaffé-von Richthofen in reply? According to the extant record, the conversation ceases, again, just as it seemed that it might finally articulate, on its own terms, something of the stakes that it held for the future of such an interlocution.

2. THE ESSAY: W. E. B. DU BOIS'S "DIE NEGERFRAGE IN DEN VEREINIGTEN STAATEN" (1906)

The essay itself is the only other extant record that seems to remain from this correspondence. And it is the only "complete" contribution thereof that is from Du Bois himself. It consists of a nine-paragraph preamble and three major sections, the latter titled "The Bondsman" (*Leibeigene*), "Ascent of the Bondsman" (*Das Aufsteigen des Leibeigenen*), and "The New Caste Mentality (*Das neue Kastengeist*).

The principal conceptual work of the essay, its theoretical sense, is accomplished in the preamble. The first and middle sections of the essay are exemplary in a superb manner of Du Bois's early empirical, historiological, contributions to a still nascent formal social science that came to be known as sociology.

Yet the third and closing section—the longest in the essay—is the locus of its most committed theoretical elaboration. That section is an account of the effects and implications of the dispositions and concomitant practices, notably among the laboring classes, of persons in America who understood themselves as categorically different from those understood as African American with regard to all major social and economic practices in the United States across the second half of the nineteenth century and the opening of the twentieth. Already in 1900, Du Bois had nominalized this problematic under the heading "the problem of the color line." His production of this statement in this essay may be understood as a timely and succinct presentation, a statement in a kind of interlocution, of this major through line of his thought, as an address to Weber, thereby also to fellow scholars who would attend to the work shared in the *Archiv*.

The first paragraph of the preambulatory passage sets in place, in two sentences, the foil that will serve as the essential background for the account of the situation of the Negro American at the inception of the twentieth century that Du Bois will describe in this narrative addressed to an audience of intellectuals in Germany and continental Europe.

> The great economic opportunities that opened up in the new North American republic at the beginning of the nineteenth century, combined with the homogeneity of its population and its institutions, let it appear not impossible that there—on the other side of the ocean—a nation would arise free of the crippling chains of the caste mentality, a nation in which social differences would be determined only by the different abilities and education of individuals. The Americans themselves did not at all doubt this development: they firmly believed that all people are created free and equal and are provided by their creator with certain inalienable rights, and that to these belong "Life, Liberty and the Pursuit of Happiness."

As was his wont, Du Bois immediately complicated this locution, simultaneously extending its purchase as a statement about the American project in this comparative context and remarking, and thus qualifying, its declarative sense:

> In many strata of the young nation, to be sure, these principles were applied with a certain *reservatio mentalis*. The good old Puritan families in New England had an aristocratic fear of the mob, and for the plantation barons of the South, they alone were the "people." Moreover, in those days of the emergence of the nation, one-fifth of the entire population was everywhere silently ignored—the one million Negroes who were mainly servants and slaves.

In the sense given here, with the idea of old Europe providing the margins or the framing reference, the American exception, as some in his projected audience might have imagined it, is called into fundamental question.

The rhythm of these two opening paragraphs announces the contrapuntal character that lends to this essay is most distinctive rhetorical force. Without sentiment, Du Bois proposes that the proscription of the Negro is costly to all concerned: to the Negro, first of all, but also to America and to the world as a whole. The Negro situation, then, is an example— one that is good to think with and one that might reveal something of the promise of America and the world for those open to a critical accounting of the historicity of their time.

In the opening section of the essay, Du Bois describes the rise of the post–Civil War social organization of the conditions of labor for Negro Americans in the rural South, the growth of the system of "share-cropping" in the wake of the failure of a national project of Reconstruction that might have engaged the Negro as a citizen of its future. It draws on the substantial and deep empirical labor on the conditions of the Negro in the rural context that Du Bois carried out in the first years of his scholarly work—that is, from 1897 through 1907. After 1907, his work with the nascent Niagara Movement and a series of professional and political disappointments, marked especially by the gradual loss of philanthropic support for his research, as the denouement of this moment for Du Bois, forced his scholarly practice to the background of his activity. Du Bois draws directly from the empirical material gathered in that early scholarly work in this section: His schematization of the organization of the post-Reconstruction system of labor as a sharecropping system is reproduced more or less verbatim from the texts published therein. And his conception of the different strata of laborers in this particular form of this system as he outlines it here had already been developed in those earlier studies (Du Bois 1904a, 1980d, 1980h).

Arguably, the second section of the essay, the shortest, is epistemically the most distinct in this context. In it Du Bois gives his account of the self-initiative of Negroes. A formal representation of such a thetic posture appears in Du Bois's texts of this time (as well as in those from other moments of his career) in such a consistent manner, even if in diverse forms (e.g., as statistics and photographs), that the gesture functions almost like a generic practice. In the strict sense, it might not bear the sanction of a discourse that would proffer itself as "scientific." Perhaps it is for this reason that the editors, especially Weber, who had published an essay on "objectivity in social science" just the year before as the premise that would guide the *Archiv* in its new projection, included a headnote whose formulation to some extent can be understood as taking slight distance from the expression of "his views" by "one of the most outstanding intellectual representatives of the American Negroes." The editors promised to return to the topic at hand and publish a more content-based or factual (*sachliche*) account of the "dimensions of the problem." Whatever might have represented such an account, it never appeared in the *Archiv*. As the end of this section reads as the least accomplished passages of Du Bois's essay, one wonders whether it was here that certain editorial cuts (mentioned in Jaffé's letter of 10 November 1905) were introduced. Yet this gesture is an irreducible part of Du Bois's practice. If he leaves it out, an impartial judgment of the Negro as degraded can remain as the only commensurate response to an account of the conditions of poverty and economic subordination. This bespeaks an epistemic circumstance: The discourse about the Negro, whatever is such, is part of the so-called Negro problems. The economy of problem that compels one to address this mode of its promulgation is as fundamental as any other demand for a study of the Negro problems. It may not be surprising, then, that Du Bois published a second essay in the European context in 1906, in French, in the Belgian journal *Revue Économique Internationale* under the title "L'ouvrier négre" (Du Bois 1906c), in which his central thematic is the *artisanal* capacity of the Negro worker.[39]

Section three of Du Bois's essay is a careful elaboration of the relations of Negroes and whites in the American South. It is an account of relations across the so-called color line, American-style. It draws directly and verbatim from two previous texts by Du Bois. In this sense, we have previous English-language versions of the passages at hand. The first half of the section reproduces the central paragraphs of chapter 9 of *The Souls of Black Folk: Essays and Sketches*, in which Du Bois outlines, in lockstep fashion, his understanding of the principal modes by which social relations among humans can be described. In its prosaic manner, it is the most akin to nascent forms of description that were subsequently routinized within sociology.[40] The second half of the section is drawn almost verbatim from a text that, while not unpublished in the strict sense, has remained virtually unknown and certainly unrecognized in its provenance in Du Bois's discourse, a text that served as the basis for a kind of stump speech that he presented several times in 1904, as I noted earlier. It is most likely the one to which Weber refers in his opening letter to Du Bois in early November 1904. Perhaps the most appropriate title for this section would be "The New Caste Spirit in America." Read retrospectively, from this section, the essay "Die Negerfrage" can be shown to announce this theme from its preamble and to sustain it throughout as the guide for all of its other thematic and topical elaborations. The issue, then, that Du Bois addressed directly and pointedly to Weber is that, in the global transformation that was afoot, of which America stood as a signal example, a turn to old forms of proscription was showing forth as a way to subtend existing orders of privilege and hierarchy, forms that had been in the process of dissolution.[41] The commitment to such retrogressive ideals threatened to compromise the whole future of America and, if practiced at a global level, the new forms of possibility that had come to show forth in the modern era. Thus, it must be emphasized that in this section Du Bois proposes not just that the "problem of the color line" is a Negro problem but that its maintenance threatens to foreshorten or delay the emergence of future historial possibility on a worldwide level.

It must be said that the mode of address throughout the essay has the character of an appeal. Yet it is an appeal that announces its own claim to authority. It does not seek philanthropy as such, for along with the sense of appeal comes the remarkably steady march of easily commanded detail, available only to one who is in the midst of *the laboring* rhythm of scholarship, the presumption of a certain skein of cordiality in discussion, and above all, the moral authority of a claim to accord with the destinal orientation of a sense of justice. It is on this register that one must catch the subtle cadences of Du Bois's closing statement: "And above all consider one thing: the day of the colored races dawns. It is insanity to delay this development; it is wisdom to promote what it promises us in light and hope for the future." In this statement, the appeal takes on the character of both a historical judgment and a warning. The movement of the discourse from one sense to the other remarks the character of the epistemic-political space traversed by the essay as a passage in this possible interlocution.

3. THE PLACE OF "DIE NEGERFRAGE IN DEN VEREINIGTEN STAATEN" IN THE WORK OF W. E. B. DU BOIS, CA. 1905

A. THE PROJECT OF THE "STUDY OF THE NEGRO PROBLEMS"

During the late 1890s, Du Bois formulated and began to carry out a program for the comprehensive study of the Negro in the United States. The project to study African Americans in the rural South developed as part of this larger program. It eventuated in a long-term project to examine the post–Civil War reorganization of rural society in the South as it showed forth in the conditions of Negro Americans. As a statement by Du Bois, "Die Negerfrage" is an extension of discourse from this project.

In the context of the commentary at hand, the rural aspect of the project must be placed in direct parallel perspective with the formative work of Max Weber during the early 1890s. While I consider this aspect of Weber's work in somewhat greater detail elsewhere in this volume (part II), it must be remarked here that it is substantially more important and deserves more interest than is usually given to it in the scholarship on his work. It not only makes legible some essential terms of the development of Weber's thought, of course, but also shows the epistemic implication of how centrally placed Weber was among the liberal intelligentsia in Germany and in relation to the dominant policy apparatuses of the state in Prussia. The same holds true a fortiori for Du Bois, with one essential divergence: Just as the so-called agrarian question in Germany at the end of the nineteenth century posed fundamental questions about the reorganization of the social and economic order facing that country, so the transformation of the organization of relations that configured the situation of the African American—first and foremost, a matter of the rural South—can be understood to have posed in its deepest and most paradoxical fashion the question of the historic transformations afoot in the reorganization of late nineteenth-century America. The question, according to a certain dominant order of problematization in each case, was: What is to be done to maintain a steady course of progress in the rise of an ambitious nation-state? At the root, in each context, was a question about the status of an historically subordinated labor force: so-called Prussian German and so-called

Prussian Polish (Prussian, Russian, and then, also, Austrian) laborers on the large estates in the eastern provinces of Prussia and historical Poland, on the one hand, and African American laborers on the large plantations, or the historical lands thereof, throughout the American South, on the other. It is thus no surprise that in both contexts, each scholar, Weber and Du Bois, would be called to this work by the agenda of the liberal intelligentsia and various policy groups, official and otherwise, that were seeking guidance through the rapid and fundamental transformations underway in their social orders. However, it must be specifically remarked, as becomes evident in part II, that Du Bois undertook his studies with far less financial and institutional support and a very different relation to the powerful institutions that could determine state policy than that which had been available to Weber in his rural studies.

In Du Bois's case, the operative question was: What happened for the Negro after slavery in the rural American South? In what way did this experience form the background of the situation of Negroes in the cities? Du Bois's investigation of conditions of the Negro in the rural South was initiated as a necessary and complimentary inquiry into the historical and social background of the groups of African Americans he was studying under the Philadelphia Negro project, which he would come retrospectively to situate in a somewhat formalistic gesture as a study of the urban and Northern Negro American. In the months of July and August 1897, Du Bois took up residence in the small country town of Farmville, Virginia, to study the rural and Southern Negro.[42] Not only are the resultant study (Du Bois 1898a, 1980e) and the documents associated with it properly part of the Philadelphia Negro project, as Du Bois declares in his preface to that study (Du Bois and Eaton 1899, iv; 1973, iv), but they also mark the first moments of his attempt to formalize a program for the study of the African American in the United States.[43] The former fact, the relation of the rural study to the Philadelphia Negro endeavor, is often overlooked: This is the first example of the fundamental linkage of rural and urban study in Du Bois's project. The latter fact, Du Bois's general project of African American studies, remains vastly underthought in African Americanist discourses and the history of the human sciences in the United States in general. Du Bois would elaborate this incipient formalization of African American studies during the early autumn when he returned to Philadelphia and would present the resultant programmatic proposal to the American Academy of Political and Social Science (Du Bois 1898b, 2015h). I consider it the founding programmatic work in the field of African American studies, because it formulated both a conception of this field as an object of study and a sense of the essential methodological premises and protocols appropriate to it (Chandler 1996, 86; 2008, 368). Across the two geographical spaces of this work from the autumn of 1896 to the winter of 1897—in Philadelphia and southern Virginia—Du Bois formulated for himself a certain conception of the project of what he called at the time "the study of the Negro problems."

The work in rural sociology also included a parallel and more detailed project on Dougherty County, Georgia, based on work initiated in the summer of 1898. While Du Bois's contribution to the Exposition Universelle (Universal Exposition) in Paris during the summer of 1900 made Georgia the key example, the work in rural sociology, so to speak, is given its first summary exposure in a testimony that he presented to the US Industrial Commission in February 1901 (Du Bois 1980h; Fisher 2005). The pivotal early essay "The Negro as He Really Is," published in June of that year, worked with the same example and empirical sources, and it operates with a comparative sensibility as its explicit frame (Du Bois 1901a). The essay was so important that Du Bois decided not only to include it in *The Souls of Black Folk: Essays and Sketches* but also to divide it and have it stand as the central seventh and eighth chapters. It gives his account of what he called the "Black Belt."

This whole historical problematic is indeed deeply indexed in "Die Negerfrage" as the theme of its opening section. Alternatively, we can easily recognize that "Die Negerfrage" as a text is of the warp and woof—of the fabric—that gathers and thus constitutes this dimension of Du Bois's early work. "Die Negerfrage" is understandable at the scholarly level only by way of reference to this matrix.

In the summer of 1906, in the months after the publication of "Die Negerfrage," Du Bois began what he later thought of as the most ambitious and well-executed sociological project of this stage of his career: a study of the Negro in Lowndes County, Alabama. With relatively substantial funding from the US Department of Labor, he worked with the assistance of two other scholars, Monroe Work and R. R. Wright, and about a dozen or more local employees as research assistants (Du Bois 1968, 226–27; 1975b, 85). The final report of the study appears to have been lost, for according to the account that Du Bois produced in his autobiographies, along with the archival record, the Department of Labor decided against its publication and subsequently claimed that the text and other documents that he had submitted had been destroyed, perhaps in a fire (Du Bois 1975b, 85–86). (When I personally conducted a search over several months of the Department of Labor Archives at the US National Archives in 1991 and 1992, I was unable to locate these documents; nor was there any extant record in those archives of their previous existence.) It can be shown that Du Bois's first novel, *Quest of the Silver Fleece*, published five years later, incorporates as its fundament a fictional account of the social and economic history that his project had otherwise proposed to bring into formal scientific and policy discourse (Du Bois 1911).

The larger project of which these three projects in rural and agrarian sociology are a part, and their role therein, could sustain a substantial reelaboration in our time. Indeed, I have undertaken such a project, of which this commentary is simply a nodal example. The scale of this larger work has seldom been fully grasped. An elucidation of its conceptual, methodological, and theoretical organization as an epistemological contribution, bequeathed to our time and as the order by which its legacy as a project of the human sciences should be understood, is still a scholastic demand posed for contemporary thought (Chandler 2008).

B. THE ESSAYS OF THE WINTER AND SPRING OF 1904–1905

We might conclude this stage of the discussion by briefly specifying "Die Negerfrage" in terms of a series of other texts that Du Bois prepared during the first six months of 1905. These were the very months of his extended— even if dormant for a time—correspondence with Weber. Their temporal proximity alone means that they should be understood as of the same contextual imprint as "Die Negerfrage."

The operative question throughout is: What are the terms of human possibility?

A set of these texts concern the matter of the limitation of human possibility. They are a series of four short essays on the history of slavery from antiquity to the end of the nineteenth century, published in the *Voice of the Negro* from February to July (Du Bois 1982a, 1982b, 1982h, 1982i). Their style suggests they were composed for a somewhat learned general audience. The questions posed across the essays concern the status of forms of unfree labor in the organization of historical possibility and outline the progressive denouement of systems of conscription as the contrapuntal rise and dissipation of the chances for human progress in general. Their explicit comparative dimension on a global scale names their collective epistemic common ground with "Die Negerfrage" and as a textual ensemble, each should be read in terms of the others.

A year earlier, in the spring of 1904, Du Bois had already published an important essay, "The Development of a People," in the *International Journal of Ethics* of Philadelphia (Du Bois 1982d, 2015b). Its conceptual organization is quite close to the historical outline that Du Bois develops in his contributions to the *Voice of the Negro*. The essay, which proposes an outline of the developmental stages by which "a people" are constituted, and thus develops a sort of schematic anthropological conception of the forms of human relation to material necessity and beyond, is oriented by a threshold concern to elucidate the ways in which the legacy of slavery precludes or fundamentally limits such a formation. Thus, it addresses precisely the relation of the history of slavery given in the *Voice of the Negro* essays to the very modern condition of the African American in the United States. On an epistemological level, although published a year earlier, it should be read as a companion piece to "Die Negerfrage" (with the former addressed in its immediate locution to a national audience, while the latter was directed to an international one), for it specifically takes one inside the "home" and internal history of the kinds of person described in the essay published in the *Archiv* while indexing it to a global level of historicity.

The other text in question here, unpublished during Du Bois's lifetime, concerns the relation of the project of science and the question of the chance or the freedom of human possibility. This text is the essay "Sociology Hesitant" (Du Bois 1980g, 2015g).[44] What is distinctive for us is that, while Du Bois does not address "the Negro question" in any direct lexical form in this text, its principal question is common to those texts by him and of this moment that do consider it: the relation of chance and necessity in the promulgation of human action. And more profoundly, perhaps, there is a discreet but fundamental relation of this text on the project of sociology to the text of "Die Negerfrage" given to the *Archiv*. While Du Bois resolutely affirms the ineluctability of chance, he was equally committed at the turn of the century to the project of a science that could recognize the operation of law in human practice. A project of a social science thus should recognize the critical limits of knowledge, yet hypothesize the possibility of such knowledge in its ultimate implication. A project of "sociology," then, would be the study of "the limits of chance in human action." If at the turn of the twentieth century "the problem of the color line" was in part a question of the status of existing forms of hierarchy and subordination in relation to an ostensible necessity, we can open a series of difficult and fundamental, apparently intractable, questions. Is this one form of Du Bois's response to the question that took shape for Weber on "the relations between the (so called) 'race-problem' and the (so called) 'class-problem'"? At its limit, Du Bois's entire meditation across the series of texts written during the winter and spring of 1905 concern the question of the relation of possibility to given forms of limitation in human social organization. If "Sociology Hesitant" appears as a kind of formal account of this question in relation to science, then it is also certain that "Die Negerfrage" examines this question with a resolute and detailed focus on a particular instance, even an exemplary one in the mundane sense of the term, at the turn of the twentieth century. Thus, we can ask: To what extent should the former essay also be understood as a legible mark of this possible interlocution of Du Bois and Weber?

These inscriptive marks—the letters, the essays of the time of this correspondence, the project from which those essays issue—thus provide a primary sedimentation of a legible provenance, a certain surround, for an initial approach to reading the essay "Die Negerfrage in den Vereinigten Staaten" sent by W. E. B. Du Bois in Atlanta to one Max Weber in Heidelberg in April 1905.

....

PART II

The Terms of the Discussion

A question has been set afoot, as announced by Max Weber in his letter to W. E. B. Du Bois in November 1904. This question was preceded by a statement. Each had been preceded by a courteous apology for being unable to accept Du Bois's invitation for Weber and his wife to visit him at Atlanta University. And both the statement and the question (entailing a request and invitation, in turn) were themselves a response to a theoretical projection by Du Bois. That projection had been given in Du Bois's work of scholarship and reflection over the previous decade, especially from 1897 to 1904. It was exemplified above all in the essays, memoir, and short story gathered in the book *The Souls of Black Folk: Essays and Sketches*, first published in 1903. Indeed—as we shall come to understand in a fuller sense and at a deeper level of reference—we already know that a certain response was proffered by Du Bois to Weber. The heart of that response was Du Bois's gathering and delivery of the essay in English in early 1905 that was then translated and published in German in 1906.

In the opening part of this study, we followed the still somewhat legible traces of the formulation of the question across a handful of months of correspondence and the discourse that followed this incipient locution. Each locution between these two scholars was given as well as received with a certain sense of mutual respect and, in all truth, a certain intellectual solidarity. However, to begin to recognize and formulate an understanding of these marks, we were required to initiate a scholastic descent into the archive—almost a subterranean declension, even though the remains in question could also yet appear rather legible above ground, according to a certain disposition for understanding and inquiry.

Yet the question announced here—this mutual locution—is, for us, more than scholastic. If we can adduce the motifs and structure of this discourse more fully—that is to say, in mapping the terrain (both above and underground) marked out by the form of the question and the form of the reply—we have yet to recognize that the question at stake is an even more deep-seated or interlaced organization of problem for knowledge and understanding. For the form of intellectual problem at stake in this question and reply is most fundamentally understood according to an epistemological order of reference. Thus, part II of this study elaborates an example of this epistemological order of problematization for situating the relation of the work and itinerary of these two thinkers.

In practical terms, this epistemological order of reference was already rendered legible by the simple interrogative posed by the archival remains: If there was this correspondence, what is it? What could the fact of this correspondence possibly mean? How ought we go about formulating an understanding of it?

Part I asked several threshold scholastic questions. Whence this correspondence? How did it come about? What is its character? How is Du Bois's essay "Die Negerfrage in den Vereinigten Staaten" situated therein? Also, beyond the matter of the circumstantial, we have begun to pose an implicit, perhaps supplementary, question—one that may perhaps eventually broach the epistemological orders of our inquiry: Why the brevity of this interlocution? Or why did it not continue?

On the basis of what we so far have been able to bring into discursive relief, we can now ask another order of question: How should we proceed in thinking through the relation of these two thinkers, both their work and their itinerary, to realize the most fundamental understanding? Should the whole matter be properly understood as an interlocution? Or, better, in what sense, according to what order of historicity, by what mode or dimension of historicity might we understand an interlocution of Du Bois and Weber to have, in truth, occurred at all? Or in what way might such possible interlocution be understood to have continued, perhaps within our contemporary historicity, not only in the previous century and more but also into our present and perhaps into the future?

How should we make sense of this moment from the standpoint of our contemporary situation? On the one hand, fundamental scholastic practice may require intrepid movement into unforeseeable discursive pathways or streams of discourse and reference, as well as the negotiation of shifts, turns, precipitous descents, or rapid escalations within the topography of the archive in general (for there are always several at stake, which may at times overlap). On the other hand, the order of an epistemological understanding requires the production of a scaffolding, for descent as much as ascent, or an architectural conception that is attentive to the articulations of available light. For this available light is not given all at once or only in an instance. It articulates according to habitations, which is also to note that such articulations arise according to temporality and duration. The archive, whatever it is, is never simply given. While it may be understood as a legible form of the historical itself, its legibility nonetheless is always marked by position and movement—always other than stasis—above all the movement of shadow (or light). In this sense, the epistemological, and the epistemic in general, is the order according to which we may begin to formulate an engagement with the archive, to render it for our own forms of critical inhabitation—that is to say, to come to a certain understanding, a kind of recognition, of the movement of light and shadow therein.

Hence, while I continue to refer to the archive in part II of this study, the commitment with which I do so seeks to discern how our guiding question—How should we understand the relation of the respective itineraries in thought and practice of Du Bois and Weber?—may allow a new or additional sense of how we may approach all that may be thought as the archival in the case of this example (this exemplary example) of two respective practices in thought that, nonetheless, may be thought in common. That is to say, this second part of the study is an effort toward an exemplary epistemological elaboration—not the only one possible—of the question of how to understand what is given to us by the archive of this epistolary correspondence of two rather remarkable thinkers.

Amid such considerations, another question becomes legible: Does this correspondence matter for us as more than an antiquarian investigation? In brief, the answer is in the affirmative.

These two thinkers, in 1904–1905, share in common a sense of a major problematization of human sociality for our time. We can properly situate this problematization in terms of an epochal sense of duration and historicity and on a planet-wide scale of geographical reference and comparative sense of emplacement. That is to say that the common sense of problem that Du Bois and Weber each inhabit as thinkers centers on a simple and fundamental problematic of the modern era: What will be the tendentious future of new forms of relation between social and historical human groups in the time to come, the future, in this so-called modern era?

In essence, the ultimate form of this question may be stated. Can we understand the relation between social and historical human groups according to a premise that is otherwise than the supposition of categorical terms of reference for distinction among them? Or must we accept as a certain truth the premise of categorical distinction for understanding difference among human groups? Or, even, must we accept the premise of some fundamental basis that is de facto determinate, even if it is historical, in the articulation of the relation of different human groups, one to another and all together?

At the year 1900, Du Bois formulates this as a term of art for his thought: "the problem of the color line" (see Du Bois 1900b, 2015e). Then, in his 1904 correspondence, both addressing Du Bois and referencing his discourse, Weber gave the phrase in English: "the 'color line' problem." Of course, we may ask whether Weber's sense of the phrase "the 'color line' problem" is the same as Du Bois's formulation "the problem of the color line."

Yet what should matter first for us is that in this correspondence the two locutions, the phrase and the formulation, each operated as two sides of one common coin, or two sides of a conceptual or theoretical coinage, that each could recognize both in common and on the terms of their own most understanding, each in relation to the other.

For Du Bois, "the problem of the color line" is a theoretical conception of modern historicity from the middle of the fifteenth century to the turn to the twentieth century. He embarks on this conceptualization to account for the historical production of matters of the Negro or African in America, at once matters of enslavement and all that it entails, and the emergence of the thought and practices of a supposed categorical distinction among human groups. The concept of race is at once the epitome of such supposed categorical distinction and only an instance of kind—one kind of the larger problematization of such ideas and practices that Du Bois formulates under the heading "the problem of the color line."[1]

The matter that is first put at issue for our understanding of Weber's thought and practice by considering the question of his solicitation by Du Bois's formulation and deployment, a certain conceptualization, of "the problem of the color line" is his understanding of modern historicity on a worldwide scale of reference—notably, as he put it at 1904, "the paramount problem of the time to come, here and everywhere in the world." Yet there is a second order of this problematization—the matter of supposed differences among groups of humans—that pertains directly to Weber's itinerary in thought and practice. As I annotate briefly later, Weber himself is also solicited within the German-speaking domains of Central Europe by political and economic questions, not to gainsay moral questions, as to presumptive and determinate claims of difference among groups of people subtended by centuries-long privilege and hierarchy—notably, with regard to land and resources, which is also to say forms of labor, directly coerced or indirectly induced or compelled. Indeed, Weber was directly solicited by the forms of world-historical problem of the relations among supposed fundamentally different groups of people within his habitations of daily life and in the itinerary of his earliest research and projections in thought (following his doctoral study, yet before the coming to full theoretical formulation of the 1904 and 1905 essays that together constitute the text we now know as *The Protestant Ethic and the Spirit of Capitalism*).

Weber, like Du Bois, is himself situated in the historical domains and within the terms of historicity that Du Bois formulated as "the problem of the color line." Although simultaneously distinct, they each inhabit in life and thought a common epistemological problematization of the supposed terms of the relations among different social and historical groups, tendentiously produced as if such difference could or ought to be inhabited as categorical in its premise and realization.

Du Bois first gave this thought a full-throated formulation late in 1899 (published in the autumn of 1900): "The color line belts the world and . . . the social problem of the twentieth century is to be the relation of the civilized world to the dark races of mankind" (Du Bois 1900b; 2015e, 112, para. 2). In early 1901, in a text later placed as the second chapter of *The Souls of Black Folk: Essays and Sketches* (published in 1903), he remarked on the telling historical example: "The problem of the twentieth century is the problem of the color-line, the relation of the darker to the lighter races of men in Asia and Africa, in America and the islands of the sea. *It was a phase of this problem that caused the Civil War*" (Du Bois 1901a, 354; 1903f, 13, chap. 2, para. 1; 2015d, 167, emphasis added).

At this juncture in our account, we are well with our rights to propose that Weber may be understood to have answered Du Bois in the autumn of 1904: "I am absolutely convinced that the 'color- line' problem will be the paramount problem of the time to come, here [in the United States] and everywhere in the world."

It is a scholastic truth, however, that before we can attend to the question of the problematization, the sense of a general problematic that solicited each of them and in common, to propose an account of the question that set in motion this interlocution between Du Bois and Weber, we must first remark an old, tenacious, and erroneous approach to thinking about the relation of their itineraries and practice in thought. For it can be shown that previous discourse on this relation, until recently, was unable to recognize or propose such a thought. Nearly two decades after I introduced the perspective that I have just adumbrated, scholarship has remained somewhat begrudging or rather partial on the matter. It thus also remains that several brief scholastic and critical annotations that I offered in my initial essay may still assist us in opening this question anew for renewed reflection.

1. THE VIRTUES OF SCHOLASTICISM: ANNOTATIONS
OF THE TWENTIETH-CENTURY DISCOURSE ON W. E. B. DU BOIS
AND MAX WEBER

A. THE LIMITS OF CONTEMPORARY SCHOLARSHIP

Throughout his two-volume biography, David Levering Lewis systematically characterizes the relation of Du Bois and Weber in a manner that obscures what is most in need of understanding: the terms of possible interlocution between these two figures. First, in part, the difficulty arises because Lewis continually places his interpretation of Du Bois in this relation, both as person and in terms of thought, under the titular heading of the premises of the biographer's own understanding of the thought of Weber. He presents the relation of Du Bois to Weber more or less under the heading of a tutelary order: Weber would be the tutor; Du Bois would be the pupil. This representation is maintained by Lewis, despite the fact that it is constructed on the basis of an engagement with the documentary record on this point that can be considered superficial, at best, and in the context of an archival deposit in which several obvious indicators could have been understood to suggest a more reserved disposition (Lewis 1993b, 131, 142–43, 159, 203, 404).[2] That such an approach moves from an unjustified premise, yielding a profoundly inaccurate, misleading, and limited perspective, should be quite legible on the basis of a reading of the actual correspondence presented in part I of this study in conjunction with Lewis's representation. Second, Lewis's account of whether or not Weber visited Du Bois in Atlanta is mistaken in the same manner as Herbert Aptheker's account (see part I).[3] Thus, Lewis writes: "Max Weber came to campus to participate in the conference on crime during his American visit in 1904" (Lewis 1993b, 225). However, he adds his own imprimatur: "The great German sociologist had no recollection of Du Bois the Berlin student, but he wrote commending the Atlanta professor's researches and hoped to run a 'short review of the recent publications about the race problem in America in the *Archiv für Sozialwissenschaft und Sozialpolitik*'; which he did" (Lewis 1993b, 225, cf. 277). As we know from Weber's first letter to Du Bois, the German scholar never visited Atlanta University.[4] Further, however, as the unfolding correspondence shows, it was Weber, at the very least, who was solicitous of Du Bois. This is regardless of the question of Du Bois's solicitation of Weber.

And, finally, at the time of his trip to the United States in 1904, Weber, while highly regarded in Germany and Central Europe more generally, was hardly famous in the United States. He was certainly not viewed in the manner that Lewis suggests. In her biography, Marianne Weber quotes from a letter she wrote to her mother-in-law on the occasion of her husband's lecture at the Congress of Arts and Sciences in St. Louis in September 1904: "In form and substance the lecture was brilliant, and there were many political points that interested the Americans. Unfortunately the audience was small, as with all foreign speakers who did not have [Adolf von] Harnack's international reputation, but [almost] all of his colleagues were there and he made many valuable acquaintances [and received invitations]" (Marianne Weber 1988, 290).[5] Among the acquaintances made on that occasion was Du Bois, who most likely invited Weber to visit Atlanta University.

Here it must be recalled that Weber was still recovering after a sustained withdrawal due to malaise and protracted (though at times intermittent) emotional depression. The congress was the scene of his first public lecture in six and a half years. The idea of a "Protestant ethic" that would make him famous in America—and, in a real sense, throughout the world after the publication of *The Protestant Ethic and the Spirit of Capitalism*, the English translation by Talcott Parsons, in 1930—was only half-written at the time. The first part was in press while Weber was in America, quite literally at the time that he initiated his correspondence with Du Bois, and the second part was still to be written, upon his return to Germany, more or less *during the time of his interlocution* with Du Bois. Moreover, up to this point in his itinerary, after beginning in the field of law in the late 1880s, which included practicing as a lawyer, Weber only somewhat ambivalently moved into scholarship as such; indeed, political ambition might have been his most self-conscious project throughout the 1890s (Roth 2002, cf. 511). Weber's earliest scholarly work had been as a political economist with deep attention to the historical character of commercial law and its relation to economic organization, not only to agriculture, as in his *Habilitationsschrift* (doctoral dissertation) on the Roman Empire, but also to the historical status of new forms of business entity and practice, as in his inaugural thesis on the emergence of joint liability in medieval business formation in Europe and his mid-1890s theorizations of the emergent forms of modern stock exchange and new international trade policy (see Weber 1984b, 61–81, 886–929; 1986; 1988; 1989a; 1993b; 1994; 2003; see also Kaelber 2003). The theoretical architecture of his lecture at the congress, which was given in the form of a comparative mode in the elaboration of economic history, was built on the premises established in the agrarian part of his studies dating from the early 1890s (Weber 1906, 1988; see also Mommsen 2005). Indeed, at the time of his visit to the United States in late 1903 and early 1904, his thematized theoretical reflection and elaboration on the general project of sociology and the human sciences had only just begun.[6]

With this in mind, it can be said that the Weber Lewis evokes in contradistinction to Du Bois did not exist at the time of the interlocution at hand.

Meanwhile, Du Bois was in full throttle. He had published *The Souls of Black Folk: Essays and Sketches* during the previous year, to almost immediate and growing acclaim, and in 1904—one of his early signal years—he was publishing almost one substantive essay a month, several of which have remained of lasting interest (Aptheker 1973; Partington 1977).

Yet of decisive bearing for the possibility that we are considering—the terms of an interlocution—is that Du Bois had undertaken his own substantive engagement, empirical and theoretical, in what can be called an approach to the "agrarian history" of the United States. The scale of that project and its importance for how we understand Du Bois's relation to the history of the human sciences, and thus a project such as that understood as Weber's, remains obscure for contemporary thought. However, it can be proposed, even if only on the basis of the sketch of Du Bois's project that I outlined at the end of part I, that Du Bois and Weber were complimentary figures on their contemporary epistemic horizon. As I show in greater detail, Du Bois and Weber had been endeavoring, each in his own way and according to the specific imperatives of their emergence as intellectuals and up to the time of their correspondence, to map and sound the depths of a terrain that was common to them in both an intellectual and a historical sense. The fundamental character of their relation remains to be thought by scholarship. The present study is only a beginning of a possible consideration.

Thus, the characterization of the relation between the two figures in 1904–1905 as given to us by Lewis can hardly do justice to the situation.[7]

B. THE MANASSE CORRESPONDENCE

Although we cannot be certain, it now appears that the source for the mistaken statement that Weber visited Du Bois in Atlanta during his visit to the United States originated in texts associated with the inquiries presented to Du Bois by Ernest Moritz Manasse concerning Du Bois's relationship to Weber.

Among the Du Bois papers is correspondence with Manasse that consists of two letters (see Du Bois 1980f, reel 57, frame 603):

Durham, North Carolina
July 18, 1945

Dear Professor Du Bois:

Several months ago, I asked you whether you are in possession of any material which would be of interest for the establishment of Max Weber's views on the American race problem. You kindly answered me at that time you could not get to your files due to the transfer of your household from Atlanta to New York.

In the meantime I have almost finished a paper which I hope to publish under the title "Max Weber on Race." I would however not finish my manuscript without having asked you once more whether you could check my material by personal records. I take the liberty to enclose the wording of a footnote of my manuscript. In case you could either confirm or correct the statements made therein, I would be very thankful. My doubt as to whether you had met Weber already in 1892 is due to the fact that at the time Weber was a very young instructor of commercial law. I have however not been able to look up a catalogue of the University of Berlin of that year.

I certainly would greatly appreciate any information you would be willing to pass on to me.

I am, dear Professor Du Bois, Sincerely yours,
Ernst Moritz Manasse

Du Bois replied two weeks later:

New York City
August 1, 1945

Dear Mr. Manasse:

I am not yet in such a position with my books and files so as to be able to use them. We are planning to move into a new building in September and I hope then to be able to get at things.

I remember the article in the *Archiv* and I am sure that it was written at the personal solicitation of Max Weber. I think he visited me in Atlanta. In Berlin, while I was in his class I did not have, as I remember, any personal contact.

Very sincerely yours,
W. E. B. Du Bois

These letters were published in the third volume of Aptheker's selections from Du Bois's correspondence (Du Bois 1973d, 44–45). It appears that there was no further communication by Du Bois to Manasse on the matter.

The essay published by Manasse two years later, "Max Weber on Race," contains a footnote that references his communication with Du Bois (Manasse 1947, 197n15). This note, along with the publication of the correspondence after the mid-1970s, may well have played a quiet but key role in the discussion about Du Bois on the point of his relation to Weber, producing an effect that could be likened to hearsay. There is little citation, if any, of either specific reference in the literature on Du Bois's early itinerary and his relation to matters German, or in the passing commentaries about his relation to Weber. Yet a certain interpretation or assessment of the implication of the ostensible facts given here is widely distributed—that is, a view that is essentially continuous with the approach proffered by Lewis.

The provenance of Manasse's essay should be remarked as the way to approach its specific bearing for us here.[8] To the extent that Weber's reputation in this domain was at issue in the aftermath of World War II, in light of his persistently avowed nationalism, perhaps it was important to name his disposition on the matter of "race" amid the growing reception of his work in the United States. In a thoughtful discussion that ranges widely and knowledgeably across Weber's texts—in which the historical question of the status of anti-Semitism, concomitant with or even beyond the question of the sociologist's consideration of Judaism, is perhaps the guiding problematic, even if the former is not thematized as such—Manasse discusses the so-called Negro question. That question amounts to a leitmotif in the essay to the extent that Manasse repeatedly suggests, in a rather vague manner, that Weber's visit to America in 1904 and his direct experience of "the American situation on race" had an impact on his thinking about such matters. Apposite to the first moment of his statements of this character, in which Weber's ostensible interest in Du Bois is presented as evidence of Weber's sympathetic disposition in this domain, Manasse writes in a footnote that "Professor Du Bois kindly informed me that, according to his recollection, Weber visited him in Atlanta" (Manasse 1947, 197n15).[9] In 1945, at the end of the war and after having completed the text of *Color and Democracy: Colonies and Peace* (Du Bois 1945), Du Bois was seventy seven and far removed in time and context from the events in question. As noted in his letter to Manasse, he did not have access to his own files on the occasion of his reply. Nonetheless, neither Du Bois's letter nor Manasse's note indicates, as stated by Lewis and Aptheker, that Weber participated in the 1904 Atlanta conference. And in any case, such participation, circumstantially, would have been impossible.

C. A NOTATION ON THE FORMS OF AUDITION

Now that we have the correspondence in question on the table, we can propose that the relation between Du Bois and Weber was of a whole different order from that which has been suggested by Lewis. His passive claim, as ambiguous and misleading as it is, that Du Bois was a student under Weber's tutelage and that this supposed relation would have persisted indefinitely, is simply a representative example, for it has become so common in the literature as to be almost a reflex.

It does need be said that, in the texts published during his lifetime and immediately thereafter, Du Bois does indicate on several occasions that he "heard . . . Max Weber." This phrase seems to make its first appearance in the signal autobiographical text *Dusk of Dawn* from 1940 (Du Bois 1975b, 38–55, esp. 47).[10] The same phrase reappears in "My Evolving Program for Negro Freedom" (Du Bois 1982e, 222), a kind of coda to *Dusk of Dawn*, the reflection on his life's work that was published just four years later. Much later, it appears in the same form in a somewhat extended discussion of the Berlin years in Du Bois's posthumously published autobiographical account (Du Bois 1968, 162).[11] It is not in the *Darkwater: Voices from Within the Veil*, the narrative of those years published at the end of World War I (Du Bois 1920, 5–23; 1975a, 15–17). It finds little (if any) direct amplification anywhere else in Du Bois's writings. In his correspondence with Manasse in the summer of 1945, Du Bois wrote of the memory of his relation to Weber in the early 1890s: "In Berlin, while I was in his class, I did not have, as I remember, any personal contact" (Du Bois 1973d, 45). However, it appears that there is no extant record of a formal enrollment by Du Bois in a course with Weber. And in the reports that Du Bois sent to his scholarly benefactors every four months or so during his time in Berlin, the trustees of the John F. Slater Fund for the Education of Freedmen, he does not mention hearing Weber lecture or attending any of his classes (Du Bois 1973c, 23–27).

When Weber was a lecturer at the University of Berlin, he was just four years older than Du Bois; he was a *Privatdozent* (junior faculty), having had his *Habilitationsschrift* accepted in 1892. With such status, Weber was allowed to lecture at the university level, and he was thereby eligible, should a chair become available, to accede to a professorship. Specifically from the winter term of 1892 through the summer term of 1893, encompassing Du Bois's first year at Berlin, Weber substituted for his ailing dissertation adviser, Levin Goldschmidt, as a lecturer in commercial and Roman law. It is certainly plausible that Du Bois might have attended some of Weber's lectures during this time. However, even if he did, it would still only present the means of asking the further question: What is the bearing of such an occurrence? Although Weber was subsequently offered a position as an "Extraordinarius professor" at the University of Berlin, a rank essentially equivalent to an assistant professor in the current American system, he remained there for just one more term. After getting married in the autumn of 1893, he accepted a chair—a much better appointment—at the University of Freiburg in the spring of 1894.

It is therefore more precise and responsible in the scholastic sense to state for the biographical record that there is *no apparent indication*, in documentation or any other form, that Weber was ever a decisive figure in the pedagogical formation of Du Bois as an intellectual or scholar, regardless of whether Du Bois attended Weber's lectures on Roman law or commercial law. This is so regardless of one's judgment as to whether it is a good or bad circumstance.

However, it seems to me that another hypothesis concerning Du Bois's audit of a lecture by Weber is just as plausible and is perhaps more suggestive, for our consideration, than that of a supposedly tutelary relationship between the two men. Perhaps Du Bois heard a presentation made by Weber to the Verein für Sozialpolitik (Association for Social Policy), a kind of early form of the present-day political lobby and the contemporary think tank in combination, and the subsequent discussion of it in Berlin on 20–21 March 1893. Du Bois records in his 10 March 1893 report to the Slater Fund that he had just joined the Verein and that the group, "which includes in its membership many well-known economists," would be meeting in Berlin soon (Du Bois 1973c, 23). It is entirely possible that Du Bois attended these sessions of the association, for even though he traveled throughout northern Germany later in the month, as he recalls in many of his later autobiographical texts, he specifically dates his departure from Berlin to 24 March in a contemporaneous manuscript text that appears to be a sheaf from a diary of that trip (Du Bois 1894[circa]b). Gustav Schmoller, the professor who led the main seminar in which Du Bois was enrolled during his first semester in Berlin—that is, "Nationalökonomie," the famous seminar in political economy and state policy—was the president of the association at that time and, in that capacity, gave the opening speech for the meeting in March 1893. The principal topic of the Verein's sessions on this occasion were the results of a massive survey that had just been completed on the status and conditions of agricultural labor throughout the country. Weber's lecture presenting the results of his part of the survey, which had focused on the eastern region, as well as a general perspective on the whole study, was a major event of the meetings. Given these circumstances, it is thus plausible, if not probable, that Du Bois heard Weber's lecture. What to make of this—if it was, in fact, one occasion (and possibly the only occasion) on which Du Bois as a graduate-level student at Berlin "heard Max Weber" lecture—remains an open question. Yet regardless of the uncertainty, the themes of the meeting, Weber's lecture, and the discussion that followed it, on the one hand, and the theme and issues of "Die Negerfrage," which Du Bois would send to the *Archiv* a dozen years later at Weber's invitation, on the other, can be understood as part of a common horizon when situated according to a certain order of attention in a general comparative global horizon. It is on an order of generality that should be named as epistemic—which is also simultaneously in every sense practical and political—that the matter of the relation of the thought of Du Bois and the thought of Weber might be productively reapproached. I consider some aspects of this matter a bit further later.

As discussed in part I, Weber, during the course of a debate at the founding meetings of the Deutsche Gesellschaft für Soziologie (German Sociological Society) in Frankfurt in October 1910, mentioned Du

Bois as an intellectual persona whose intellect and character provided an exemplary contradiction of the views of his interlocutor Dr. Alfred Plötz (whose ideas of "racial hygiene" would later be taken up by Adolf Hitler and thus serve as a primary orientation for the National Socialist regime's policies on "race" in the 1930s). In the 1910 debate, Plötz posited "intellectual and moral inferiority of the Negro" as an imagined basis for a withdrawal by white students from contact with Negro students in a hypothetical American college context. Weber responded in a form full of a resonate irony that could apparently belong to him, certainly in his correspondence, even if not so often in his public discourse. I quote at some length, as this text has had almost no recognition in the literature on Du Bois:

> Nothing of the kind is proven. I wish to state that the most important sociological scholar anywhere in the Southern States in America, with whom no white scholar can compare is a Negro[,] Burckhardt [*sic*] Du Bois. At the Congress of scholars in St. Louis we were permitted to have breakfast with him. If a gentleman from the Southern States had been there it would have been a scandal. The southerner would naturally have found him to be intellectually and morally inferior. We found that the Southerner like other gentlemen would have deceived themselves. (Weber 1911, 164; 1971; 1973, 312)

Also recall the changing forms of Weber's salutation to Du Bois across the time of this correspondence, from his initial address of "Dear Sir" to the final one that we have extant at this point: "My Dear Colleague!"

Thus, we know from Weber's recollection some six years after the event that the first, and apparently only, in-person meeting of the two scholars was over breakfast at the Congress of Arts and Sciences in St. Louis during the third week of September 1904.[12] We know of this meeting only from Weber's recollection in 1910, caught in the archive due to the polemical occasion of the dialogue. We can suppose that since it appears that Weber had planned to visit Atlanta University, as I noted earlier, it is likely that an invitation for such a visit was extended to him directly by Du Bois at their meeting in St. Louis. But from our present, this can only be inferred. As Weber stated in his initial letter, he regretted that the circumstances required him to forgo acceptance of the invitation. His action was to extend an apology, a solicitation, and a form of invitation in turn.

In this way, according to our archive, it is Weber who proposed the terms of an interlocution.

2. THE SCHOLASTICISM OF THE VIRTUAL: A PROBLEMATIZATION FOR TWENTY-FIRST-CENTURY DISCOURSE ON W. E. B. DU BOIS AND MAX WEBER

How, then, might we adduce volume for this possible interlocution? Was there dimension to this commonness? Are there passages—subterranean, perhaps—whose form might have been able to sustain a resonance of the distended concatenation that is utterance, such that we might be allowed to retrace something of its character and thus resound, as a form of recoding in our own locution, the virtually illegible marks of its passage?

Moving from the documents at hand as legible mark, then, we can say that the titular frame or form of passage for this interlocution is given in Weber's initial letter to Du Bois: the question of "an inquiry about the relations between the (so called) 'race-problem' and the (so called) 'class-problem' in your country" (Weber to Du Bois, November 1904, reproduced in part I). We know from Weber's reply that Du Bois, in his now lost reply of 8 November, accepted the invitation in a general sense *to engage this question with* Weber, even as we cannot know whether he proposed in that reply an emendation of these specific terms (Weber to Du Bois, letter, 17 November 1904, reproduced in part I).[13]

Yet by way of Weber's reply we are able to adduce something about the epistemological depth terms of this interlocution. Weber declared: "I am sure to come back to your country as soon as possible and especially to the South, because I am absolutely convinced that the 'color line' problem will be the paramount problem of the time to come, here and everywhere in the world" (Weber to Du Bois, letter, 17 November 1904). In this reply Weber stated an affirmation of his own sense of the importance of this general horizon of problematic in America, particularly in the South. And it is stated in a formulation that one can reasonably presume Weber would have anticipated that his interlocutor would have recognized as issuing from a kind of symbolic currency common to both of them at that point, even if not itself comprising a coin or inscription of obvious, known, and designated, precisely shared epistemic value designed for this specific exchange. Thus, quite apart from the question according to which we might adjudicate this sentence, it can be said that, in his opening letters from the autumn of 1904, Weber announced himself on that part of the epistemic and political terrain of their common historical situation that he knew was already inhabited by Du Bois. And, further, Weber announced himself in the specific idiom—metaphoric and conceptual—to which Du

Bois had already given a distinctive stamp, impress, or valuation in his writings of the previous seven years.

Can we outline the respective immanent forms of passage by which each thinker came to the question at issue here: *the question of historical relation in general*, the relation of groups supposed or understood as different in some essential sense (practical and existential, whether understood as social and historical or otherwise), as a fundamental problematic of thought such that we can then begin to rearticulate *the terms of a relation of intellectual and symbolic exchange* between them? If so, it might assist us by directing us to specific historical and epistemological terrain in which such a mark, a certain question, acquired its legible imprint. Therein, one might productively undertake an effort in a kind of theoretical de-sedimentation that is breaking up the epistemic bedrock in which the supposed relation of the practice in thought of these two thinkers has been encrusted.

After rendering legibility to such scattered forms of mark, might not these apparently only graphic forms of concatenation assist us further in tracking and then listening according to a certain silence or sounding for certain kinds of fault lines in the sedimentation that surrounds and runs through this discursive archive? Might we not then be able to track lines of possible intersection that might, in turning, as a turning, take form as an apparent hollow or subterranean passage, suggesting the space of a possible resonance or even a locus of possible interlocution between these two figures? Might we try to resound or recode certain forms of question according to the impress or depress or the displacements of such forms?

And further, is there not a certain dimension of historicity—the time of inscription of the mark, the time of writing in the most general sense—in which an idiom or idiomatic remainder can be rendered available for critical thought, critical thought of the social, as the articulation of relation? For is not relation in its historical apparition simultaneously the sign of the common and the mark of differentiation—that is, as a differential inhabitation of the otherwise common?

Let us thus attempt to sketch a sort of surface map of the epistemic terrain (which might also be at stake, with resonance, in its subterranean dimensions) at issue here as a guide for later attempts that we may undertake toward a sounding or resounding of the organization of epistemic sedimentation—initially in terms of the thought of Du Bois, but later in terms of the discourse of Weber.

While it is the case that, even as early as the autumn of 1904, *The Souls of Black Folk: Essays and Sketches* had become the signal textual locus for the hearing of Du Bois's promulgation of the statement that "the problem of the twentieth century is the problem of the color line," it was, in fact, neither the occasion of the first enunciation of such by him nor the text by him whose semantic horizon could carry in translation the most resonant echo or the most legible impress of the potential value of the statement offered by Weber in his 17 November letter.

Du Bois began to announce the theme of the problem of the color line in his writing of the mid-1890s.[14]

As specific and nodal examples one can cite the opening sections of "The Afro-American" (Du Bois 1980a), a key unpublished essay dating perhaps from the fall of 1894, during Du Bois's first months at Wilberforce University as a young professor (it was most likely prepared just months after his return from Europe), and "The Conservation of the Races" (Du Bois 1897a), a lecture that was presented at the founding meeting of the American Negro Academy during the time of his first sociological research at Philadelphia. In those two texts, the matter of "the problem of the color line" appears as a theme under the force of the guiding problem of how to recognize and organize a Negro American group as an articulation of historical possibility. Many decades later, in *Dusk of Dawn* (1940), in a phrase that is repeated in his posthumous *Autobiography*, Du Bois wrote about this time: that upon his return to the United States, following his years abroad, he "was casting about" for some three years trying "to find a way of applying science" to the study of "the race question" (Du Bois 1968, 208; 1975b, 54–55). The time in question stretches between the events of his formulation of the Negro question in "The Afro-American" of 1894 and "The Conservation of Races" of 1897 (see Du Bois 1894[circa]a, 1897a, 2010, 2015a, 2015b).

Sometime over the course of 1897, we can then propose, Du Bois came to a clarification for himself about how to pursue his vocation: a social-science study of the so-called Negro question. It is my judgment, thus, that "The Conservation of Races" would come to stand for Du Bois at the end of a time of relative theoretical uncertainty and at the head of a new stage of his itinerary marked by an initial critical clarification of concepts and a first decision about a general methodological practice. It was then, in the autumn of 1897, that Du Bois produced the essay "The Study of the Negro Problems" (Du Bois 1898c, 2015h), which can now be understood as both the epistemological clarification for himself of how to study the so-called race question, or the so-called Negro question, as a practice of science in general and as the epistemological blueprint for the elaboration of the Philadelphia Negro project in particular (both retrospectively, offering an account of the empirical work, which he had carried out more or less completely from September 1896 to November 1897, and prospectively, sketching the premises according to which he would construe a textual representation and interpretation of the whole empirical archive over the subsequent eighteen months or so) (Du Bois and Eaton 1899, 1973).

It is thus on the apparent margin of the sociological work on the Negro question in the United States in the context of the social systems that organize the situation of the group called by the name Negro American, or a variation thereof, that the first thematic statement of the thought of the "problem of the color line" on its own terms is announced in Du Bois's discourse. Yet the statement bespeaks the most general and fundamental historical frame of Du Bois's conception of the so-called problem of the Negro in the United States and of which the situation of the Negro in Philadelphia was simply a part or a relatively local instance.

The central thetic judgment of this epistemic statement already appears in the afterword of *The Philadelphia Negro* text, written most likely in the late spring of 1899, after Du Bois had left Philadelphia and had been working at Atlanta University for some eighteen months (Du Bois and Eaton 1899, 385–97, esp. 385–89; 1973, 385–97, esp. 385–89). The immediate audience for his study were the sponsors of social reform in the city of Philadelphia. In the only textual scene in which a direct address and appeal to them might be acceptable, according to a presumptive norm of scientific objectivity, Du Bois proposed to situate this apparently very local and very specific circumstance—that of the conditions of the Negro American in a ward in Philadelphia in the late 1890s—in the most general comparative context that might be thematically relevant. Beyond the specific forms of social condition, the matter for Du Bois in these pages was the sense of relation among humans. The question was posed directly and starkly. While it is formulated as a matter of judgment, Du Bois names the terrain on which it takes shape as coextensive with the organization of social hierarchy as a form of the control of land and labor. The problem itself is given only by way of history. In the past and present, Du Bois proposed, not all human groups have been considered of equal moral status (at once in the traditional sense of the supposed ontological status of human beings) and, hence, of equal political status. The question thus was: Who will be considered human in the centuries to come? Or, better, what would be the exact meaning of such a consideration? With such temporal markers, Du Bois gives historicization, and thus a sense of relative status, to the situation of the present. The "problem of the color line" should be understood as a historical condition. While claims about human difference might be proposed within a traditionalized sense of a supposed ontology of the human, for Du Bois the determination of such difference did not issue from an ostensibly ontological ground.

Six months later, on December 27, 1899, in Washington, DC, Du Bois made his presidential address to the third annual meeting of the American Negro Academy under the title "The Present Outlook for the Dark Races of Mankind" (Du Bois 1900b, 2015e). In the address, the formulation is fully exposed in Du Bois's thought in an epistemic sense as a theoretical proposition of a dimension of historicity that would be geographically global and temporally coextensive with all that might be understood to make up the modern era. Du Bois named the problematic in a deft formulation whose apparent simplicity nonetheless exposed a deep and enigmatic complexity: "the relation of the darker to the lighter races of men" across the whole of the modern world (Du Bois 1900b, 2015e).[15] According to this text, "the problem of the color line" acquired shape in the modern historical period as an antagonistic, violent, and destructive devolution of an age-old problem: the relations among different human groups within one political and economic horizon. In a sense, that might be understood to pertain to a dimension of the question called metaphysical in general; a fundamental character had been attributed to various lines of apparent or putative difference among groups of humans for millennia (e.g., that of the so-called religious in recent centuries). Following Du Bois's thought, it can be proposed that what was distinctive in the most recent passage in the modern period—specifically, the eighteenth and nineteenth centuries—was the new sense of the ontological claims for the status that should be given to such differences in the context of a new question and a new thought: the critical thought of man (or humankind) as a whole and the possibilities of the human, in general, in common. In a historical sense, the actual forms of relation—in particular, the status of labor within modern forms of political and economic organization and imperial relations in the form of enslavement, colonialism, and capitalism—took shape as a conflict over the promulgation of new systems of hierarchy, exploitation, and privilege, on the one hand, and the attempt to announce and sustain a new sense of the originary value and capacity of all forms of human ingenuity—from all groups and from any strata—in the production of practical well-being for the future, on the other.

Yet if this is the general order of Du Bois's thought in the "Final Word" of *The Philadelphia Negro* and "The Present Outlook for the Dark Races of Mankind," it must be understood that by adducing such an order of reference, he also proposes a specific conjoined relativization and generalization: the situation of the Negro, particularly in the United States, is one example among others, yet it is an example of a fundamental problematic and thus bespeaks in an exemplary way the most general order of problematization of the human in our time, this modern era. In this way, the American situation and the global horizon of "the problem of the color line" were indissolubly linked in a *historical* conception and historiographical narrative frame of the actual making of what had become the present at the turn of the twentieth century, however schematic its factual reference.

By way of this sense of the present, an account of the historicity of the future could then be proposed. In Du Bois's terms, at the end of December 1899 all of this would acquire a new exemplification in the century to come: the twentieth. There would be two aspects of this new historical stage, or phase, of modern historicity. On the one hand, the historical movement would yield an irreversible production of the heterogeneity of populations within a dimension of relation that might otherwise be understood as a domain of commonness—specifically, that of the state as a project of nation but also of contexts of so-called race, so-called social class, and even so-called culture. Any presumptive principle of purity would be rendered utterly obsolete in all matters of the social and the historical. On the other hand, it would pose a general question of the status of *ideals* in the articulation of such relation. Without ontological presumption on his part, Du Bois saw the matter at the turn of the century as a question of the relation of the groups that might be understood as more historically developed, according to the norms of his time (even as he does operate at this point in his itinerary with an idea of the universal and a general sense of social evolution as not reducible to any traditional sense of the natural as biological or as an all-determining form of necessity), or groups that are socially supraordinate in various contexts, to those that are socially subordinate and less realized in their capacities in the sense of a specific historical epoch of possibility. In both aspects, for Du Bois, the situation in the

United States, as exemplified by the questions pertaining to the situation of the Negro American—in Philadelphia, for example—was an example, exemplary as a type, of the situation that he thought was to become globally general during the twentieth century:

> The expansion and consolidation of nations to-day is leading to countless repetitions of that which we have in America to-day—the inclusion of nations within nations—of groups of undeveloped peoples brought into contact with advanced races under the same government, language and system of culture. The lower races will in nearly every case be dark races. German Negroes, Portuguese Negroes, Spanish Negroes, English East Indian, Russian Chinese, American Filipinos. (Du Bois 1900b, 107, para. 18)

The decisive line of questioning would thus become: What will the character of the relation among groups in this historical situation—these transformed and hence new, social horizons and contexts—be? What form will these relations take? Who will take the lead in defining the terms of such relations? For Du Bois, these questions marked the inception of a new form of social problematic, a transformation of one historical phase to another, perhaps to the inception of a new stage or phase in modern historicity.

The indication of the development and the fundamental place of this conception in the thought of Du Bois must be given further precision, however brief. (Please note my complementary considerations of Du Bois's thought on "the problem of the color line" in Chandler 2021, 2022b.) For our commentary here, the key reference is to the opening paragraphs of an essay that Du Bois originally published in July 1901, "The Relation of the Negroes to the Whites in the South" (Du Bois 1901e, 2015f, 189–208).[16] The temporal proximity of its publication to that of both the "Final Word" of *The Philadelphia Negro* and "The Present Outlook for the Dark Races of Mankind" already suggests its epistemological locus in Du Bois's thought. Indeed, it is woven from the same epistemic cloth as those two, slightly earlier texts. Yet on its other side, it pertains directly to his contribution to the interlocution with Weber in the form of "Die Negerfrage," for that 1901 essay was later republished as the chapter 9 of *The Souls of Black Folk: Essays and Sketches* (Du Bois 1903f). From its position in that collection of essays, as a primary textual scene therein for a direct lexical address of the question of the terms of relation of groups of people in the United States according to "the problem of the color line," the central thought of this essay came to supply—through extended verbatim quotation by Du Bois—the principal argument for the closing and longest section of the essay that he would send to Weber in March 1905. That is to say, the text that would be published under the translated title "Die Negerfrage in den Vereinigten Staaten" in 1906, the last and longest of the three sections of the German-language essay reproduced almost verbatim across its elaboration the central paragraphs of the 1901 "Relations" essay as they appear in chapter 9 of *The Souls of Black Folk: Essays and Sketches*. The verbatim quotation forms the first half of the third section of "Die Negerfrage," while the second half of the section was taken from the text of the 1904 speech "Caste in America" (Du Bois 1980b, 1982c). However, the opening two paragraphs of *the chapter* version of the essay were *not* excerpted or reproduced in the text sent to Weber. (And since the opening paragraph of *the original essay* was set aside by Du Bois in its republication as a *chapter*, the two paragraphs in question are the second and third paragraphs in the original essay.) Yet it is these two paragraphs as they open the chapter version of the essay in *The Souls of Black Folk: Essays and Sketches* that declare in proper rhetorical register—as a heading for thought and action—the terms of the question as understood by Du Bois at the turn of the twentieth century. Their pertinence to an elucidation of the epistemic terrain of the conversation between Du Bois and Weber demands that they be quoted in full. They formulate the question in all of its relevant dimensions: of history, politics and economics, morals, and science:

> The world-old phenomenon of the contact of diverse races of men is to have new exemplification during the new century. Indeed, the characteristic of our age is the contact of European civilization with the world's undeveloped peoples. Whatever we may say of the results of such contact in the past, it certainly forms a chapter in human action not pleasant to look back upon. War, murder, slavery, extermination, and debauchery,—this has again and again been the result of carrying civilization and the blessed gospel to the isles of the sea and the heathen without the law. Nor does it altogether satisfy the conscience of the modern world to be told complacently that all this has been right and proper, the fated triumph of strength over weakness, of righteousness over evil, of superiors over inferiors. It would certainly be soothing if one could readily believe all this; and yet there are too many ugly facts for everything to be thus easily explained away. We feel and know that there are many delicate differences in race psychology, numberless changes that our crude social measurements are not yet able to follow minutely, which explain

much of history and social development. At the same time, too, we know that these considerations have never adequately explained or excused the triumph of brute force and cunning over weakness and innocence.

It is, then, the strife of all honorable men of the twentieth century to see that in the future competition of races the survival of the fittest shall mean the triumph of the good, the beautiful, and the true; that we may be able to preserve for future civilization all that is really fine and noble and strong, and not continue to put a premium on greed and impudence and cruelty. To bring this hope to fruition, we are compelled daily to turn more and more to a conscientious study of the phenomena of race-contact,—frank and fair, and not falsified and colored by our wishes or our fears. And we have in the South as fine a field for such a study as the world affords,—a field, to be sure, which the average American scientist deems somewhat beneath his dignity, and which the average man who is not a scientist knows all about, but nevertheless a line of study which by reason of the enormous race complications with which God seems about to punish this nation must increasingly claim our sober attention, study, and thought, we must ask, what are the actual relations of whites and blacks in the South? and we must be answered, not by apology or faultfinding, but by a plain, unvarnished tale. (Du Bois 1901e, 121–22; 1903d, 163–64; 2015f, 189–90)

The frame is historical and comparative in a fundamentally global sense. The modern past, in the perspective that Du Bois proposed here, has so far been a form of destruction and limitation of possibility (even of the possibility built on the terms of exploitation). And this limit shows in two general forms: in moral development (it can sustain no justification) and in the production of genius or ingenuity (it is a historically untenable restriction to the few, with no basis in the truth—in particular, the truth of science). For Du Bois, this is a question about the whole of the possibility of the modern world, its present and its future. What will be the future relation between human relation and possibility? He speaks about hope in this passage. The problem of realizing this hope poses a form of responsibility. And the first action in response is a form of study—of inquiry, critical discussion, and judgment.

It is just such a frame that provides the line of connection to the inquiry posed in Weber's question. The whole thought of the essay from which these two paragraphs are taken will be placed by Du Bois as the guiding question of the third and final section of "Die Negerfrage." It can then be proposed that, from such a positioning, it in fact guides the construal of the later essay as a whole. While we cannot know whether Weber ever read any of the earlier texts by Du Bois mentioned earlier, and thus we cannot know whether he responded to any specific textual elaboration of Du Bois's thought of "the problem of the color line" other than *The Souls of Black Folk: Essays and Sketches*, it is certainly not implausible to think through the implications of the hypothesis of a certain interlocution of Weber with Du Bois within the general horizon of the problematic named therein.

B. MAX WEBER AND THE FORMS OF SEDIMENTATION OF "THE PROBLEM OF THE COLOR LINE"

It can be said, then, that Weber's November 1904 inquiry of Du Bois takes shape on the epistemological terrain named here. Yet to what extent, and in what sense, is this terrain inhabited by them as a question in common? Whence this question for Weber? What is the depth organization of the epistemic ground in question? What, in fact, are the lines of intersection, if any? What is the depth character of this proposed interlocution? What are the possible terms of exchange?

1. Historicity and Problematization: On an Example of the Formation of a Question for Thought

Even in our contemporary moment, it is not so well understood in general discourse that Weber had his own form of the "problem of the color line." The question of "the relations between the (so called) 'race-problem' and the (so called) 'class-problem'" announced itself as a constitutive epistemic horizon in the itinerary of Weber almost from the inception of his intellectual practice in the late 1880s. During the early years of the 1890s, from 1892 to 1895, it acquired a definitive shape and organization internal to his discourse.

What was its character? How can it be understood? What concepts and theoretical perspectives are necessary for a critical engagement with its terms? What are its implications for how we understand the possibility of this interlocution?

In brief, leaving the elaboration to follow as its substance, it can be stated here that the announced character of Weber's "problem of the color line" took the form of the so-called Polish question in late nineteenth-century Germany. This question, in turn and in layers, was sedimented on the bias across the so-called eastern question in general in Prussia, which in its turn formed a definitive layer in the general "labor question," not only in the German Reich but in Europe as a whole. In its latter articulation, the question stood at the heart of the general *Soziale Frage* (social question) of the second half of the nineteenth century in Germany, into which, interlaced on additional strata, the so-called Jewish question was also interwoven.

The matter of the "problem of the color line" as it came to Weber can be conceptualized as a part of a generalized questioning of the commonness of the social.

Analytically, we can elaborate the matter as twofold. Yet each dimension is articulated in the other. In this historicity, forms of hierarchy and forms of horizontal concatenation are everywhere an instance of the other. In this sense, they are always relative to each other. A theoretical perspective that might allow us to approach this matter must maintain this unstable yet persistently heterogeneous and always previous relative concatenation of the terms of historicity.

And then, by way of such an approach to Weber's problematic, *we* might then be able to think the thought and itinerary of Du Bois and Weber, respectively, according to the same movement of a problematization that constitutes the epistemic horizon of our situation—both our past and our historical present.

On one level, "the problem" in question was the historical articulation and devolution of new forms of hierarchy by way of and in terms of old forms. The whole historical problematic that specifically concerns us here had been unfolding for some half a millennium, involving the major differentiated but overlapping groups of German, Polish, and Jewish *Prussians* (Hagen 1980, 2002). It entailed the promulgation, perpetuation, or reconstitution of feudal forms of exploitation and political domination (both of which were interlaced with the question of religious forms of domination) across these centuries, in which the principal economic distinction articulated the difference between those who could sustain a superior claim to land and those whose claim would become derivative or subordinate thereof, primarily as laborers in support of the former. The Polish nobility, which was the most powerful class for centuries in this devolution on the territory that I call historical Poland, might well be described as moribund even at its height. A decisive rearticulation of these forms unfolded by way of the partition of historical Poland during the last half of the eighteenth century by Prussia, Russia, and Austria, inducing a fundamental destructuring of the relatively traditional indigenous forms of sovereignty. Across the contrapuntal contestations of the nineteenth century, the beginning of the dismantling of seigneurial authority in Prussia in general, and of Prussian Poland in particular, that followed in the wake of the Prussian defeat by Napoleon at Jena in 1807; the compromised devolution of the revolutions of 1848–49; and the unification of the German states in 1871 by Otto von Bismarck, a new form of the question of the relation of the differences among groups—economic and political and now, too, the so-called cultural (or racial)—to any supposed common project of nation, or even a transnational class, was set afoot. Old relations were set at a disjoint but not completely disarticulated. The problem of the status of *a* putative nation as state took on a new and definitive shape as the imperial process of its composition—its possibility as such—confounded the supposedly supreme form of sovereign interest that would announce its historical form. That is, the proposition of such interest always announced therein—even if in an illegible form or in a form that was not strictly decipherable—the strife that was its very condition of possibility. This historical devolution can thus be understood to have rendered the question of who counts as a Prussian, or a German, or a citizen, for example, as susceptible to new forms of problematization—which remain ongoing in our time—in a manner that was much more fundamental than the apparent (and long-sought) forms of resolution.

On another level, the general problematization was the concomitant articulation of these forms with structural transformations in the organization of the world economy as this "color-line problem" (to recall here Weber's phrasing) devolved on the terms of a regional- and state-level situation.

In this case, the region straddled the eastern border of German Prussia and Prussian Poland and entailed both Russian and Austrian Poland (Hagen 1980, 2002). However, before naming a bit further the specific historical domain at hand in Weber's problematization, it might be apposite to offer a note pertaining to a line of possible comparison as a kind of foil that would begin to suggest the possibility of a whole other theoretical approach to this epistemic horizon.

The fundamental rethinking of the history of Atlantic slavery, especially the development of a comparative problematic, that has taken discursive shape over the past three generations posed the question of the relation between the large, landed estates of Prussia and those of the American South. This question itself has antecedents in two early twentieth-century discourses that were almost directly theoretically opposed: that of Vladimir Lenin and that of Weber. (They spoke, respectively, from opposite sides of the agricultural hinterland of Russia, historical Poland, and German Prussia.) In 1897 and again in 1907, Lenin essayed the thesis of the difference of the Prussian and the American way to a form of capitalist agriculture (Lenin 1962; 1974, 32–33). It is not well remarked that in his Congress of Arts and Sciences lecture in 1904, Weber specifically elaborates a comparative interpretation of the same historical problematic, also posing a distinction between a new land such as America or the United States and "an old civilized" one such as the Prussian state and the German Reich understood in its image (Weber 1906, 1998). However, in both of their conceptions of the American situation, the *legacy* of slavery is not conceptualized as of the essence of the post–Civil War era. It is on exactly this track that Du Bois makes a contribution from the outset of his work, a moment that would be *contemporary with the work of both Lenin and Weber*. Two examples can perhaps assist in clarifying Du Bois's theoretical projection. In an essay only recently published, "The Afro-American," dating most likely from the months following his return from study in Germany (the late autumn of 1894 or early 1895), whose signal importance has yet to be recognized in the criticism of his work, Du Bois specifically links the postemancipation situation in the United States to that of both Russia and imperial Prussia. Naming three schools of thought in the American context on what should be done with the Negro as freedman, the dominant one in his interpretation, which he called "Ricardian," proposed a laissez-faire or "free" competition idea. Du Bois goes on to criticize this approach and makes an explicit comparative reference to the respective topoi at stake in the work of Lenin and Weber. "Russia, to whom America has often thought fit to read lectures on national morality," Du Bois writes, "gave the emancipated *serfs* a part of the land on which they and their fathers had toiled: not an inch was given America's freedmen; the builders of the monarchic Prussian state took care that the ignorant German *bauer* was in a condition to compete before he was left to 'free competition': the democratic American state did not give its freedmen so much as a spade" (Du Bois 1894[circa]a, 1980f, reel 82, 1232–42; 2010; 2015a, emphases added). The pertinence of this formulation for our critical recognition of Du Bois's theoretical perspicacity holds here regardless of one's historiographical judgment of his account from some perspective other than his own. To give brief reference to another example, it is the precise burden of chapters 7 and 8, on the "Black Belt," in *The*

Souls of Black Folk: Essays and Sketches to establish the historical character of this legacy as simultaneously immediate and of long-standing duration, across centuries (Du Bois 1903b, 1903c). Barbara Jeanne Fields, whose signal essay "The Advent of Capitalist Agriculture: The New South in a Bourgeois World" (1985, 80) was issued three generations ago in the course of the debate on the comparative horizon of slavery in North America, is the only scholar, it seems to me, who has recognized the fundamental conceptual pertinence of Du Bois's contribution here. It can be shown that this thought is elaborated virtually everywhere in Du Bois's writings of the turn of the twentieth century. Later, Du Bois's historiographical magnum opus, the astonishing essay *Black Reconstruction* (1935; see also Du Bois 1976), offered a fundamental intervention on this terrain.[17]

As the specific domain or site in question in the case of Weber's problematic—the East Elbian region of German Prussia—was historically agricultural, the matter at issue was a transformation in the organization of the relations of the landowners (proprietors of large estates) and the laborers who worked on this land. The landholding class, especially the Prussian Junkers of the late eighteenth century, had operated there as essentially seigneurial lords. The old, persisting feudal or semifeudal relations between landholder and peasant or laborer passed through a contrapuntal and contradictory process in the relief of seigneurial authority for some two centuries or more up to the mid-nineteenth century. While the right of lordship was dismantled in part, the landlord class was nonetheless successful in the enclosure of much land that had previously been in the hands of the peasant and laborer. For a time, a kind of "second serfdom" was maintained. Yet by the last quarter of the nineteenth century, the estate form of social and economic organization in Prussia was undergoing legal and practical dissolution as the changes in the general forms of economic organization at the national and international levels induced a regional transformation. Thus, the old forms of estate organization, usually summarized under the heading of patriarchalism, which historically had been oriented toward an economy of domestic self-sufficiency rather than production for the market, had become unsustainable. In the same historical instance, as the extra-economic mechanisms (especially a kind of police order) that had restricted the movement of workers were loosened (in particular by way of a series of laws in Prussia at the time of the new German Reich in 1870 that degraded the previous forms of sanction by which the breaking of contracts by workers had been criminalized), laborers began to emigrate in large numbers—some seasonally; some semipermanently or permanently—to the west and south of Germany and overseas, especially to the Americas (north and south). This process tended to produce an increasingly acute seasonal shortage of labor on the large eastern estates. In response, throughout the nineteenth century but especially in the 1870s and 1880s, the estate owners began to recruit labor, primarily migrant workers from farther east, from both Prussian Poland and Russian Poland, as well as from parts of Austria, on a seasonal basis. The cascading ensemble of effects had taken shape both as a deep historical—irreversible—transformation in the general internal form of agricultural organization in the region and as a rearticulation of the position of this regional system of agriculture within both the state- and global-level processes of capitalist industrialization.

2. Problematic and Institution: On the Passage from Question to Knowledge

In the late nineteenth century, academic and policy concern with the effects of these transformations were manifest at a number of levels in Germany. One of these articulations was the growth of various organizations, dominated by a middle- and upper-class intelligentsia, that sought to intervene by way of study and advice in the promulgation of reformist policy at the level of the state on a regional and national basis (Rueschemeyer and Van Rossem 1996). Later, such groups would be more or less supplanted by the development of special interest lobbies (Krüger 1987, 71–72). One of the most important examples of such a group was indeed the Verein für Sozialpolitik, founded at Eisenach in October 1872, after a preliminary meeting in July of that year, by Gustav Schmoller, Georg Friedrich Kapp, and Lujo Brentano (Hagemann 2001, cf. 152–55; Lindenlaub 1967).[18] The moment of its formation coincides with the founding reorganization of the German-speaking states into the new Reich by Bismarck. Although ambivalent in its attempts at direct intervention, the association's dominant political commitment was reformist policy that would support this new state-level entity.

A different institutional response from that of this liberal reformist group was the foundation in 1863 of the Sozialdemokratische Partei Deutschlands (German Social Democratic Party [SPD]), which has its own complicated and widely known history (Fairbairn 1997; Lidtke 1966). Of fundamental importance with regard to the terms of his interlocution with Weber is the fact that Du Bois commented on this political topography in two texts from the mid-1890s that remained in manuscript form during his lifetime but were recently published (see Du Bois 1998a, 1998b).[19] One of those texts specifically proposed a historicization of both Germany of the 1890s in general and the project of the Verein in particular, mentioning both Schmoller and Adolph Wagner (who was also a key figure in the Verein) by name as "Socialists of the Chair" or "Katheder Socialists" (Du Bois's phrasing). The other text places the question of modern German history and the history of the United States in a comparison. Given the depth of direct pertinence and complexity of the *Soziale Frage* and the question of "socialism" in general (including here the proposal of a kind of communism) in late nineteenth-century imperial Germany, and the scholastic obscurity concerning Du Bois's engagement with it that only now is being diminished, I leave this dimension of the problem to be addressed in another context.

This project as a practice of knowledge production came to be known within the academic discourse, both then and now, as the German historical school of political economy (Grimmer-Solem 2003; Herbst 1965; Koslowski 1997; Shionoya 2001), even as it should be remarked that its status as a "school" of thought should remain an open question (Grimmer-Solem and Romani 1998). Yet such nominalization would name it in the German context as distinct from both the discourse and projects of laissez-faire economics, often situated by way of a reference to the Manchester School, which the "historical school" displaced as the dominant discourse in German policy circles over the course of the second half of the nineteenth century, and the discourses of socialist thought, above all in the form of Marx and his followers, whose projection on the Russian historical terrain, for example, already from the turn of the twentieth century became of deep and abiding concern. In an epistemic sense, the group proposed variations on a historicism that understood a liberal path of inclusiveness—economic and political—as its interpretive premise.[20]

The Verein as a political projection of this production is especially pertinent in our instance, for its whole project came to play a key part in the intellectual formation of both Weber and Du Bois. This private association of scholars and policy makers might well be understood then as a key scene for the formative epistemic habitation of the two scholars that occupy our main attention here. Several figures were of import. Schmoller was perhaps the key persona in the early history of the association, often defining the terms of its discussions during its first two decades and holding its presidency from 1890 until his death in 1917 (Hagemann

2001; Krüger 1987; Peukert 2001). At the University of Berlin, he directed the "Nationalökonomie" seminar with Wagner. These scholars were principal teachers for both Weber and Du Bois. Along with several other figures who were part of the intellectual scene at Berlin, including Alfred Meitzen, an older figure, and Max Sering, a younger one, they were quite active in the Verein. Not only was there no radical divide between the academic and policy halls in this specific context, but the question of policy was a fundamental reference in the organization of scientific investigation. The Verein was a key institutional form, serving as a conduit, joining these two arenas of specialized practice. Weber prepared his dissertation on the history of medieval business organizations, which was presented formally in August 1889, as an associate of the seminar on state policy and statistics; his *Habilitationsschrift* in Roman commercial law was also prepared in this context (Riesebrodt 1989, 143–45). His next major intellectual project, a study of agricultural labor in the eastern provinces of the Reich, was rendered possible through his principal mentors at Berlin, who were not only members of the Verein but, arguably, its most important leaders. Likewise, barely four years later Du Bois entered the same pedagogical scene at the University of Berlin. After a semester there, he wrote in his quarterly report to the Slater Fund, his sponsor, that "most of my time was spent in the seminary of Economics under Professor Gustav Schmoller." In addition, he recorded that he had "attended two sets of lectures by Professor [Adolph] Wagner," and that this professor had "expressed himself as interested in my work." Wagner would indeed subsequently admit Du Bois "to membership in his seminary [for] the next semester." Working in the "Nationalökonomie" seminar with these two professors over the course of some fifteen months, from October 1892 until December 1893, he would indeed complete a study that could have served as an inaugural doctoral thesis in the German university system of the time, making a presentation of his work in early December 1893. According to Du Bois's report to the Slater Fund dated 29 March 1894, the study was eventually titled "Die landwirtschaftliche Entwickelung in den Südstaaten der Vereinigten Staaten" (Du Bois 1973c, 27).[21] In this context, it should be noted that Du Bois would open the first section of "Die Negerfrage" with a summary of the statistics on the changing size of farm holdings among African Americans from the Civil War to the turn of the century. This question regarding the scale of agriculture was in fact an ongoing, if not perennial, question in the seminar at Berlin, within the association, and throughout Germany during the last quarter of the nineteenth century.

As previously indicated, the March 1893 meeting of the Verein took place in Berlin. While Schmoller gave the opening address as president (Verein für Socialpolitik. 1893, 1; see also Tribe 1989, 98, 126), it appears in retrospect that Weber presented the key lecture in outlining an interpretation of his part of the association's project on the agricultural labor question in Germany, which was focused on the eastern provinces (Weber 1993c). Weber's report, the main part of which had been prepared in 1892, was his third major research project and marked a turning point in the formulation of his interpretation of Germany's situation in its historical present. That is to say that, for Weber in 1893, the present was understood as a time of fundamental transformation in German agriculture and society in general, a change that was being wrought by the accelerating growth of capitalism (Weber 1984b).

Around the same time, in his quarterly report to the Slater Fund dated 10 March 1893, Du Bois indicated that he had recently joined the Verein (Du Bois 1973c, 23). Thus, although we do not now have at hand any documentation that can confirm that he was present at the sessions, it is not unreasonable to suppose that Du Bois, as a member of the "Nationalökonomie" seminar at Berlin and as a new member of the Verein, hoped to attend this meeting. This accords with the tenor of his report to the Slater Fund. Yet beyond this factual uncertainty, which remains after consultation with the archive, what is more decisive is a general epistemic dimension in which Du Bois could find a certain common intellectual habitation with the scene of the seminar and the project of the Verein.

Beyond these contemporaneous references, Du Bois himself gives us a legible passage to this epistemic horizon in *Dusk of Dawn*: "I wrote on American agriculture for Schmoller and discussed social conditions in Europe with teachers and students. Under these teachers and in this social setting, I began to see the race problem in America, the problems of the peoples of Africa and Asia, and the political development of Europe as one" (Du Bois 1975b, 47).[22]

The commonness that Du Bois adduces is a historical dimension in which a fundamental transformation in the organization and status of labor had taken shape as a matter of state policy and thereby was announced within science and politics as a problem for thought. For both the seminar and the Verein, the implications of the changing character of labor that was afoot during the last quarter of the nineteenth century for Germany (in German domains and forms of the polity as a whole) could be understood as the pivotal problematic. Likewise, for Du Bois, perhaps in part through the pedagogical dialogue of these scenes, the question of the status of the relation of the laborer to land in the African American situation in the context of the United States would come to announce itself at this early stage in his itinerary. It should be recalled, however, that Du Bois had already begun his research in economic history at Harvard in the seminar of Albert Bushnell Hart and had focused on a problem that should be understood as a dimension of the history of labor relations—namely, the legal and political processes of "suppressing" the slave trade to the United States. He would, of course, complete this study as his dissertation in 1895 when he returned to the United States (Du Bois 1973d). The formulation of this general question in Du Bois's locution would always sustain a comparative reference. In the course of its eventual construal over the 1890s, beyond the apparent titular question of the policy of the national state, this question of labor took shape in his discourse as the most decisive issue that emerged in the aftermath of the Civil War and the failure of Reconstruction. This historical dimension as an epistemological horizon remains to be fully thought with regard to *both* Du Bois and Weber and rendered more tractable in the critical reengagement of the so-called German historical school in general. And such, an inquiry, if it proposes a cut on the bias and across the vertical grain of its layers of sedimentation, should render legible in the depth of their respective particularity that each situation—that of Du Bois and of Weber—can be carefully understood only by way of a certain reference to the other *beyond the given or so far conventional theorizations of the forms of epistemic horizon.*

Across its internally heterogeneous positions, the Verein, in general and as a group, engaged the transformations in the organization of German society as a problem of the risk that the excesses of capitalism posed for the social order as a whole. Such excesses were marked especially in the intensified exploitation of laborers who were increasingly rendered proletarian—that is, without any rights to land, rural as well as urban. Within that general concern, the problem was yet formulated as a question of the stability of labor relations. This concern was not on the terms of the interests of labor as such. More simply, the concern of the Verein was the appropriate policy for the maintenance of labor as a stable factor in the enterprise of the owners of industry and agriculture. The self-initiative of ostensibly "free labor," including the formation of labor unions, was understood across the spectrum of different opinions within the association as a risk to the organization of both the economy and the state. Thus, the question was understood within the Verein as a matter of the best policy by which such risk could be limited. Study of the organization and conditions of labor was a necessary step in the development of an approach.

On two occasions during the 1880s, in 1883 and 1887, the Verein attempted studies of labor. However, both were understood even within the association as profoundly limited on methodological and technical grounds (Tribe 1989, 98). While there were certainly multiple factors that motivated the attempts that these studies represented, the status of agricultural labor in the eastern provinces, and especially the increasing importation-immigration of workers from both Prussian and Russian Poland onto the large estates of the Junkers, was a defining one. In 1885–86, this immigration was stopped, and some thirty thousand or more Polish-speaking workers and their families were forcibly deported, some 30 percent of whom may well have been Jewish (Blanke 1981, 43–47, 55–91; Hagen 1980, 2012, 2018). In 1890, after pressure as exerted by the estate owners, a compromise was reached that provided an initial three-year trial policy to allow the resumption of such immigration, limited to unmarried workers from Russian Poland and Galicia (i.e., Austrian Poland) into the eastern parts of German Prussia between April and November of each year (Herbert 1990b, 19). This new policy no doubt played a major role in the decision by the Verein's leadership to undertake a new study, an idea formally suggested by Max Sering, an agriculturist economist and intellectual friend of Weber's who was already concerned with such questions in the region, including its situation in relation to a new international context, especially the role of US agriculture in this situation. (Indeed, Sering had written a book on American agriculture as a competitor in a global market for cereals [see Barkin 1970, cf. 147, 174, 179; Tribe 1989, 98). Conducted in the form of a survey of some 2,600 landowners on the "local conditions" pertaining to labor, it was thereby compromised both in terms of its point of view and its imprecise focus. Yet its sheer volume provided some possibility to cross-check its direct statistical contributions. Thus, despite its profound limitations, the study remains an empirical landmark in the German discourse on the conditions of agricultural organization (Tribe 1989, 99).

3. Sovereignty and Historicization: On the Theoretical Example

As a rising young member of the Verein and the political and social circles attendant to it, Weber was chosen as an interpreter of that part of this general study that had the highest profile, the part that focused on the status of such relations in the eastern provinces of the Reich: East and West Prussia, Pomerania, Posen, Mecklenburg, Brandenburg, Silesia, and Lauenberg (Weber 1984b, 61, 109–829). All were east of the Elbe river. (In Anglophone historiography, the region is usually referred to as East Elbia.) Not only is this the historical domain of the giant estates of the Junkers, but it was the high-status scene of the Prussian military tradition and the defining source of the modus operandi of much of the Prussian state civil service.

While the titular question for the Verein as a whole had been the status and condition of labor relations, Weber reformulated the question such that the epistemic heading was a question of "state interest." As he would come to formulate it across his writings from 1892 through 1897, the eastern question for Weber was primarily the historically privileged scene of a question about the German state: its possibility, its essence, and its historical position within Europe and in the new international scene. For Weber, the apparent question of the situation of labor in eastern Germany was, in fact, a question about the relation of the two key historical classes in play there—the large estate owners and the laboring groups therein—to the future of the German state that had taken shape by way of the Bismarck-led and Prussian-defined unification. On the one hand, Weber saw the Junker landowner class as historically moribund and generally reactionary in terms of the present and future interest of the German Reich, despite the Junkers' defining role in the Prussian state, supplying much of its civil corps and its military leadership (especially since the late eighteenth century) and its bequest of the same to the new German Reich after 1871. To the extent that the world economy generated a new playing field—as given, for example, in the availability of grain on the international market (especially wheat from the United States) that was cheaper than the cereal coming from German wheat and rye production in the eastern provinces—the simultaneous call for protectionism by the Junkers to shield their costly products and their demand for the right to import cheap seasonal labor from historical Poland and Russia, despite the impact of that practice on the structure of the region's overall political, social, and economic order, represented a national-level cost that simply favored their regional and class-based attempts to maintain a specific historical form of economic and political privilege. Yet not only was such a form of privilege doomed historically in Weber's terms; it also contradicted the German state's "national" interest (Weber 1984b, 68–108, 889). Thus, a question was announced in the Verein with a particular organization of titular and secondary epistemological headings—respectively, first, the status of labor in the midst of the brutal processes of Germany's rapid capitalist transformation during the nineteenth century; and second, the proper state policy to ameliorate it. Weber redeployed this question with another one—the interest of the state in formulating a policy that would secure its future—making this the lead question and the conditions and organization of the relations of the different classes secondary.

At this juncture, while recalling the outline of Du Bois's rural studies given at the end of part I, the relation of the disposition of Du Bois and Weber on "the labor question" can be usefully remarked on two fundamental axes: their respective thoughts about the dominant classes and the laboring class. On the one hand, there is a parallel to Weber's criticism of the Junkers in Du Bois's assessment of the antebellum planter class in the American South as historically moribund, a circumstance that, paradoxically, was shown in even greater relief in the decades after Reconstruction. This thesis was already present in the Du Bois's essay "The Negro as He Really Is" (1901b), which became chapters 7 and 8 of *The Souls of Black Folk: Essays and Sketches* two years later (Du Bois 1903b, 1903c). It was then elaborated across all of Du Bois's writing on the nineteenth-century American South, perhaps most fully in his study of Reconstruction in the 1930s (Du Bois 1935, chap. 3; 1976, chap. 3). On the other hand, though, from the inception of his itinerary through to World War I, the question for Du Bois of the status and condition of the laboring class—not only that of the Negro American freedman in North America, even though this was a necessary first reference, but also that of the colonial laborer, in particular throughout the African Diaspora and on the continent of Africa—was formulated as the guide to a deep understanding of modern historicity not only in the United States and in Europe but throughout the world (Du Bois 1900b, 2015e). It can be said, then, that a given interest, even if understood under the heading of reasons of state—for example, that of the United States—could not preempt the status of the historical truth that might be exposed in the elaboration of such a question.[23] A pivotal aspect of this theorization was a conception of a problematic that, by the time of World War I, Du Bois had attempted to both specify and generalize on a worldwide scale of reference as "the problem of the color line" (Du Bois 1909, chap. 13; 1915; 1973c, 254–73).[24]

In terms of Weber, this dimension of his work is certainly well known among scholars. His work on the so-called eastern question from 1892 to 1897 has long been prominently treated in the English- and

German-speaking contexts, dating at least from the second chapter of Reinhard Bendix's pioneering intellectual biography and in the course of Wolfgang Mommsen's study of politics in Weber's intellectual itinerary, both of which were issued more than sixty-five years ago (Bendix 1960, 13–48; Mommsen 1984, 36, 53).[25] And from more than four decades ago, and across a dozen years of debate, the Weber scholarship sought to come to terms with its epistemological position within an understanding of Weber's work as a whole (Käsler 1988; Mommsen 1984, 43; Riesebrodt 1989; Tribe 1989).[26]

However, in precise terms, that aspect of Weber's early work that in his own itinerary might be understood to have given dimension to the question that he posed to Du Bois remains in the shadows or muted in this scholarship. It is usually discussed in a rather presumptive fashion or, that is to say, it is named by way of an always already effective pre-comprehension of the question, if obscurely recognized at all. According to this scholarship, the question as we might translate it here, following the terms of Weber's question to Du Bois, of "the relations between the (so called) 'race-problem' and the (so called) 'class-problem,'" had virtually no standing in the dominant critical inhabitations of Weber's discourse two decades ago and remains profoundly obscure for such scholarship.[27]

Yet such a question may well be shown to have taken shape as the nodal articulation of a constitutive dimension of Weber's thought.

The question, especially as it would later be articulated and put at stake in the interlocution with Du Bois, can be summarized this way: What analytic status within a scientific discourse should be attributed to the ostensibly manifest differences articulating among the social groups configured in a situation or horizon that otherwise might be understood as common? Or, translated further, what is the status of the historical differences among groups in their relation to one another within a defined national-or state-level context? And we will allow further translations as we proceed to formulate a conclusion of our inquiry into the sedimented terms of this interlocution. Weber, that is, wondered out loud at the turn of the century whether there might be some determinate relation between the production of a hierarchical order that yields so-called classes and the elaboration of the differences that one might call national, cultural, or "racial." This is a question that remains operative within contemporary thought even at the end of the opening quarter of the twenty-first century. Yet the question issues from an order of presumption that is seldom explicitly acknowledged or engaged. That Weber placed it in circulation, despite our critical disposition toward his inhabitation of it, stands in our service in a project for the de-sedimentation of the problem for thought that we can still usefully approach by way of the concept-metaphor of "the problem of the color line."

Let us attempt a critical de-sedimentation of the problematization (at once social and historical and epistemological) encrusted for the dominant forms of scholarship in place here. We do so even if only provisionally, engaging some dimensions of the organization of this problematic for Weber. I make brief reference to three early texts—*Die Lage der Landarbeiter im ostelbischen Deutschland,* his first formal engagement with the so-called eastern question in the form of his written report to the Verein für Sozialpolitik completed in 1892 (Weber 1984b); "Die ländliche Arbeitsverfassung," his lecture in Berlin at the March 1893 meeting of the Verein delivering an interpretation and account of the results of the 1890–92 labor inquiry, with sustained and primary reference to the East Elbian scene (Weber 1893; 1993c); and "Entwickelungstendenzen in der Lage der ostelbischen Landarbeiter" ("Developmental Tendencies in the Situation of East Elbian Rural Labourers"), a key thematic elaboration that followed in 1894 (Weber 1989a; 1993a)—from among his many subsequent serial elaborations of an interpretation of this problematic in 1893 and 1894. This restricted focus is maintained here despite the fact that this whole movement of Weber's thinking calls for a reengagement with his work in the contemporary moment along the track that I am outlining.[28]

Weber's 1892 interpretation of the Verein's survey results from East Elbia proceeds from a fundamentally historical premise (Weber 1984b, 68, 86–89). Rather than directly pose the question of policy or give an account of policy, Weber's approach, as in his *Habilitationsschrift* of the previous year (Weber 1986, 2003; see also Kaelber 2003), took as its task an attempt to show the emergence of a form of problem as such (see also the 1896 essay on the agrarian problematic as a decisive scene for tracking the decline of imperial Rome [Weber 1988]). Yet the disposition of the young Weber is also toward the inductive nominalization of a "tendency." The relation of such a process to the idea of scientific law was distinguished in his theoretical construal from that of a tendency to the extent that a tendency remained articulated by factors that could announce a local influence that would be stronger in its effect at the level of the instance in relation to the processes named tendentially.[29] Tendency would certainly announce a general process but would remain at issue in the instance.

For Weber, the historical present of agricultural organization in Germany in the early 1890s showed the general form of a structural economic and political-legal change from a patriarchal organization of production, with limited reference to the market, to a capitalist organization of agriculture. This entailed the proletarianization of the estate worker, who in some areas historically had been able to sustain some hereditary rights to land and even to production from the estate in general, but who were in this transformation eventually being dispossessed of any such claims.[30] Weber's conceptualization of the different strata of estate laborers and the historical form of their constitution remains exemplary even in our time. Whereas in the estate order that existed prior to the advent of a capitalist problematic the laborer might receive some provisions and a share of the harvest, under the changing organization of labor relations (*Arbeitsverfassung*) over the course of the previous century, such claims had been progressively withdrawn. There had thus been a gradual erosion of this "community of interest" (*Gemeinschaft*) (Weber 1984b, 68–108; see also Käsler 1988, 55).

Here there is a direct parallel with the work of Du Bois, for in "Die Negerfrage," as well as in his other work in rural sociology, he would produce a detailed account, with nuance, of the strata of Negro agricultural workers in the post-Reconstruction South and describe an absolute absence of common material "interest" in the outcome of the production process. Likewise, Du Bois's attention here remains exemplary, especially in his sense of a comparative horizon for the social organization that he was observing. A key difference between the two, and one that remains to be explored elsewhere, is that Du Bois undertook the empirical work directly, in the field with his various assistants, whereas the conceptualization of the survey and its results were delivered to Weber. Another key difference is that Du Bois did not make a fundamental distinction of kind between himself and the principal group that he made the object of his study, while Weber understood himself as of a fundamentally different root or horizon from the group of East Elbian laborers whom he understood to pose the deepest historical question of the situation that he was studying.

The thematic that can be shown to guide Weber's interpretation across the sprawling pages of this large-boned study, constructed of voluminous statistics and multiple texts, is the problem of the premises for an approach that could recognize *both* the historical determination of the social "interest" of the different groups, respectively, and the capacity for that interest to be transformed so as to reinstitute a historically previous, supposed form of common interest. While the acutely wrought methodological reflection of Weber's text justifies patient engagement, such a consideration must be developed elsewhere. Yet across the premise of an essential asymmetry of social interest and a telic structure of its determination, he adduces another order of interest, a certain sense of the historicity of the present, and deploys it as the basis for his formulation of the place of "the eastern question" in a comparative global historical future. In this latter order of interest, or historical sense, as it is announced in the study, a theoretical disposition that would in its epistemic possibility stand beyond the limits of the different social groups in relation is joined to the authority of a political and legal project that, according to Weber, must always supersede the interests of any given class. While withholding for the moment any statement on the epistemic premises operative in his stated theoretical disposition, it can be quite directly understood at this juncture that the political project is the production of the coincidence of an idea of the German nation (sometimes called a race or a culture across these early texts) with the German Reich in the form of the Second Reich, the German Empire. It is the premise of the possibility of recognizing and affirming this order of historical "interest" that leads Weber to his most decisive statement with regard to our own order of attention here:

> The dynasty of Prussian kings is not destined to rule over Slavic nomads [*slawisches Wandervolk*] along with Polish sharecroppers [*polnischen Parzellenbauern*] and depopulated latifundia, as will eventuate if the current development in the East is neglected any longer; but instead [to rule] over German peasants alongside a stratum of large landowners whose workers bear in themselves the consciousness that they can find their future in their own homeland through ascending to an independent existence. (Weber 1984b, 928–29 [804 in the original text])[31]

The premise of a "homeland" of the "future" stands, then, as an epistemic-political horizon in terms of which the tendencies of the historical past and present can be interpreted and given their proper meaning.

The theme of interest is rendered more directly still in "Die ländliche Arbeitsverfassung," Weber's lecture to the Verein in March 1893, as the name of the problem that must be addressed by *policy*—both economic and political—in the eastern region.[32] Despite the fact that a proletarian status might not show as an objectively better economic position, according to Weber, the *sense of freedom* that followed the release from legal patriarchal or seigneurial authority was so great that laborers from the east were led to migrate in hopes of realizing a better life. For Weber, such fragmentation of interests could not have "produced the political organization and the formation of political spirit which have created the unity of the *Reich*" (Weber 1893, 65–66; 1993c, 169). Yet Weber assessed not only that the old estate organization under the Prussian Junker class was in terminal decay, by way of the ongoing and irreversible shift to a capitalist organization of agriculture, but also that in its death throes, its actions to stave off its finality were contrary to the proper new order of interest: the young German Reich. For Weber, the prime example of this ongoing dissolution of a certain historical *Gemeinschaft*—and he had no strictly romantic sense of the old order but, instead, an idea of the depth of a material community of interests—was the importation of seasonal workers from the German, Russian, and Austrian Polish territories (a practice that had been disallowed in 1885–86 but was reinstated on a provisional three-year basis in 1890; hence, it was very much at issue in the policy-making halls of Berlin in the spring of 1893 [Herbert 1990b, 19]). Such importation of labor, for Weber, exacerbated the ongoing dissolution of order instead of inducing a resolution: It accelerated the reorganization of the estates as capitalist enterprises, thus yielding *more* emigration of German-speaking laborers and calling for *more* seasonal immigration of Polish-speaking Catholic and Jewish agricultural laborers from historical Poland. In its eventuality, in Weber's analysis, the weight of his most committed historical judgment would thus come to fall on the sense of the latter group. The immigrant Polish estate worker, in his view, thus represented the emerging *inner* limit to the effective elaboration of the new Reich as the expression of a *German* nation. From this standpoint, Weber's statement at the Verein sessions of March 1893 that the large estates of the eastern provinces "is our *greatest Poloniser*" was proposed as a devastating epithet and thus led to his judgment that the projection of the class interest of the conservative Junkers in this form had emerged as "the most dangerous enemy of our nationality" (Weber 1893, 72, 1993c, 177).

Keith Tribe has noted that this is the first appearance in Weber's discourse of the "so-called Polish question" as the fundamental form of "the eastern question" and the "labor question" in his historical present (Tribe 1989, 111).

If this was so, then it might not be simply circumstantial that Weber turned in the March 1893 lecture to introduce the most decisive gesture of his approach to this ensemble of questions: He declared that the ultimate or fundamental *epistemic position* from which he moved in his interpretation was the standpoint of "Staatsraison" (reasons of state interest). He wrote:

> I view the question of the rural [or agricultural] laborer exclusively from the viewpoint of *Staatsraison*. For me, it is not a question about the rural [or agricultural] laborers themselves, not whether they are doing well or poorly, and how are they to be helped. On the basis of the [inquiry by the Verein] we can only conditionally answer these questions, and it is in any case not the viewpoint from which I approach this matter. And freely, it is for me even less the question: How are the large landholders of the east to find laborers? The interest of the state and of a nation can differ from that of each individual social estate [*Das Interesse des Staates und einer Nation kann differieren von dem Interesse jedes einzelnen Standes*]—not just from that of large landed property which is occasionally forgotten, but also from that of the proletariat, likewise often forgotten. The interest of the state in the question of rural labor in the east is only properly formulated in the question of whether the fundamentals of social organization are so arranged that the state can in the long run be maintained if it commits itself to the solution of those political tasks which it will confront in the East in the immediate future. This question must in my view be answered in the *negative*. (Weber 1893, 74; 1993c, 180–81)[33]

The "fundamentals of social organization" in the east would need to be rearranged by way of state intervention, according to Weber, for the existing organization could not sustain the state's interest in the situation—not only its interest in the maintenance of a specific idea of sovereignty (the Junker weakness in the context of a global market was an example of the limits of the present economic forms), but, more fundamentally, its capacity to project itself onto an unfolding new imperial global horizon (not only figurations of empire "overseas" such as those promulgated at the Berlin Conference of 1884 in the "partition" of Africa, but also, and in particular, its expansion within Europe into the so-called eastern frontier of Prussia and its historical ambitions of expansion in the Polish-speaking lands and along its "borders" with Russia). What matters for us at this stage of Weber's discourse on the eastern question is the form by which it joins the epistemological and the political: A theoretical disposition toward an inductively derived sense of historicity is, nonetheless, sutured to the premise of a possible horizon of values and judgment that ostensibly would declare itself as ultimate. And such a horizon is not just political in the immediate sense. It is the epistemic presumption—the sovereign capacity of an ultimate historical vision—of the future possibility of the co-incidence of a singular horizon of interest as the very form by which a conception of the state in the present can be adduced that is decisive. It is the "future of the nation," as Weber says to the assembled members of the Verein, in the "evening of our days" and beyond, that should guide thought and thus policy in this domain (Weber 1893, 86; 1993c, 197). In one gesture then, the epistemic capacity to stand beyond any given interest and the political claim of the state to the position of a sovereign legal authority are brought together as the ground or horizon for an interpretation of the historicity of the present.

But how might this be linked to the eruption of the so-called Polish question in Weber's discourse?

In a word, according to how one approaches questions of historicity, both in general and with reference to a sense of the modern era on a worldwide scale of reference as a whole. Or it is about the historical in general. I propose that the issue is a conception of the historical in general. The historical ought to be understood here as a horizon of emergence and realization—in time and place, most certainly—but neither is given. In the case here, Weber's thought of the early 1890s, the thought of the historical, is rooted in a conception of a supposed genealogy at once of a possible historical emergence and the putative existential arrival of its most complete realization, its fulfillment.

Weber conceptualizes the Polish according to the logic of the possibility of a fundamental limit in historical possibility and historical becoming. Astride the 1890s, he seems reluctant or unable to conceive of the Polish migrant in general (immigrant or not, long-term or temporary) in the German Reich, and perhaps beyond, as acceding to any form of historicity that could be understood as ultimate. That is to say, the Polish could not announce for him, for example, the future form of an ultimate accomplishment of possibility within the German Reich. The pivotal issue here is an understanding of the matter of capacity or the sense of ability as possibility. Then it must be recognized that the basis of this limit as historical is theoretically no different from any other presumption of categorical necessity. Its determination for any interpretive judgment would be as decisive as any presumption of a traditional concept of race that would move from the premise of a given physical organization of the human—that is, as a natural or a biological entity—as the indication of a fundamental and a priori limit (supposed as rooted, grounded, or expressive of the essence of a form of human historical being).

It is in this sense that in "Developmental Tendencies in the Situation of East Elbian Rural Labourers" (Weber 1989a, the English-language translation of 1894's "Entwickelungstendenzen in der Lage der ostelbischen Landarbeiter" [1993a]) Weber moves far more forthrightly in specifying the character of the problem and in elaborating a proposed intervention. Whereas in the two earlier texts on the eastern question considered earlier the issue was the changing historical form of labor organization and its implication—that is, the announcement of the *problem* of the construction of a new horizon of common interest—the matter had now devolved within his stated discourse such that the difficulty could be specified as yielding what he called in 1894, a year after his Verein lecture, an economic struggle for existence (*Kampf ums Dasein*) (Weber 1993d; 1994, 2) and a little more than a decade later still (i.e., in 1904, during his lecture at the Congress of Arts and Sciences in St. Louis) he would reference it as a kind of "cultural contest" (Weber 1906, 1998).

The question is truly one of how we conceptualize possibility in human doing, how we think of possibility and limit, with regard to supposed essential differences among and between the appearance of diverse groups of humans.

The premise of the capacity to *stand at the limit* of historicity, in the sense of *being the singular historical form of the passage beyond limit*, is what would make possible the theoretical declaration of such limit. This idea of singularity is the key. Indeed, it authorizes the promulgation of radical force, a certain ferocity, for it is ultimate. Such a premise is thus the other side of the postulation of a Polish limit. It is this presumption of the capacity to stand, or move, beyond any such limit—epistemically and politically—that alone makes it theoretically coherent to declare that the "eastern question" as the "Polish question" is a matter of "reasons of state."

If the Polish could be understood to be or become a full citizen of the Reich, in equal measure to anyone, then they would be welcomed. If the rendering legible of the fundamental heterogeneity of the "German" nation was understood as remarking an expansion of historical possibility, then Polish immigration, no matter its form, would be seen as posing no risk to the German state.[34] That is to say, such immigration could perhaps be understood on the contrary—as an inestimable affirmation and possibility for the future.

Across these texts from 1892 to 1894, Weber will avow a claim of the superiority of "German" "culture," not only that issuing from the "noble" class but also that issuing from the middle and laboring classes, in the historical devolution of hierarchy in an eastward expansion of the historical Prussian state into Polish-speaking lands (Weber 1989a, 1993a). A decade later, as noted earlier, in his lecture at the Congress of Arts and Sciences, he would maintain this premise without any modification in its *theoretical* determination at the level of an assessment of *relative* group character (Weber 1906, 1998). In the same theoretical breadth, he would speak of the threat of a "Slavic invasion" (*slavische Überflutung*) posed by the ostensible capacity, as he saw it, of the immigrant Polish laborer to subsist on a lower standard of living due to the group's generally lower "culture." That would lead to a general degradation of culture in Germany, a "cultural repression of major proportions" of the "German" nation, and threaten to limit a priori the future horizon of the state (Weber 1989a, 1993a).

The obvious critical question, of course, even or especially according to the protocols that have since become canonical from Weber's own formulations, is poignant: Does not the name "German," whatever that could mean, then or now, confront the heterogeneity of its *always already* historical formation? We can leave all of the weight of the answer to the very possibility of the question.

Thus, we can turn the question to its other side: Is not the so-called Polish question then announced within Weber's thought as a form of a general problem of the constitution of something that we can usefully call "the problem of the color line" in Du Bois's sense, maintaining and affirming all of its unstable metaphoric properties? What is "the problem" of the "color line" if not the practical operation of a judgment that a given historical form of existence is but the expression of an always already given limit (Chandler 2021, 29–32)? (In terms that reference general contemporary philosophical discourse, such a limit might be construed as ontological.) If so, then it is in this form that it certainly crosses and indexes, on the bias, and is thus interwoven with the whole of the problematic of the so-called Jewish question (*Judenfrage*) as it had already taken shape, especially since the eighteenth century, in Prussia and historical Poland.[35]

And then, is this not a major question on the continent of Europe, now, in our own time and in our future, in a new—yet persisting—guise? Would it not be exemplified in the ongoing immigration of foreign workers into Germany, especially, for example, from Turkey (Herbert 1990a)? At the start of the twenty-first century, traversing the massive upheavals in German society in the twentieth century, has not this question returned a fortiori by way of new forms of the problematic of nation that call for another thought of possibility (Adelson 2005)? And, indeed, has it not become a question general to the question of the "union" of the "European" states—posed even for philosophy (Balibar 2004; Chandler 2021, 55–58)?

Was this not the prediction first given on the eve of the year 1900 by Du Bois in a discussion that gave substantial reference to a putative "Europe" (as quoted, for example, in extenso in my account of his critical concept of the problem of the color line) (Du Bois 1900b, 2015e)?

Was it not this naming of a problematic that Weber replied in the affirmative from New York (and later from Heidelberg) in his letter to Du Bois in Atlanta in the late autumn of 1904?

If it is only now, more than a century (indeed, nearly a century and a quarter) after the fact, that we can begin to render into legible relief the tracks of a prior discursive step, or to resound the resonances from the contours of such a passage in thought, in interlocution (for all appearances previously subterranean), or recognize and remark such strata or trace the outline of the seams and hollows of a possible discursive interlocution, then such a circumstance simply gives one form of name to a theoretical demand of our own time.

We understand our epistemic ground and horizon otherwise than according to the presumption of a relative and given—hence, tendentiously categorical—distinction of epistemological ground or an inherited thought of the status of relation among human social groups and historical possibility as the condition of our own thought. We must think the question of the status of relation and possibility otherwise than according to such a presumption. We must think the matter of the supposed common among the human otherwise than according to any simple presumption of difference—that is to say, according to any presumption of hierarchy.

In my own reflections, this imperative pertains to both historicity in general and the history of contemporary thought—not only matters of politics and power, but matters of epistemic limit and possibility.

With regard to the specific example at hand, we must think both sides of the limit. On the level of historicity in general, although it is certain that the "problem" named under the heading of "the problem of the color line" can be understood to acquire legibility for thought as a particular form of its devolution, as the so-called Polish question or the so-called Jewish question, in nineteenth-century Prussia and the German-speaking states, for example, or as "the half-named Negro question," as Du Bois termed it in the opening chapter of *The Souls of Black Folk: Essays and Sketches*, in nineteenth-century America, it is the case that a particular form of this problematization would remain only one historical example among others. On the one hand, in the generalized sense proposed in this study (as well as elsewhere [see Chandler 2021, 29–32; 2022b]), was not Du Bois right when he theorized "that the problem of the twentieth century" would be "the problem of the color line"? On the other hand, in terms of our discussion, have we not been able to recognize in this study that within Weber's early discourse was a fundamental layer of sedimentation that constitutes the organization of an irruptive problematization of a putative "*problem* of the color line" (emphasis mine) in the sense we have recognized from the discourse of Du Bois? And then, such a question is always and everywhere as much a question of freedom or liberty as a question about the relation of possibility and limit.

With regard to the specific orders of *the historicity of thought*, we must recognize that thought arises as the always already agonistic relation that constitutes its internal organization. It thus always announces within itself both limit and possibility. This issues as a fundamental demand: Critical discourse must remark, rather than simply repeat, the existing forms of limit within thought. It can attempt such remarking with a certain effectiveness, if it all, only if it can allow its own relation to such historicity to remain at stake. If so, then, I can propose that we have only begun to name the terms of a fundamental order of possible interlocution, not only in the time of the projections of Du Bois and Weber, or in the time of the most contemporary of our discourses, but also for those inhabitations of thought that are still to come. We, too, in thought, are of the historicity in question. It is precisely this sense of "we" in thought that is at stake for us—whoever this "us" is—in thought. Allow me to reformulate the question on the bias: We, whoever "we" are, must understand in just what way Du Bois's thought (namely, his thought of "the problem of the color line") remains at stake for us (whoever "us" is) as our own most problematization. It is our thought that remains at stake by way of this possible interlocution.

In the instance at hand, we can say without hesitation that, despite the considerable difference in respective initial formal projects for Weber and for Du Bois (the inaugural dissertation of the former was on the emergence of joint liability in medieval business organizations and the latter's initial dissertation study was on the history of laws and statutes promulgating the suppression of slavery), there was a fundamental intersection, a certain common as I have nominalized it, of their problematizations. It occurred precisely at the epistemic-political conjuncture that took shape as old forms of hierarchy, subordination, and exploitation were announced within the projection of new or so-called modern forms of relation. It is this common epistemic horizon of intellectual labor, however different their orientations, habitations, and commitments, that most compels our attempt to the think the work of Du Bois and Weber together—that is to say, in relation. Indeed, my suggestion here is that to think of one on this order of problematic ought necessarily to entail or implicate how we might think of the other.[36]

Since the question—in its historical form—is about how we think of possibility, I suspect that Weber knew all too well that he shared a common horizon of problematic with Du Bois. And for Du Bois, Weber's solicitous formulation, "the relations between the (so called) 'race-problem' and the (so called) 'class-problem,'" might well have been understood to bespeak a sense of genuine shared question to the extent that an answer was not presumptive.

Yet all cannot be thought at one go in our own time of thought. We must remain with the threshold question given within the archive: What is the "common" of this common problematic? More precisely, what is the common that we share with this problematic? It is proper that this remain as a problem for thought, for it remains at stake for us (whoever is "us" if there even is an "us") in the eventuality of its possible devolution. We can recognize such eventuality by reference to a later moment of this possible interlocution, which, even if it could appear as actual, might well remain almost impossible.

In the moments just after the end of World War I, in the context of the sense of a stunned world as a whole, Weber and Du Bois each felt compelled to offer some account of the status of European civilization in the century that was still so young. The divergence of theoretical inhabitation within this problematization is instructive. Whereas Weber would produce a stark proclamation at the end of World War I of the absolute singularity of the West in the figure of "Europe" in the introduction to his *Collected Essays in the Sociology of Religion* (2002a)—a thought fundamentally interlaced with his early idea of the singularity of the German state—Du Bois, in the reflective introduction to *Darkwater: Voices from Within the Veil* of 1920, in the aftermath of the same war, would write of the sense that "Europe" had betrayed the inheritance bequeathed to it from the history of civilization throughout the world (Du Bois 1920). We recall Weber's formulation first, noting in advance that the whole of the "prefatory" statement from which we call this statement should be understood as implied in this passage: "The heir of modern European civilization [*Kulturwelt*] will inevitably and justifiably approach problems of universal history from the standpoint of the following problematic [*Fragestellung*]: what chain of circumstances led to the appearance in the West, and only in the West, of cultural phenomena which—or so at least we like to think—came to have universal significance and validity?" (Weber 2002a, 356). Undertaking a critical reflection during the height of the war, under the title "Of the Culture of White Folk" (Du Bois 1917), Du Bois wrote, in a manner that appears as an anticipatory reply to Weber's formulation of the problematic:

> The greatness of Europe has lain in the width of the stage on which she has played her part, the strength of the foundations on which she has builded, and a natural, human ability no whit greater (if as great) than that of other days and races. In other words, the deeper reasons for the triumph of European civilization lie quite outside and beyond Europe,—back in the universal struggles of all mankind. Why, then, is Europe great? Because of the foundations which the mighty past have furnished her to build upon: the iron trade of ancient, black Africa, the religion and empire-building of yellow Asia, the art and science of the "dago" Mediterranean shore, east, south, and west, as well as north. And where she has builded securely upon this great past and learned from it she has gone forward to greater and more splendid human triumph; but where she has ignored this past and forgotten and sneered at it, she has shown the cloven hoof of poor, crucified humanity,—she has played, like other empires gone, the world fool! (Du Bois 1975b, 40)[37]

If in the passage of address from 1904–1905 these two figures could be announced to each other as of the same formation and as colleagues in a common project of inquiry, then in the aftermath of the silences that rose up around their correspondence in the first decade of that century, a transformation that was perhaps already afoot at the change of one century to the next, yielded respective premises of address that, a generation later, in the time of war and its aftermath (1919–1920) left almost no ground for common future orientation.

How could the *common* of such a differentiation occur? Also, how could the differentiation of such common problematization find its way, come to distinct articulation? Engagement with this question is a task for contemporary critical thought.

Reading such locutions from the standpoint of our present, at the end of the first quarter of the twenty-first century, the question has necessarily become: Does a form of common possible interlocution remain that might still proceed for us, for future thought, under the respective headings of W. E. B. Du Bois and Max Weber? This commentary has sought to suggest in what way the possible form of an interlocution remains open and at stake: indeed, as a question of relation—of the relation of relation and possibility in history as such. I have sought to propose by example the necessity of its elaboration as the form of a question about such relation and such possibility in our own time and in the future, the time that is yet to come. As I regard the order of attention attempted here as calling for the talents and commitments of an ensemble of scholars, the foregoing has been proposed as a gesture for a possible discussion. And, of course, the form of this proposition remains only one possible example among others.

....

PART III

Coda—Or, Available Light
and the Terms of Discourse

All this—the articulation of the apparition of forms of difference among human, as groups—is a problematization that has articulated itself across the globe as fundamental to our time, our era, perhaps our epoch. That is the historicity that we share with both W. E. B. Du Bois and Max Weber. So, too, we share it with them as a problem for thought, as also our own (Chandler 2021).

Yet for recent contemporary scholars and commentators on the work of Du Bois who have also remarked his relation to Weber, or his relation to matters of German thought and culture at the end of the nineteenth century, the full epistemological and theoretical status of Du Bois's formulation "the problem of the color line" within his problematization as a scholar (also, thereby, its status in his practical theoretical projection in social thought, what is often understood as his activism) has remained obscure (Appiah 2014; McAuley 2019; Morris 2015). The integrity of the theoretical sense of the thought named by that phrase and its epistemological status within Du Bois's itinerary in general—his thought as given in his writings and his practice—has remained without substantial critical engagement by those scholars. The paradox is that even if there is a disposition to approach Du Bois's discourse with regard to the worldwide scale of his conception of historicity in the modern era as a whole, the adjudication seems to concern the extent to which he accords with a presumptive horizon. That Du Bois may have cultivated a conception of that historicity in a general sense that might, in turn, render relative in a general sense the very premises of such contextual horizon (the privileged examples explored in part I and II all are ideas of the historicity of modern capitalism, but one may note also ideas of liberalism and its conventional avatars, whether domestic or international) is hardly available in such scholarship. That Du Bois's formulation of the thought of "the problem of the color line" may be understood as a general theoretical production, at once sociological and historiographical, is hardly accessible for thought in even the most ambitious of such work (McAuley 2019). Of course, it also appears that those same scholars have adjudged it suitable to forgo the status of this problematic for a critical engagement with Du Bois's thought as I have sought to propose it my own engagement with his legacies in part II of this study and elsewhere (entailing both matters of German thought and the discourses of the human sciences; see Chandler 2022b, 145–220).

In likewise manner, scholars of the work of Weber also appear to have judged that they could forgo (or have remained unaware of) the problematization of his thought in relation to the work and itinerary of Du Bois. As new scholarship of the past decade and more has brought to new light Weber's itinerary during the last years of the 1890s and the first years of the twentieth century, it seems that most scholars of Weber's work could scarcely imagine his thought and practice as solicited by the work of Du Bois. This, for all appearances, is the case with an otherwise meticulous relatively recent intellectual biography of Weber (Ghosh 2014). Or scholars have simply refrained from engaging the problematic, even within a rather anachronistic annotation and remark of Weber in relation to Du Bois, such as articulated in work by the major commentator on Weber in relation to matters American (Scaff 1998b; 2011a, 100–108). Notably, one can note a perhaps studious nonengagement in the somewhat perfunctory and theoretically obscure, if not misleading, acknowledgment of my own contribution (as it was presented in 2006 in essay form), in which that commentator precisely reproduced (more by a somewhat patronizing and presumptive tone in his account of Du Bois's itinerary and work) the perennial inaccurate and misleading attribution of Du Bois's thought to that of Weber and did so while citing, but not actually engaging, the integrity of the archive and the theoretical axes and the efforts at elucidation given in my elaborations (specifically, what is now the opening of part II of this study) and my proposition of just how matters of "the problem of the color line" were at stake for Weber, both within his itinerary and as a thinker and scholar in relation to another scholar, Du

Bois, who was both an exemplary practitioner (who might be understood to have distended all premises of a categorical distinction between himself and Weber) and whose theoretical projection in thought had solicited him (Scaff 2011b, 280–82). Any consideration of this proposition would, for that scholar of Weber's work and others, almost certainly have entailed an engagement with my further theoretical positioning of the question of just how this problematization may be recognized as at stake within the very premises of Weber's most general projections of a sociology, whether historical or theoretical.

With the methodical accomplishments of the past decade and a half, and more, in the production of Weber's *Gesamtausgabe* (Complete works) (Weber 1984a)—that is, with regard to the discourses of the two originating essays of 1904–1905 and other texts proximate to or concerning those essays, as well as the 1920 book version of *The Protestant Ethic and the Spirit of Capitalism*, and the letters and fragmentary texts of the 1903–1905 period (Weber 2015, 2016)—the sense of the density of sedimentation in thought and the forms of refraction that may become available for critical thought, according to Weber's itinerary of inquiry, would reposition the questions posed in this study a fortiori for what we receive in our time from his work and legacies.

For in this problematization, our own, all of those questions that inscribed both Du Bois and Weber bear on our thinking now according to discreet but distinct lines of force, bearing greater force than ever, shall we say, with regard to contemporary engagements of matters of the apparition of historical difference among human social groups of all kinds.

In 1993, Karl-Ludwig Ay of the Bavarian Academy of Sciences, who had served for some time as editor-in-chief of the *Max Weber–Gesamtausgabe*, was led to undertake a formulation and gather references that pertain to (but do not encompass, according to any measure) this horizon of problem in his discourse (Ay 1993). For us to gather and work with Ay's scholastic bequest in the context of considerations concerning Weber's thought, we need not assume that we know what is "race" (*Rasse*), an assumption that, in Ay's text, was somewhat common in the discourse that attends his work of the 1980s and early 1990s.

For, indeed, with Du Bois's thought at hand we can now understand that matters under the heading "race," at once the idea and the concept of race, as well as tendential practices operating in this whole historical semantic domain—that is, racisms, including brute material violence—ought be understood as only *one node or one instanc*e, or one line of problematization, of "the problem of the color line" in the general and epistemological, sense that I recognize (here and elsewhere) in Du Bois thought and practice.

It is my critical judgment that the sense of "problem"—as in a problem for thought, a practical theoretical problematization of existence for knowledge, judgment, and all manner of practice (policy, political organization, institutional promulgation)—is what we should underscore in the way we receive this problematic from within the scholarly and theoretical practice, the discourse, of Du Bois. It is not only the more complete engagement with Du Bois's thought and practice that becomes possible by way of the understanding proposed in this study; the being at stake of Weber's practice in thought is also rearticulated in the context of our understanding of this problematization in a manner that is more precisely and profoundly consistent with the sense of his own commitment to fundamental thought.

Yet beyond such cautionary considerations, allow me to reaffirm the status of a future interlocution among practitioners and scholars in contemporary thought, especially students of the work of Du Bois and Weber:

1 In a manner that has yet to be understood, matters of Europe were at stake for Du Bois from the inception of his itinerary and throughout his practice—indeed, until its denouement. The same is true with regard to the extent to which he was a profound thinker of the possibilities of Europe, both its historical emergence and its pertinence for the future for the world in general. Although scholars and activists on the European continent and in England engaged periodically with Du Bois across the twentieth century—including a rich, variegated response from intellectuals who staked themselves as of African (continental and diasporic) reference, as well as from intellectuals of the colonial and postcolonial context from across the globe but based in the European context—the question of the implication of Du Bois's thought for understanding Europe has yet to be fully engaged in our time. Since 2005, a possible shift in perspective has begun to emerge. Yet thinking Du Bois's proposition of "the problem of the color line" as engaging how we conceptualize the historical production of the modern era in general, including the constitution of Europe as idea and practice, and not as pertaining only to those understood as other than European, may be understood to remain at stake, yet to be fully engaged, even in these recent accomplishments (Bessone and Renault 2021; Mezzadra 2010).

2 Most directly, Du Bois's thought on "the problem of the color line" proposes a general fundamental problematic for thought about modern historicity in a sense that pertains to the whole planet, most certainly from the incipit of all that we might reference as modern in the fourteenth and fifteenth centuries through to our own century, the twenty-first, in its opening decades. The devolution of all that is Africa is central here, especially, but not only, by way of modern systems and practices of enslavement and its implications across the globe, for it has entailed all that is the Atlantic Basin in the modern period, north and south. It thus implicates the historical formation over more than two millennia of what we call the Indian Ocean (known by some in the early modern period as Oceanus Ethiopicus) as articulated as a certain world-historical domain in the modern period and, for Du Bois, inscribing all that we now know as Asia. So for Du Bois, the domain may also be understood to articulate what we sometimes remark as the transpacific.

3 This worldwide and general implication may be not only *indicated* to interpolate the Weber's work and itinerary, as I proposed in 2006 and as is given in this study. It may also be *elaborated* in our time by way of new forms of interlocution as a question that could produce variegation in our theoretical sensibilities so that a previously unrecognized luminescence, perhaps several, might arise for us as we inhabit in our own time the archival, perhaps subterranean, dimensions of the problems that so far has determined the sense of Weber's legacies for us. It is my considered judgment that this work of elaboration still has not been undertaken, with patience and precision, on its own terms.

It may now finally be said that the epistemological formulation for thought that one can gather under the heading "the problem of the color line" subtends and guides a singular through line in Du Bois's major work. Elsewhere, I have proposed an elaboration of the incipient stage of Du Bois's formulation of "the problem of the color line" (Chandler 2021, 29–32; 2022b). That work was realized in tandem with my archival research for this study. On a more general order of reference, this problematization was at stake throughout all of Du Bois's mature thought and practice, his itinerary, from the turn of the twentieth century through the denouement of his itinerary in the early 1960s. It is nascent in his signal essay "The Conservation of Races" (Du Bois 1897a) and in *The Philadelphia Negro: A Social Study* (Du Bois and Eaton 1899). It is the guiding thought, explicitly declared, for the gathering of *The Souls of Black Folk: Essays and Sketches* (Du Bois 1903f). It is the matrix of the bio-historiographical study under the eponymous heading *John Brown* (Du Bois 1909). Two exemplary essays attend to the world-historical reference and implication, respectively, of an African American situation: "The Present Outlook for the Dark Races of Mankind" (Du Bois 1900b, 2015e) and "The African Roots of War" (Du Bois 1915); each issues from this epistemological formulation of the problem. Likewise, the two volumes of writing that bookend the 1920s for Du Bois—*Darkwater: Voices from Within the Veil* (Du Bois 1920) and *Dark Princess: A Romance* (Du Bois 1928)—were prepared from this same epistemological emplacement. Above all, the massive historiographical and theoretical contributions of the 1930s and 1940s are formed out of this epistemic sedimentation—importantly, his magnum opus *Black Reconstruction: An Essay Toward a History of the Part Which Black Folk Played in the Attempt to Reconstruct Democracy in America, 1860–1880* (Du Bois 1935). The same is true for its epistemological and theoretical sequel (although it is not generally understood as so related), the jointly conceptualized *Color and Democracy: Colonies and Peace* (Du Bois 1945) and *The World and Africa: An Inquiry into the Part Which Africa Has Played in World History* (Du Bois 1947; see also Chandler 2021, 59–74). And it would not be too much to say that only an index of Du Bois's thought on "the problem of the color line" could make possible a critical approach that might be commensurate with the fictional epic issued by him as *The Black Flame: A Trilogy* (Du Bois 1957–61), the concluding volumes of his major work.

For reason of this breadth and the depth of a lifetime of commitment, nearly a century of living, and more than six decades of his mature thinking and writing, which form essential referents for our engagement of the legacy of the practice of Du Bois, the possible future forms of the interlocution that I have sought to affirm amount to a solicitation to contemporary scholarship toward forms of habitation and thought and practice that can only acquire volume, gather available light, enable resonance anew, if we approach our common domain of questioning as if it is not yet all given. The archives, whatever they are, are in general only a condition of possibility for our thinking.

Thoughts of architecture as they have come to me from three astonishing practitioners—one from the middle decades of the twentieth century and two from the era that straddles the twentieth and the twenty-first—have guided my efforts in preparing this book and the theoretical dispositions I have shared herein.

From Tadao Ando, notably his Chichu Art Museum of Naoshima island, in Japan's Seto Inland Sea, I came to understand the architectural bearing of the existential understanding that underground there is no given orientation (Ando 2005). Toyo Ito, by way of his approach to the Sendai Mediatheque, also in Japan, made clear for me a sense that forms of habitation are always at stake, in a future sense, for they are never simply given, in their incipit or in any remainder (Ito 2016; Witte 2002). Yet it was Louis Kahn who formulated the central thought—perhaps six decades or more in the past (which I first heard in reference to his Salk Institute for Biological Sciences on the Pacific Ocean, in the San Diego suburb of La Jolla, California)—that architecture is light (Kahn 2003; McCarter 2005). Or, as I am wont to phrase the thought, that architecture is all about the possible inhabitation of available light. In the understanding that has come to me through their examples, architecture is fundamentally about the articulation of time. Or better said, for Kahn, as I understand him (as also for Ando and Ito), architecture is about the articulation of available light—which is given as time.

If this is so for architecture, perhaps it is also so for a careful new kind of scholasticism, for a self-questioning thought in a general sense, for fundamental work in thought. With reference by analogy to what Ando has taught me (that underground there is no orientation); to what Ito has taught me (that what matters for living is the making of place, a habitation, for a time); and hence, also, to what Kahn has enabled for thinking (that architectural practice is about the inhabitation of available light), we can recognize that fundamental thought is the commitment to being at stake on the terms of that which remains yet to come. If so, for practitioners in thought, in scholarship, our problematization is to understand the terms, virtual and otherwise, of the available light rendered by way of the vagaries, fault lines, shifts, declensions, and elevations of the archive. In just this manner, the archival always entails, solicits, and produces anew revised practices of inhabitation. If the archive, like architecture in general, places us at stake in our practice, it does so, virtually and otherwise, according to available light.

That is to say that the form of recollection in scholarship and reflection of a possible past interlocution of Du Bois and Weber that I have proposed in this study has unfolded otherwise than by given orientation.

Likewise, it has been carried out with the hope that the epistemological bearing for practice in critical social thought will be recognized and understood, pertaining to both then and now, with the available light rendered by way of a certain inhabitation of the archive. Such light was decisive then, at the time of a possible interlocution of one W. E. B. Du Bois and one Max Weber, each in relation to the other, together, and in difference (one might suppose). The question of such possible interlocution can and must be rearticulated now. It, too—this possible future locution—is always according to available light. And such light is never only given. For in the terms that I propose here, it is always at stake as both habitation and inhabitation. We ought not presume orientation or take for granted the requirements and possibilities of future habitations. Any supposed memorial sense poses for us the unceasing epistemological task, at once scholastic and theoretical, to cultivate anew forms of habitation and practices of inhabitation in thought, as this is at stake in our own time—that is to say, in the *future* sense of our time.

APPENDIX

....

W. E. B. Du Bois, "Die Negerfrage in den Vereinigten
Staaten" (The Negro Question in the United States)
(1906)

TRANSLATED BY JOSEPH FRACCHIA

1   The great economic opportunities that opened up in the new North
American republic at the beginning of the nineteenth century, combined
with the homogeneity of its population and its institutions, let it appear
not impossible that there—on the other side of the ocean—a nation
would arise free of the crippling chains of the caste mentality, a nation
in which social differences would be determined only by the different
abilities and education of individuals. The Americans themselves did not
at all doubt this development: they firmly believed that all people are
created free and equal and are provided by their creator with certain in-
alienable rights, and that to these belong "Life, Liberty and the Pursuit
of Happiness."

2   In many strata of the young nation, to be sure, these principles were
applied with a certain *reservatio mentalis*.[1] The good old Puritan families
in New England had an aristocratic fear of the mob, and for the plantation barons of the South, they alone were the "people." Moreover, in those
days of the emergence of the nation, one-fifth of the entire population was
everywhere silently ignored—the 1 million Negroes who were mainly servants and slaves.

3   In those days of turning inward that followed the French Revolution, the Negro Question too was pondered back and forth in America;
the general view was that with the cessation of the African slave trade the

Negro population would gradually disappear.[2] Calmed by this assumption and by the rapid progress of Negro emancipation in the North and even in the South, the nation no longer concerned itself with this question, and the development of democratic ideas followed its quiet course over 30 years.

4   The internal history of the Union from 1800–1830 exhibits a decisive leveling tendency—political life had descended from John Quincy Adams to Andrew Jackson, social life obtained a utilitarian flavor, people were proud of a mean birth and a poor childhood.[3] These tough people were admirable in their struggle with the world and, despite the coarseness and the general lack of cultivation [*Bildung*] of the America of those days, that was nevertheless the time of the building, the strengthening of the nation.[4]

5   It would have been strange if in the striving toward a new and powerful economic development a new stratum of people had not been suppressed and burdened, thus preparing the way for a new caste difference. In America, too, this happened, and the suppressed class was the Negro slaves. Under the liberal influence of the first years of the nineteenth century, they had slowly begun to rise up out of slavery. Of the million Negroes, 60,000 were free in the year 1800, already 320,000 in 1830. Before the Revolutionary War all states were—legally—slave states, in the year 1830 only the Southern states. Nevertheless only a few concerned themselves with the improvement of the situation of the slaves, while defenders of the system, on the contrary, occasionally stepped forth. The reason for this obviously lay in the growing yield of the cotton plantations. From 1822–31, the harvest was doubled and yielded 1 million bales, 1.5 million in 1838, 2 million in 1840, 3 million in 1850, and 5 million bales in 1860. That meant that an industry of world importance was already by 1830 based on slavery, and the enormous significance of this industry increased by leaps and bounds while political parties dodged this question, and moralists and churches enlisted the arts of casuistry.

6   In other words: in the heart of the nation that had laughed about social prejudices and that had set itself the goal of erecting a state with the least conceivable class differences, there existed from the very beginning the worst of all caste differences that, unheeded, grew to a threatening girth, namely a slavery based on race and color.

7   How could the nation get rid of this evil and remain true to its democratic task? In the 20 years between 1830 and 1850 the leading minds of the nation found no passable way out. Then they saw the dilemma with

ominous clarity: if the industries of half of the nation were based on slavery and caste differences, then free labor in the other half of the nation would quickly disappear.

8   In a bloody four-year Civil War the nation decided that the agricultural laborer should be a free man. With what result? With the sole result of suppressing the *slave trade*; in the South workers could no longer be brought to the public market and sold.[5] Otherwise the emancipation basically altered little. In the long and hard school of slavery the Negroes had become an unfree caste of laborers. No law changed any of this. The only way out was to use extraordinary means to bring Negroes up to a height such that they could enter into competition with the free American laborers or to distance them one and all from the country. The latter plan was unrealizable for three reasons: first, it would have meant the economic ruin of the South; second, the Negroes would not have liked to abandon the only fatherland that they knew; and third, the entire deportation would have failed because of, so to speak, its technical impossibility.

9   Thus the only remaining possibility was to uplift the Negroes. But this process was lengthy and expensive, the resolute opposition of the ruling stratum stood against it, and before it could be fully carried out, a new caste mentality had emerged that not unhappily looked upon "lower classes" and "inferior races" in the country.

10   Thus we must attend to three things: first, to the opposition of the former slave states against the improvement of the freedmen; second, to that which the freedmen managed to achieve with the help of their friends; third, to the new caste mentality that hindered the sons of the freedmen in their struggle for a more dignified human existence.

1. THE BONDSMAN

11   Slavery continued in the Southern states in two forms and under different names: as peonage and as convict slavery.[6] Let us glance at the historical development after emancipation in order to understand the former.

12   Before the war the Southern plantation owner possessed 20 to 200 slaves and several hundred acres of land.[7] Directly below the master stood an overseer who with the help of several slave foremen [*Obersklaven*] called "drivers," presided over the work. The regular slaves were

divided into domestic servants, artisans, and field workers. Anyone over 12 years old had to work in some manner; children, the aged, and the infirm received a half-day's work.

13   The main crop of the plantations was cotton, but in South Carolina rice was frequently planted, in Louisiana sugar, and in the more northern states tobacco. Grain was less often considered and the yield of hay, fruit, and vegetables barely covered the plantation's own need.

14   Characteristic of these plantations is their large area. Although exact figures are not available, one can assert with certainty that from 1820 to 1850 the plantations steadily increased in size. The more the old lands were exhausted, all the more did the demand for virgin soil push the large farms to the south and west.

15   The first available exact numbers derive from the census of 1850 and from that of 1860. The intervening decade witnessed the high point and the beginning of the decline of the plantation system. The history of those years is the history of the struggle of the landowners for their economic predominance. The cotton market was favorable, the prices increased and remained high. The zone of large landholdings stretched more and more toward the west and south, and the depleted lands of the border states became slave-breeding farms in order to cover the growing demand of the cotton districts. Thus, Maryland, Virginia, North Carolina, Kentucky, Tennessee and Missouri became the seat of an expanded interstate slave trade. The average estimated value of the slaves (that was one-third to one-half less than the real value) rose from $324 in the year 1840 to $361 in 1850 and $505 in 1855. As a consequence, the forbidden *foreign* slave trade increased significantly in the years before 1860.

16   Between 1850 and 1860 the average size of the plantations in the Southern cotton states grew from 427 to 431 acres; not counting Texas, whose livestock ranches were still not yet real farms, the increase was from 353 to 408 acres, or 15.7 percent. But during this same time in the border states, where the land was exhausted and the plantation system was given up in favor of slave breeding, the average size fell from 282 to 258 acres.

17   Still more characteristic than the growth of the area of the great plantations of the Deep South was the fact that most of the slaves of the South were concentrated on them. The slaves made up about one-third of the population of that region, but the owners of these slaves made up only five or six percent of the white population and approximately three to four percent of the total population.

18   This economic system was destroyed by the Civil War. The land devastated by the armies declined in value, the 1.5 billion dollars of capital invested in slave ownership completely disappeared, and the population remained poor and severely in debt.

19   In almost all states the post-war development took a similar course. The old system of large-scale operation was partially rejuvenated with contract laborers and borrowed capital; but the system soon fell apart because the freedmen refused to work under the conditions offered. The result was a compromise between the landowners and the landless through which a kind of sharecropping system [*Halbpachtsystem*] was introduced.[8]

20   This system assumed many different forms. Already in 1866 in South Carolina a plan devised by a Negro was implemented. The workers were supposed to work five days a week for the landowner. In return they were supplied with a house, provisions, three acres of land, and every second Saturday a mule and plow, and additionally $16 in cash at the end of the year. This sum was supposed to represent the value of an extra half day per week, so that one-and-a-half days per week or a quarter of his labor time were devoted to the worker's own purposes and profit; his remuneration was thus calculated as equal to his room and board and one-quarter of the yield of his labor. This system was quite successful. In the second year several of the workers proposed to work only four days, to nourish themselves, and to receive in return twice as much land and use of mule and plow, but to renounce the money. In the third year the three-day week was proposed. The workers also supplied part of their own team and, because many others paid off the rent on their house and on one acre with two days of work weekly, one often found on the same plantation different classes of workers who worked for the owner between two and six days weekly.

21   The most frequent kind of the sharecropping system consisted in giving a piece of land to the freed family—usually 40 to 80 acres—and taking part of the yield as rent. The size of this part depended on what the worker himself supplied. If he supplied nothing but his own labor and that of his family members, while the owner provided the tools, the draft animal, and the provisions, then the latter received two-thirds of the harvest; if the worker supplied his own provisions, the owner received half of the harvest. If the worker also supplied tools and animals, then the owner received one-quarter to one-third of the harvest. The details of this agreement naturally varied according to the situation, fertility and the harvest,

and also according to the character of the parties concluding the contract; if the worker was lucky and industrious, the total rent of the land was eventually set at this or that much cotton or money, and then the true tenant or renter [*Pächter*] replaced the sharecropper [*Halbpächter*].

22   This system had as its natural consequence the disintegration of the great plantations of the South.[9] The virtually constant decline in the size of the landholdings can be seen in the following table [4.1].

23   The average area of the farms in the South fell from 335.4 acres in 1860 to 138.2 acres in 1900, that is 58.8 percent. The decline was considerably greater in the coastal states than in the central states. This change was largely caused by the fact that the large plantations were no longer worked by the owner with slaves or wage labor as a united enterprise; rather they were rented in the small parcels to tenants and thus, according to the mode of payment, each of these pieces represented an individual farm.

24   Another result of the sharecropping system in the South was the emergence of the system of mortgaging the harvest. A closer look at this system is absolutely necessary to the understanding of the situation of the Negro tenant.

25   Let us assume: *A* is a landowner with 1,000 acres of land in one of the agricultural districts of Georgia, *B* is a merchant and *C* is a Negro with a wife and several half-grown children.[10]

26   Before the emancipation the relations of these groups would have been as follows: *A* was the owner of *C* and his family; he provided them with a home, food and, in given intervals, with clothing; whatever supplies he did not have on hand, he bought from *B*, usually on credit, and paid after the harvest. At that time *B*'s business was primarily a wholesale business which he carried on at some centrally situated place like New Orleans or Savannah.

TABLE 4.1. AVERAGE SIZE IN ACRES OF ALL FARMS OF THE SOUTH, 1860–1900

Census	Entire South	South Atlantic	South Central
1900	138.2	108.4	155.4
1890	139.7	133.6	144.0
1880	153.4	157.4	150.6
1870	214.2	241.1	194.4
1860	335.4	352.8	321.3

27   Immediately after the abolition of slavery the relations between these three main factors at first changed as follows: *A*, the previous white owner, who was almost or completely bankrupt, divided his land and let *C*, the black freedman, and his family work—let us say—80 acres for part of the yield. *A* still provided room and board, tools, working capital and maybe even clothes; *C* was supposed to cultivate the land and receive in return one-third to one-half of the net yield after *A* was reimbursed for the food and clothes. *B*, the merchant, from whom *A* bought the commodities on credit, was no longer a wholesaler, but a retailer in one of the neighboring market towns of 500 to 1,000 inhabitants who possessed a small fund of cash capital and a large supply of various goods.

28   This system proved to be very unsatisfactory. The end of the season usually found the freedman without surplus or in debt; furthermore, under the mild laws concerning debt collection current at that time, the merchant *B*, caught between the landlord and the worker, was in constant danger of losing everything. Because the freedman was the real producer of the harvest, it was obviously in the merchant's interest to enter into a direct relationship with him, if he [the merchant] could only acquire some kind of legal claim on him [the freedman]. On the other hand, the freedman, who readily attempted to escape from a relation that was hardly better than the old slavery, gladly applied directly to the merchant. The previous master for his part was inclined to approve of any agreement that guaranteed him a satisfactory income from his land. Thus the economic situation changed between the years 1870–80 as follows. *A* provided the land, lodging, and animals. The rent amounted to either a precisely delineated part of the harvest, a certain number of pounds of cotton per acre, or a specific cash sum. *C* bought his supply of food, clothes, etc., directly from *B* on credit. New laws that gradually emerged favored *B* who could insure himself through a promissory note that represented a second mortgage on *C*'s ripening crop, the rent to be paid to *A* being the first. *B* was now a hawker who understood how to attract and to hold his black customers.

29   A study of this system based on the census of 1880 showed that a growing number of workers attempted to obtain credit in order to make themselves independent as renters, and that they wrote out their promissory notes mainly for their daily need, but to a certain extent also for fertilizer, draft animals, and farm implements.[11] The effect of this new debt-peonage system on the freedman depended on the circumstances. Some few proficient Negroes who were in the hands of well-meaning landowners and honest merchants could well become independent property owners; indolent

and unknowledgeable Negroes who found themselves in the power of un-scrupulous landlords and merchants certainly sank to a lower level only a bit higher than that of slavery. The destiny of the mass of the Negroes lay in the middle between these two extremes and depended on chance or the weather. A good year with good prices regularly freed a few from their debts and made them into property owners; a normal year made slaves of most of them. Bad weather or unfavorable prices ruined almost all.

30   The agricultural population in the black belt shows today, 40 years after emancipation, four sharply separated economic classes that represent the different stages on the way to free property ownership.[12]

31   The *renter* [*Pächter*] who paid a specified cash rent formed the highest stratum. His only advantage is that he can himself determine how he wants to work his land and that he must himself bear the responsibility for his mon-etary affairs. While several of the renters [*Pächter*] are almost comparable to sharecroppers [*Halbpächter*], they are generally, however, a more clever and a more independent class; from them the independent property owners eventually emerged. We are interested, however, in the three other strata.

32   There is first of all the *agricultural wage laborer* who receives at the end of the year a stipulated wage of $30–$60 for his labor. Several are also provided with a house and garden plot; their supply of clothes and food is advanced to them; in this case the advance with interest is deducted from their money wage. Several of them are contract laborers, i.e., labor-ers who are paid yearly or monthly and whose maintenance is defrayed by the landowner. In the season they receive 35–40 cents daily; they are usu-ally unmarried persons, among them many women; if they marry, they be-come sharecroppers [*Halbpächter*] or eventually renters [*Pächter*].

33   The second category, the *"croppers"* possess no capital at all, not even in the sense that they can support themselves from sowing time to the harvest; they only perform the labor, while the property owner sup-plies the home, land, animal, tools, and seeds.[13] At the end of the year the cropper receives a stipulated part of the harvest, but he must pay out of his part, with interest, for the food and clothes that were supplied to him in the course of the year. Thus we have a worker without capital and with-out wage and an entrepreneur whose capital consists primarily of the food supplies, etc. advanced to the workers. This arrangement is unfavorable for both parties and is usually found on poor lands with indebted owners.

34   Above the cropper stands the *sharecropper* [*Halbpächter*] who cultivates the land on his own responsibility; he pays the rent in cotton; the system of mortgaging the harvest supports him. The great mass of the

Negro population belongs to this class. After the war this system tempted the freedmen because of the greater freedom that it offered and because of the possibility of obtaining a surplus. If the predetermined rent remained within reasonable boundaries, then the sharecropper was motivated to do his best; but if the rent was too high or the land exhausted, then the sharecropper became demoralized and his labor remained fruitless.

35   The tenant mortgages his mule to the merchant and his cart for seed corn and for a week's rations.[14] As soon as the green cotton leaves appear above ground, the crop is mortgaged.[15] Every Saturday, or in longer intervals, the tenant picks up his rations from the merchant: a side of bacon and several bushels of grain each month. In addition, shoes and clothes must be obtained. If the tenant or his family is sick, there is a bill for the druggist and doctor; if the mule needs shoeing, a bill for the blacksmith, and so on. If the tenant is an industrious worker and the harvest promising, he is often encouraged to buy more—sugar, better clothes, perhaps a small wagon—but he will seldom be advised to save. Last autumn as cotton rose to ten cents, the clever merchants in Dougherty County, Georgia, sold 1,000 wagons in a season, most to blacks.

36   The security that was offered for these transactions—the mortgaging of the crop and movable possessions—at first seemed little and thus the merchants related many a true story about deceptions that occurred and about the simple-mindedness of the population; how, for example, cotton was secretly harvested at night, how draft animals escaped and the tenants disappeared. But on the whole, the merchant occupies the most favorable position in the region of the black belt. He pulled the meshes of the law so cleverly and so narrowly around the tenant that only the choice between misery and crime remains open to the black man. All advantage that the law accorded to the homestead owners were circumvented in the contract. The Negro was not able to touch his own mortgaged crop which the law placed almost entirely under the control of the landowner and the merchant. The merchant watches over the ripening crop like a hawk; as soon as it is ready for the market, he takes possession of it, sells it, pays the landowner the rent, deducts his bill for that which he had delivered, and if—as sometimes happens—there is still a surplus, this is given to the black bondsman for the Christmas celebration.

37   The first result of this system in agriculture is the exclusive cotton culture and the chronic bankruptcy of the tenant. The currency of the black belt is cotton; it is a fruit of the field that is at all times saleable for cash money, that usually is not subjected to any large yearly price fluctuations,

and one that the Negro knows how to handle. For that reason the owner demands his rent in cotton and the merchant does not let any other crop be mortgaged. There is therefore no sense in suggesting a rotation system to the black tenant—he simply cannot introduce it.

38   As cotton prices fell in the year 1898, 175 of 300 tenants in a county in Georgia were indebted up to $14,000; 50 had no surplus and the remaining 75 had together a profit of $1,600.[16] In the entire county the black tenants with their families must have had at least $60,000 in debts. In more favorable years the situation is better; but on the average, most tenants close out the year with no surplus or with debts, that is, they work for naked subsistence. Such an economic organization is wrong from the ground up. Whose fault is it?

39   The causes that lie at the bottom of this situation are complicated, but explicable. And one of the main ones, aside from the thoughtlessness of the nation that let the slave begin his free life with nothing, is the viewpoint widespread among the merchants and employers of the black belt that the Negro can only be brought to work through the pressure of peonage. In the beginning a certain amount of pressure was doubtless necessary in order to keep the simple-minded and sluggish at work; and still today the mass of Negro workers need more stringent control than most of the workers of the North. But this honest and widespread opinion can also be the cover for much dishonest and many-sided exploitation of the ignorant worker. On this issue one must point to the evident fact that the enslavement of their ancestors and the system of unpaid hard labor improved neither the performance capacity nor the character of the mass of Negroes. This is not only true of Sambo; history shows us the same with John and Hans, Jacques and Pat, with all oppressed peasants. This is, today, the situation of the Negroes in the black belt—and the unavoidable fruits of their reflection about this situation are crime and a superficial and dangerous socialism. I see still an old gray-bearded Negro sitting along the wayside and giving an echo to the words of many generations: "White man does nothing all year long, nigger works day and night, nigger has hardly any bread and meat, white man takes everything: It is *not* right."[17]

40   And what do the better situated Negroes do in order to improve their situation? If at all possible, they buy land; if not, they move into the city. As it was no easy matter centuries ago for the serf to flee to the free air of the city, so too still today difficulties are made for the agricultural worker. In many parts of the gulf states, and especially in Mississippi, Lou-

isiana and Arkansas, Negroes are, so to speak, forced to work on the plantations of the bottom-lands without wages. This is especially true of the districts where the farmers themselves are poor and uneducated whites, and where the Negroes stand beyond the influence of the school and interaction with their advancing fellows. When such a bondsman escapes, one can be sure that the police official, appointed by the whites, will catch him, bring him back, and not ask any further questions. If he escapes into another county, then one can be sure that an easily supported accusation of a petty theft will bring about his extradition. Even if an uncomfortably duty-bound official insists on a hearing, then the friendly jurors take care of the conviction, and the master can then buy cheaply the convict labor to be performed for the state. Such a system is impossible in the more civilized parts of the South or in the large cities. But in those extensive lands not reached by the telegraph and the newspaper, the sense of the 13th Amendment is severely disregarded.[18]

41   Even in the better-administered rural districts of the South the farm workers' freedom of mobility is hindered through the laws regulating emigration agents. Some time ago the "Associated Press" reported the arrest of a young white in south Georgia who was an agent of the Atlantic Naval Supplies Company and who was caught as he lured away workers. The crime for which this young man was arrested carries a fine of $500 in every county in which he intended to bring together workers in order to contract them outside of the state in question. Thus the Negro's unfamiliarity with the situation of the labor market outside of his immediate vicinity is perpetuated by the laws of almost every Southern state.

42   The unwritten law of the hinterlands and the small towns of the South, according to which a white man must vouch for every Negro not known in the locality, has a similar effect. Here we have the reappearance of the old Roman idea of the patron under whose protection the newly freed man was placed. In many cases this system was fortunate for the Negro and very often, under the protection and the leadership of the family of his previous master or that of another white friend, the freedman could improve himself in moral and economic respects. But the system usually had the consequence that entire localities refused to acknowledge the Negro's right to move about freely and to self-determination. Thus, for example, an unknown black in Baker County, Georgia can be accosted everywhere on the highway and made to talk and answer about his plans to any curious white.[19] If he does not give a satisfactory answer, or if he appears too self-confident, he can be arrested or simply forced across the border.

43 Thus it comes about that in the rural districts of the South written and unwritten laws have imposed over broad reaches a system of villeinage, binding to the soil, patronage domination. In the countryside, too, the opportunity for illegal oppression is much greater than in the city, and almost all serious collisions between the two races in the last decade originated as conflicts between landlords and workers.[20] The peculiar appearance of the "black belt" developed out of this situation and it also caused the emigration toward the city.[21] The black belt does not, as many assume, owe its origin to a migration toward regions climatically more favorable for work. It was a crowding together of the black population out of a survival instinct, an assembling for mutual protection in order to find the peace and security necessary for advancement. This movement took place between emancipation and 1880, and only partially fulfilled its purpose. Since 1880 the move toward the city is the counter-current of those disappointed by the economic possibilities of the black belt.

44 In addition to peonage, the treatment of black *criminals* became a means to secure the bondage of blacks. The two labor systems that still blossom in the South are the direct descendants of slavery: these are the just-sketched system of mortgaging the harvest and the system of renting convicts.[22] Through this latter system persons who are juridically convicted of crimes and transgressions become slaves in the hands of private individuals. Before the Civil War crime in the South was actually punished just as in the North. Except in a few states the number of crimes was lower than in the North; the situation was naturally modified by slavery. Only in exceptional cases could a slave be seen as a criminal in the eye of the law. The investigation and punishment of almost all usual offenses and crimes lay in the hands of the masters. Consequently, the state hardly had to busy itself with any kind of serious crimes by Negroes. Criminal justice was almost exclusively tailored for whites; as usual with a dispersed population, it had predominantly aristocratic tendencies, it was indulgent in theory and lax in execution.

45 On the other hand the need to provide ordered conditions and surveillance of the slaves effected a cautious common procedure among the masters. The South was never rid of the fear of an insurrection and the fateful attempts of Cato, Gabriel, Vesey, Turner and Toussaint transformed this fear into an ever-present specter. Thus, a rural police force was developed that was at its post primarily at night and whose task it was to prevent nightly wanderings and meetings of slaves. This organization was usually very effective and held the slaves in fear. All

whites belonged to it and had to fulfill their precisely defined service in specific intervals.

46　This system was destroyed in a single blow by the war and emancipation. Simultaneously, respect for the law among the whites became even weaker as a result of the unavoidable influences of inner conflicts and of social revolution; the freedman found himself in a particularly anomalous situation. The power of the slave police was based on that of the masters; as the power of the masters was broken, their police became an illegal criminal band that history knows as the "Ku Klux Klan." At that time the first and probably most unfortunate of that series of attempts was made through which the South sought to ward off the consequences of emancipation. The moralists will always disagree about the degree to which a defeated people must subordinate itself to the victor; under such conditions it is difficult to withhold a certain degree of sympathy from the resisters. But the South made the mistake that its kind of resistance in the long run weakened its moral feeling, destroyed respect for law and order, and little by little imparted a fateful predominance to the worst elements. The South believed in slave labor and was convinced that free Negroes would not work steadily and productively. Thus extensive and cleverly formulated laws were passed about apprenticeships and vagrancy in order to force the freedmen and their children to work for their former owners for practically no wage. These laws were rationalized by pointing to the unavoidable inclination of many former slaves to the life of a vagabond as soon as the fear of the whip was taken from them. Nevertheless, the new laws went much too far and fully overlooked the existence of that large class of freedmen who wished to work and to gain their own property; they made an end to any competition of the workers among themselves and exploited the labor-power and freedom of children. As I have said, these laws saw in the Emancipation Proclamation and in the 13th Amendment only stipulations about the cessation of the slave trade.

47　The intervention of Congress in the reorganization of the Southern states prevented the implementation of these plans, and the "Freedmen's Bureau" consolidated and expanded different attempts to employ and guide the freedmen, in many places under the protection of the army.[23] This guardianship of the government introduced free wage labor with the help of the army, supported by the ambition of the best blacks and the collaboration of many whites. The Bureau failed, however, when it came to the issue of regulating legal relationships. To be sure, it did institute Bureau Courts that consisted of one representative of the former masters, one of the freedmen and an assessor; but they never won the trust of the population. As the regular courts gradually regained their currency, they had to define through their decisions the changed position of the freedmen. It was perhaps just as natural as fateful that in the chaos of that time the regular courts attempted to bring about through their decisions that which the special laws had originally intended: namely, to make the freedman into a bondsman. This had as its consequence that the petty offences of a thoughtless, ill-bred class were punished with heavy sentences. The courts and prisons were filled with the simple-minded and the ignorant, with those who wanted to enjoy the newfound freedom, often enough with the innocent victims of oppression. The testimony of the Negro had little or no value in court, while the accusation of a white witness was usually decisive. Thus the criminals in the South seemed suddenly, at a single stroke, to increase acutely; so large was the increase that the state could not reduce or control it, even if it had wished; and the state did not wish. In the entire South laws were immediately passed according to which the officials had the right to hire out convict labor to the highest bidder. The bidder assumed the care for the prisoners and let them work according to his own discretion under nominal control of the state. Thus a new slavery and a new slave trade was introduced.

48   There has been much discussion of the misuse of this system. It was as bad as slavery, but without [slavery's] good sides. Innocent, guilty and downcast were crowded together; children and adults, men and women were completely given over to the discretion of a person who was in no way responsible and whose only purpose was to earn as much money as possible. The innocent became bad; the guilty worse; women were abused and children corrupted. Beatings and torture were routine and the cases of death as a result of the cruelties increased mightily. The overseers of such contracted prisoners usually belonged to the lowest class of whites and their encampments were often very distant from human settlements. The prisoners seldom even had clothes, they were miserably nourished with rye bread and fatty meat and they worked 12 or more hours per day. After work, everyone had to cook his own meal; shelter was poor. As late as 1895 in a camp in Georgia, 61 people slept in a room that was 17 by 19 feet and 7 feet high. The hygienic arrangements were pitiful; medical care was hardly, if ever, to be had, women and men were not separated at work or for sleeping, the former often wore men's clothes. In Camp Hardmont in Georgia a young girl was raped several times by the overseers and finally died in camp in childbirth.

49   These facts illustrate the worst sides of the system as it existed in almost all Southern states and still exists today in parts of Georgia, Mississippi, Louisiana and other states. It is difficult to say whether it is more ruinous for the whites or the Negroes. For the whites it reduced respect for the courts, allowed illegality to grow and gave the states into the hands of those who filled the prisons. The courts were subject to the politics of the moment, the judges were elected for ever shorter terms, and a public opinion developed that was no longer capable of judging a criminal as such, without consideration of the color of his skin. If the criminal was white, only in the most extreme cases did public opinion allow him to be sentenced to forced labor. Thus it came to the point that still today in the South it is difficult to apply criminal law against whites. On the other hand, it had become so customary to convict a Negro on the basis of a mere accusation that the public no longer wanted to give an accused black a real trial and often fell to the temptation of playing the judge. Furthermore, the state became a merchant in crime and profited so much by this trade that it had a yearly net income from its prisoners; those who used convict labor also made a great profit. In these conditions it was almost impossible to free the state from this corrupt system.

50   The effect of this form of forced labor on the Negroes was most deplorable. In their views the concepts of crime and slavery were inseparably linked as equivalent forms of oppression by whites. Thus punishment lost a great deal of its deterrent effect and the criminal was pitied rather than despised. The Negroes lost faith in the integrity of the courts and the impartiality of the judges. And what was still worse was that the bands of convicts became schools for criminals that soon called into existence the *habitual* black criminal. It was indeed unavoidable that emancipation had a certain degree of criminality and vagabondage as a consequence. A nation cannot systematically devalue labor without corrupting the laborer, but the manner in which the Southern courts handled the freedmen after the war without a doubt enormously increased the criminality and vagabondage. There are no reliable statistics according to which the growth of criminality among the freed slaves can be established with some certainty. About 70 percent of all prisoners in the South are black; but this is partially explained by the fact that still today accused Negroes are easily convicted and given long sentences, while whites still easily avoid punishment. Nevertheless, there can be no doubt that in the South since the war a stratum of black criminals, vagabonds, and good-for-nothings has emerged that means a danger for their black and white fellow citizens.

51   As the real black criminal appeared, the South became deeply agitated. For a long time the whites had used the criminal courts to force Negroes to work, but vagabondage and petty theft were really the only offences that had occurred, no crimes out of insubordination, violence or evil intent. As such crimes increased after times of financial depression, like for example 1893, the wrath of the people who were not used to an ordered system of penal law knew no more bounds and expressed itself in strange barbarian acts of revenge and cruelty. Instead of focusing the attention of the best people of these states and of the nation on the problem of Negro criminality, such occurrences discouraged and alienated the higher Negro strata and filled the better white Southerners with shame.

2. THE ASCENDANCE OF THE BONDSMAN

52   In the beginning most people, especially Europeans, certainly held as utopian the notion of raising the African Negro to the level of the modern white worker. Regarding the West Indies and Africa they would have said: this race is not ripe for such a development and such responsibility. Thus they see in the persistence of the Negro question in Africa only proof of the accuracy of this assumption. Thus they conclude that in a civilized country the Negro must be a pariah because he is too backwards for anything else.

53   When, however, one studies without prejudice that advance of the American Negro on the basis of reliable information, then one finds surprising results. First, the vitality of the race, even under very difficult circumstances, is evident through its steady increase [as shown in table 4.2].

54   The birth- and death-figures are both high, but as far as reliable censuses are available, they gradually decline. In the course of the decade from 1890 to 1900, the latter has fallen from 32.4 per thousand in 1890 to 30.2. The number of deaths is probably lower in the rural districts where the Negro population is most dense.

55   This people, almost 9 million strong, has made rapid intellectual progress; the number of children above ten years old who can read and write has increased as [shown in table 4.3].

56   If it continues in this manner, the next generation will have just as low a percentage of illiterates as the most favorably situated European nations. The number of academically educated is indeed small, but is steadily growing and has today reached some 3,000.

TABLE 4.2. GROWTH IN THE NEGRO POPULATION
IN THE UNITED STATES, 1750–1900

Year	Population Size
1750	220,000
1780	462,000[1]
1800	1,002,037
1820	1,771,656
1840	2,873,648
1860	4,441,830
1880	6,580,793
1900	8,833,994

[1] [AN] According to Bancroft's estimation. [EN] See Bancroft 1844–75.

TABLE 4.3. GROWTH OF LITERACY AMONG NEGROES
IN THE UNITED STATES, 1860–1900

Year	Percentage Literate
1860	9
1870	20
1880	30
1890	42.9
1900	55.5

57   Forty-five percent of the population ten years and older is employed; the main occupations and their growth since 1890 can be grouped [shown in table 4.4].

58   For historical reasons most of the Negroes are farmers and most Negro farmers sharecroppers. But here too there is obvious progress. Between 1890 and 1900 the number of farms cultivated by Negroes increased about 37 percent.

59   In the year 1900 there were in the United States 746,717 farms cultivated by Negroes; of these 716,514 with buildings. These farms encompassed 38,233,933 acres or 59,741 (English) square miles, that is an area that is only a little smaller than half of Prussia; 23,362,798 acres or

TABLE 4.4. DISTRIBUTION OF OCCUPATIONS OF WORKING NEGROES
IN THE UNITED STATES, 1890–1900

Kind of Work	Working Negroes of Both Sexes at Least Ten Years of Age				Distribution of Working Negroes Among Jobs, 1900
			Index of 1890–1900		
	1900	1890	Number	Percent	
Total	3,992,337	3,073,164	919,173	29.9	100.0
Jobs with more than 10,000 Negroes	3,807,008	2,917,169[1]	869,095	29.86	95.4
Agricultural workers	1,344,125	1,105,728	237,397	21.5	33.7
Farmers, planters, overseers	757,822	590,666	167,156	28.3	19.0
Workers not reporting their jobs	545,935	349,002	196,933	56.4	13.7
Servants and waiters	465,734	401,215	64,519	16.1	11.7
Laundry workers	220,104	153,684	66,420	43.2	5.5
Drivers, coachers, etc.	67,585	43,963	23,622	53.7	1.7
Railway workers	55,327	47,548	7,779	16.4	1.4
Mine and quarry workers	36,561	19,007	17,554	92.4	0.9
Sawmill workers	33,266	17,276	15,990	92.6	0.8
Porters, shop boys, etc.	28,977	11,694	17,283	147.8	0.7
Teachers and professors	21,267	15,100	6,167	40.8	0.5
Carpenters and cabinet makers	21,113	22,581	1,468	6.5	0.5
Turpentine farmers and workers	20,744[2]	—	—	—	0.5
Barbers and hairdressers	19,942	17,480	2,462	14.1	0.5

(Continued)

TABLE 4.4. (*Continued*)

Kind of Work	Working Negroes of Both Sexes at Least Ten Years of Age				Distribution of Working Negroes Among Jobs, 1900
			Index of 1890–1900		
	1900	1890	Number	Percent	
Nurses and midwives	19,431	5,213	14,218	272.7	0.5
Ministers	15,528	12,159	3,369	27.7	0.4
Tobacco and cigar workers	15,349	15,004	345	2.3	0.4
Stable hands	14,496	10,500	3,996	38.1	0.4
Masons	14,386	9,760	4,626	47.4	0.4
Tailors	12,569	7,586	4,983	65.7	0.3
Iron- and steelworkers	12,327	6,579	5,748	87.4	0.3
Seamstresses	11,537	11,846	309	2.6	0.3
Doormen and vergers	11,536	5,945	5,591	94.0	0.3
Maids and concierges	10,596	9,248	1,348	14.6	0.3
Fishermen and oystermen	10,427	10,071	356	3.5	0.3
Machinists and stokers (excluding railway)	10,224	6,326	3,898	61.6	0.2
Smiths	10,100	10,988	888	8.1	0.2
Other occupations	185,329	155,995	50,078[3]	32.1	4.6

[1] [AN] Excluding turpentine collection.
[2] [AN] Not counted separately in 1890.
[3] [AN] Including turpentine collection.

61 percent of the total area was prepared for new cultivation. The total value of these farms amounted to $499,943,734, of which $324,244,397 represented the value of the land and of the improvements, $71,903,315 that of the buildings, $18,859,757 that of the machines and implements, and $84,936,265 that of the livestock. In the year 1899, the gross value of all products of Negro farms amounted to: $255,715,145. In these totals, however, the sum of $25,843,443 is included for the products fed to the animals and which then reappears in the given value of animal products like meat, milk, butter, eggs and poultry, that is, this sum is given twice. If we subtract it, we thus have a yield of $229,907,702 or 46 percent of the total value of farms cultivated by Negroes. This sum represents the gross yield of the farms. In 1899, a total of $8,789,792 was spent on Negro farms for labor and $5,614,844 for fertilizer.

60   Of the 746,715 farms cultivated by Negroes in 1900, 21 percent belonged completely, and 4.2 percent partially, to the farmers who cultivated them; in other words: 40 years after emancipation, 25.2 percent or one-quarter of all Negro farmers had become property owners.

61   Of all Negro farming families 120,738 or 21.7 percent were owners of their farms in 1890. In the year 1900, there were 187,799 farms that belonged to Negroes and 190,111 Negro families with private farm ownership. Thus the number of Negro farmers increased from about 36 percent to 38 percent, but that of property owners more than 57 percent and the percentage of self-ownership 3.5 percent. Although these percentual relations are based on numbers that are not completely comparable, they are exact enough in order approximately to establish the degree to which Negro farmers in the last decade have neared ownership of their own operations.

62   In the following table [4.5] the Southern states are arranged according to the percentage of farmers with their own operations and indeed in declining order.

63   The total landed property that found itself in the hands of Negroes is worth some $230 million. If we add the estimated value of total movable property, we thus have about $300–350 million of wealth that has been accumulated in a single generation by a multitude of black bondsmen.

64   In 1890, Negroes had 23,462 church organizations with 2,673,977 members and $26,626,448 in property. In 1899, 5,000 businesses led by Negroes existed with a capital of almost $9 million. These were primarily grocery stores, small shops, printing businesses, funeral businesses, drug stores, and so on. There existed 3 banks, 13 building and credit unions,

TABLE 4.5. DISTRIBUTION OF FARM OPERATION AMONG NEGROES IN THE UNITED STATES, 1900

Negro Farms in the Year 1900 Run by: State or Territory	Property Owners (Percent)	Foremen (Percent)	*Pächter* [Tenants]		
			Total (Percent)	Renters (Percent)	Sharecroppers (Percent)
West Virginia	72.0	1.1	26.9	9.1	17.8
Oklahoma	71.2	0.3	28.5	7.6	20.9
Virginia	59.2	0.5	40.3	15.4	24.9
Maryland	55.8	1.8	42.4	9.6	32.8
Indian Territory	55.4	0.3	44.3	7.1	37.2
Florida	48.4	0.7	50.9	40.7	10.2
Kentucky	48.0	0.6	51.4	7.0	44.4
Delaware	40.5	1.8	57.7	9.2	48.5
North Carolina	31.2	0.2	68.6	19.0	49.6
Texas	30.7	0.1	69.2	12.9	56.3
District of Columbia	29.4	11.8	58.8	58.8	—
Tennessee	27.8	0.2	72.0	32.2	39.8
Arkansas	25.4	0.2	74.4	33.7	40.7
South Carolina	22.2	0.2	77.6	49.7	27.9
Mississippi	16.3	0.1	83.6	44.5	39.1
Louisiana	16.1	0.1	83.8	36.5	47.3
Alabama	15.0	0.1	84.9	59.7	25.2
Georgia	13.7	0.3	86.0	41.9	44.1

and several consumer associations. There are also many philanthropical institutions led by Negroes for the best for their comrades, among them 7 hospitals, 20 or more orphanages, and at least 100 insurance funds against accidents and illnesses.

65   Negroes are responsible for many of the crimes in the United States, which is indeed understandable for a recently emancipated race. Their previous and present conditions of life have, as we have said, contributed to the increase of this tendency. From emancipation until 1880, criminality slowly increased. Then it grew more rapidly and reached its highpoint around 1890 to 1895. Since then it has slowly declined. Most of the crimes were such as are characteristic of a class with an unclear concept

of property and little sense of ordered life, namely theft and assault. Negroes are especially accused of crimes in the sexual area; this is not correct. Even of the 2,000 Negroes who have been lynched in the United States since 1885, less than one-quarter were accused of rape and one can be certain that a large part of them were innocent. Marital infidelity and births out of wedlock naturally occur very frequently among the Negro masses, and that is only too natural for a race whose women were 300 years long the unprotected victims of the lusts of white Americans; have not today some 3 million—if not more—of the 9 million American Negroes mixed blood? And still today Negro girls of the South are little protected by the law and hardly by manners.

66   In the veins of many prominent Americans flows Negro blood. Alexander Hamilton, one of the most prominent fathers of the constitution, was born in the West Indies and probably had Negro blood, although it is the mode today in America to deny it. Frederick Douglass, a mulatto, was one of the main instigators of freeing the slaves. The Negro actor Ira Aldridge was honored in all of Europe and made a member of the Prussian Academy for Art and Science. The paintings of the artist Henry O. Tanner, a mulatto, were hung in the greatest galleries of Europe including the Luxembourg. A Negro invented the system employed for lubricating the machines of most American railroads. And in the whole world today, telephone parts are used that another Negro invented. A Negro literature has appeared that describes the struggles and hopes of the race and exhibits such works as [David] Walker's *Appeal*, the *Autobiography* of [Frederick] Douglass, the history of [George Washington] Williams, [Booker T.] Washington's *Up from Slavery*, [Paul Laurence] Dunbar's [poetry] and [Charles Waddell] Chesnutt's novellas.[24] Must I also speak of the wonderful "sorrow-songs," the most beautiful contribution of American Negroes to world literature?[25]

3. THE NEW CASTE MENTALITY

67   One should suppose that, if a mistreated and oppressed class within a nation, after it has been given several chances to work itself up, has within a generation increased in intelligence, has in large proportion become economically active, has been able to dam up the criminality and lawlessness that followed from a sudden liberation, earns some 4 million marks of wealth yearly,[26]—that then this race should at least receive

respect, sympathy, and assistance, especially from a nation that is suppos-edly as democratic as the United States.[27]

68   To be fair, one must say that many classes in the United States have performed admirably in the social education of the freedmen. Churches and mission societies have spent millions for the education of the Negroes and self-sacrificing men like [Edmund Asa] Ware,[28] [Erastus Milo] Cravath,[29] and [Samuel Chapman] Armstrong[30] have given their lives to this work. But this movement was never a national one and today it is limited to the churches and a certain group of philanthropists. The nation as such has done practically nothing for its wards, and there exists today a directly hostile tone of public opinion toward the Negro. This at-titude is naturally the result of the tough opposition to the Negro in the former slave states, and it is necessary to clarify precisely of what this pub-lic opinion consists and from what it draws its nourishment.

69   In the cultural life of the present, social conflict and the rela-tions of people among each other may be presented according to some few viewpoints: in the first place one must mention the spatial proximity of the homesteads and places of residence, the kind of group formation among neighbors and the points of contacts of those so grouped.[31] Sec-ondly, and above all in our time, economic relations are important— the kinds of cooperation among individuals for supplying goods, for the satisfaction of needs and for the creation of wealth. Then come the political relations, the common participation in political life, in govern-ment, and administration. Fourth come the not so visible, but especially important forms of intellectual contact and interaction, of exchange of ideas through conversations and meetings, through newspapers and li-braries and above all in the gradual formation of that remarkable *tertium quid* that we call "public opinion."[32] Closely related are the different forms of social contact in daily life, while traveling, in the theatre, in domestic interaction, through marriage, etc. Finally, one should also mention the different forms of religious undertakings and organizations for mutual benefit.

70   Primarily in these different ways members of the same com-munity are brought into contact with one another. For that reason I would like to indicate how the common life of blacks and whites in the United States and above all in the Southern states is formed in these respects.

71   In terms of *living together* it is possible in almost every Southern community to draw a color line on the map which separates the homes

of the whites from those of the blacks. The geographical course of this line is naturally different in the various communities. I know several cities where one can draw a straight line through the middle of the main street which separates nine-tenths of the whites from nine-tenths of the blacks. In other cities the older settlements of the whites are surrounded by a broad ring of blacks, in still other cases small settlements of blacks emerged directly amidst the whites. Usually every street of a city has its pronounced color and only occasionally are the colors mixed in closer community. Even in the countryside something of this separation can be seen in the smaller regions, above all, of course, in the more significant phenomenon of the black belt.

72   This separation according to color does not depend on that natural amalgamation of social equals. A Negro back street can be suspiciously near to a white villa-quarter; especially often, however, white "slums" are found in the center of a respectable Negro quarter. One thing above all seldom occurs: the upper class whites and the upper class Negroes almost never live in any proximity. So it happens that in practically every Southern locality whites and blacks get acquainted with one another from their worst side. This is a great difference from earlier where through the common life of the masters and house slaves in the patriarchally-led great house the best of both races came into close contact with one another, while the dirt and the monotony of the working life of the other slaves lay outside of the horizon of the family. It is easy to understand that someone who thus knew slavery from the living room of the parental home, and today gets acquainted with freedom in the streets of the large city, has no understanding of the new picture. On the other hand, the mass of Negroes firmly believes that the whites in the South have no goodwill toward the blacks and this belief has been strengthened in the last years through the constant daily contact of the better Negroes with the worst elements of the white race.

73   The *economic* relations of the races seem to be well enough known through several studies, many discussions and not to be underestimated philanthropic efforts; and yet several essential points in the common work and business life of the Negroes and whites are easily overlooked or not correctly understood. The average American imagines the Southern states as a wealthy land impatiently awaiting development and populated by black workers. For him the problem of the South lies in making industrious labor power out of this material through the necessary technical education and through the investment of sufficient capital. The prob-

lem is, however, not so simple, because these workers had just been raised centuries long as slaves. They show the advantages and disadvantages of this upbringing: they are willing and good-natured, but not independent, scrupulous and careful. If, as seems probable, the economic development of the South demands their intensive utilization, then we will have a mass of workers who must subject themselves to a merciless competitive struggle with the workers of the rest of the world without having enjoyed the education of the modern independent democratic worker. The black workers need careful, personal guidance, they must be led in small groups, by men who have a heart for them, in order to educate them to reflection, precision, and honesty. There is also no need of ingenious theories about racial differences in order to prove the necessity of such education after the mind of the race has been killed by a 250 year long education to subjection, thoughtlessness and dishonesty. After the liberation of the slaves it was a public duty to take over this guidance and education of the Negroes. Here I do not want to inquire further about whose duty it was, whether that of the former white masters who had enriched themselves through unpaid labor, or that of the philanthropists of the northern states whose tenacity brought the crisis to a head, or that of the national government whose edict freed the slaves. I only want to express here that someone should have been concerned with preventing these working people from being left alone and without leadership, without capital and land, as completely without skills, without economic organization, as they were; even the protection of law and order was denied them. They were left to themselves in this large land—not in order to grow peacefully in a slow and gradual development, but in order almost immediately to take up the competitive struggle with the best modern workers—subjected to the rule of an economic system where everyone struggles only for himself and often without any consideration for his neighbor.

74   For we must not forget that the economic system that has succeeded the old one in the South today is not comparable to that of the industrial North, of England or France which have their trade unions, their set of protective laws, their written and unwritten modes of interaction and their long experience. It is rather a likeness of England in the earliest years of the nineteenth century before the passing of the factory laws—that England that moved the intellectuals to sympathy and inflamed [Thomas] Carlyle's anger.[33] The scepter that was taken from the gentlemen of the South in 1865, partially through force, partially through their own evil will, has never been given back to them. It has rather gone

to those men who had come to take into their hands the industrial exploitation of the South—the sons of poor whites who were driven by a new hunger for wealth and power, ambitious and greedy Yankees, clever and unscrupulous Jews.[34] Into the hands of these men fell the workers of the South—white and black—and not to their own good fortune. These new leaders of industry felt neither love nor hate, neither sympathy nor romantic empathy, for the workers as such. For them it was a matter of cold cash and dividends. Every working class must suffer under such a system. Even the white workers are not yet intelligent, ambitious, and disciplined enough to defend themselves against the powerful encroachments of organized capital. The result for them too is long working hours, low wages, child labor, and lack of protection from usury and fraud. But for the black workers the situation is aggravated, first of all by racial prejudice that wavers between the doubt and mistrust of the best white elements and the glowing hate of the worst, and secondly by the miserable economic legacy that the freedman inherited from slavery. With this preparation it is difficult for the freedman to learn to seize the opportunities already offered to him—and new opportunities seldom open up for him, rather they offer themselves preferentially to whites.

75 This unfortunate economic situation does not mean an obstacle to every advance in the black South, nor the complete absence of a class of black landowners and artisans who despite all disadvantages accumulate property and become good citizens. But it results in this class not being at all as numerous as it could be under a just economic system, it impedes so much those who survive the competition that they achieve much less than they deserve, and above all it leaves the selection of the successful to chance and not to a well-considered choice or a rational method of selection.

76 The relations of the Negroes to their fellow white workers and especially to the trade unions is of special interest:

77 The Evans brothers, who came as agitators from England in 1825, took up among their 12 demands the following: "10. The abolition of slavery."[35] From 1840 to 1850 social reformers were in many cases upright abolitionists; thus one of them said in the year 1847: "In my opinion the great worker question will, when it arises, surpass all others in importance and the factory workers of New England, the peasants of Ireland and the workers of South America shall not forget the slaves of the South."[36]

78 And the anti-slavery agitation and the organization of workers in the United States proceeded apace; both were revolutionary in character

and although they struck out on different paths, they had the same goal: namely the freedom of the working man.[37]

79   Several worker disturbances that had economic causes accompanied this movement, especially the series of uprisings in Philadelphia from 1829 until after the war, in which Negroes had to endure much from white workers. The Civil War with its accompanying evils weighed heavily on the working classes and called forth expanded agitation and many attempts at organization.

80   Especially in New York the workers found that the conscription was unjust, for the wealthy could buy themselves free for $300. Loyalty to the Union declined and a bitter feeling toward Negroes emerged. Dockworkers and railroad employees went on strike from time to time and attacked non-organized workers. In New York Negroes replaced dockworkers and were attacked.[38]

81   The struggle reached its highpoint in a three-day long uprising that to a certain extent became a war of extermination [*Ausrottungskrieg*] against Negroes.

82   Before the Civil War a number of trade unions existed, among others: the Boilermakers/Boilermen of Boston (1724), the Shipbuilders of New York (1803), the Carpenters of New York (1806), the Typographical Society in New York (1817). There was also an attempt to unite the trades and workers in general organizations, like, for example, the Workingmen's Convention of 1830 in New York, the General Trade Union of New York in 1833 or, earlier, the National Trade Union in 1835, among others. Negroes had no part in any of these movements and were either silently or expressly excluded. The trade unions then began to develop from local to national bodies. The print workers came together in 1850 and formed a national union in 1852; the iron founders banded together in 1859; the machinists in the same year and the ironworkers in the year before. Before and soon after the war the railway unions emerged and the cigar workers and masons founded organizations; almost all excluded Negroes from their membership.

83   After the war attempts were renewed to organize all workers and to unite the trade unions, and under the influence of the Emancipation Proclamation the tone against blacks became less hard-hearted.

84   On August 19, 1866, the National Labor Union stated in its proclamation: In this so difficult hour for the working class we call all workers, whatever their nationality, whatever their faith or whatever their color, whether they are skilled or unskilled, trade unionists or not

organized, to reach to us their hand in order to abolish poverty and all evils that accompany it.[39] On August 19, 1867, the National Labor Congress in Chicago (Illinois) assembled; 200 delegates from the states North Carolina, Kentucky, Maryland, Missouri were present. Among other things in his report, Z. C. Whatley, the president, said: the emancipation of the slaves has put us in a new situation and the question now arises: what position should they assume within the working class? They will begin to learn and to think for themselves, they will soon become wage laborers and thus come in contact with white workers. But it is necessary that they do not work against them; for that reason they can do nothing better than to form trade unions and thus work in harmony with whites.[40] But not until after the organization of the Knights of Labor did the joint action of workers show success. The Knights of Labor was founded in Philadelphia in 1869 and held its first national meeting in the year 1876. For a long time it was a secret organization, but from the very beginning it was not supposed to have recognized any differences, "neither of race, nor of faith, nor of color."[41]

85   Nevertheless, admission had in all cases to depend on the vote of the local meeting to which the candidate had applied, and initially three black balls sufficed to reject an applicant. Actually, therefore, Negroes in the northern states were mostly excluded. On the other hand, the shadow of black competition gradually arose on the horizon. Most expected it very soon and the exodus of Negroes in the year 1879 greatly alarmed working class leaders of the North. Signs of the workers' movement also became visible in the South and in 1880 the Negroes of New Orleans went on strike in order to win a daily wage of a dollar, but they were suppressed by the militia.

86   Such considerations induced several trade unions at the beginning of the 1880s, for example, the iron and steel workers and the cigar makers, to eliminate the word "white" from the statutes that limited their membership and at least in theory to open admission to Negroes. The Knights of Labor also began to proselytize in the South and could report from Virginia in 1885: "The Negroes stick with us with body and soul and have organized here (in Richmond) seven conventions, and in Manchester one, with many participants."[42]

87   Around 1886, The Brotherhood of Carpenters, that had black branches in the South all the way to New Orleans and Galveston, also expressed similar sentiments: "In the Southern states the coloreds who work in trades have applied themselves to the organization with zeal, so that the

Brotherhood in the South encompasses fourteen trade unions of colored carpenters."[43]

88   Even the anarchists of that time (1883) declared themselves "for equal rights for all without differences of sex or race."[44] In the year of the great worker uprising, 1886, working class leaders declared that the color line was broken and that now blacks and whites work together for the same cause.[45] In the same year, however, at a meeting of the Knights of Labor in Richmond, shadows of evil forebodings arose. One Negro delegate, R. I. Ferrell, sent by District Assembly 49 of New York, confronted multiple difficulties in the hotels and theatres and at the introduction of Governor Fitzhugh Lee to the assembly.[46] It was necessary to turn to the chief of police for protection, the press became excited and the "Grand-Master Workman" published the following defense of his position in the *Richmond Dispatch*:

> You are confronted with a vital, inescapable fact—with a responsibility that cannot be avoided. The Negro question is as important today as ever. The first fact that confronts us is the following: The Negro is free; he is here and will remain here. He is a citizen and must learn to take care of his own affairs. His labor and that of the white man will be offered on the market and no human eye can discover a difference between an object produced by white and one produced by black workers. Both lay claim to the same amount of protection that is accorded to American labor, and both must set aside their disputes or become a prey of the slave labor that is now being imported into this land.
>
> Does someone want to explain to me why the black should work for starvation wages? As long as many capable black workers in the South are not educated enough to demand sufficient wages, it is not difficult to predict that as long as this race increases in number and ignorance, prosperity will never knock at the door of the Southern worker and even much less enter into his home.
>
> On the labor market and as American citizens we know no lines of separation, neither of race, nor of faith, nor or politics, nor of color.[47]

That was a high point for a leader of the workers, probably too high a one for his constituents, for the history of the workers' movement from 1886 until 1902 shows us a gradual retreat from these just views on the position of the Negro.[48]

89   After a brilliant career—they probably had at one time more than a half- million members—the Knights of Labor began to decline as a result of inner dissension and have today maybe 50,000–100,000 members.[49]

With the decline of the Knights of Labor, the advance of a greater and a more successful movement fell apart. That success now went to the American Federation of Labor [AFL] with some million members. This organization was founded in 1881, at a meeting of discontented members of the Knights of Labor and other workers. From the very beginning this movement represented the particularist notion of trade unionism against the all-encompassing, centralizing tendencies of the Knights. And although the central administration has recently grown in power and influence, the AFL is however above all a federation of autonomous, mutually independent trade unions—a federation intended to lead them [the autonomous unions] to concerted action and mutual understanding. The expressed racial politics of such a body is less important than that of the Knights of Labor, for it gives advice rather than regulations to the individual trade unions. The attitude of the Federation has been summarized as follows: "It was always one of the main principles of the Federation that 'workers must stand together and organize themselves without consideration of faith, color, sex, nationality, or politics.'" Earlier the Federation expressly rejected every trade union that in its written statutes excluded Negroes from admission. For this reason the International Association of Machinists was held at arm's length for several years until it crossed out the word "white" from its qualification for membership.[50] It has been said, too, that at that time the color line was the main obstacle to the unification of the Brotherhood of Railway Firemen with the Federation.

90   Nevertheless, the Federation seems to have modified its views. The Railway Telegraphers and Tracklayers were accepted though they limit their membership to whites.[51]

91   One can say that the American Federation of Labor has gone through the following stages.

1   "The workers must band together and organize themselves without consideration of faith, color, sex, or politics." That was the earliest declaration, but it was not written down in the statutes. In 1897, it was again confirmed, though with some opposition. Bodies that only accepted white members could not join [the AFL].

2   For central trade unions, local unions or federated trade unions, that have exclusively black members, special statutes can be passed. This statement was accepted by the General Assembly of the year 1902; it recognizes the admissibility of the exclusion of Negroes from local unions, central workers unions and so on.

3 A national trade union that expressly excludes Negroes by stat-
ute can join the AFL. This changed policy was not expressly announced, but it became obvious with the above-mentioned cases
of the Railway Tracklayers and Telegraphers among others.

4 A national trade union that has already joined the AFL can change
its statutes such that Negroes are excluded. The Stationary Engi-
neers did this at their meeting in Boston in the year 1902, and the
Molders attempted the same thing in the same year. The AFL took
in these cases no public steps.[52]

92 Thus unfolded the struggle for the maintenance of high and just
ideals that ended in defeat; more broad-hearted workers' leaders like Samuel Gompers had to give in to narrow prejudices and selfish avarice.[53]
These struggles are similar to those of Negroes for their political and civil
rights; just as they were temporarily defeated in that case, so they have en-
countered resistance in the search for economic independence. Nevertheless, there is probably a greater number of Negroes who are members of
unions today than ever before; a renewed inclination to industrial activity
is becoming visible, and at the same time a better understanding of the
workers' movement. On the other hand, the economic growth of the South
has brought into leading positions a number of white workers who since
birth have looked at Negroes as inferior and who only with the greatest
difficulties can be brought to see in them brothers in the struggle for better working conditions. These are the forces that confront each other in
mute struggle.[54]

93 Of great interest is the *political history* of the Negroes in the South.

94 In many colonies in the earliest times free Negroes had the suffrage if they were in all other respects qualified, but later this right was
taken from them as, for example, in Virginia in 1723. After the Declaration of Independence they received the right to vote, but it was later
often limited by qualifications as, for example, in New York in 1821, or
through the limiting of suffrage to whites, as in Pennsylvania in 1838. The
14th Amendment to the Constitution of the United States, passed after
the Civil War, sought to punish states that limited the suffrage, and the
15th Amendment declared illegal differentiation of voters according to
race and color. These declarations were made necessary by the resistance
of the South to the Freedmen's Bureau and through the obvious intention
of Southern legislation to make the freedmen again into slaves through
the restriction of citizenship rights, laws against vagabondage and special

laws. Through these amendments the government of the Southern states during the years 1866 to 1876 was put in the hands of the freedmen. In any community such a sudden expansion of the suffrage would have brought discontent and difficulties, but under good leadership the final result could have been different. As the situation was, dishonest politicians interested only in their own advantage, in the North as well as the South, exploited unknowledgeable Negro voters for their own purposes and the consequence was much waste and in places bad government. Despite that, it was correctly said about these governments:

> They obeyed the Constitution of the United States and annulled the debts of the states, counties and cities resulting from the bonds issued to conduct the War of Rebellion and to maintain armies in the field against the Union. They introduced a public school system where previously public schools were unknown. They made the ballot box and the jury bench accessible to thousands of whites who until then were kept from them because of their lack of property. Self-administration was introduced into the South by them. They abolished public whippings, branding, the pillory and other barbaric forms of punishment that were prevalent until then; they reduced the crimes punishable by the death penalty from about twenty to two or three. In a time inclined to waste, they were wasteful of the sums that were set aside for public works. In the entire period the human rights of no man were limited by law. The life, house and hearth and the business of every democrat were safe. No one obstructed a white on his way to the polls, limited his freedom of speech or boycotted him because of his political views.[55]

And a Negro legislator of that time said in defense of his race that those who criticized the indiscretion of the time between 1869 and 1873 forgot to mention:

> those imperishable gifts that were given by Negro voters to South Carolina between 1873 and 1876—the finance laws, the erection of penal and welfare institutions and above all the introduction of a public school system. We began in 1869 as children in lawmaking and thus did not consider many a wise measure and uncritically accepted many a law. However, because we learned the consequences of bad laws through experience in the administration of business during the next four years, we immediately passed modifying laws for every branch of the state, county or communal administration.[56]

These laws are *still in force today* in South Carolina. They are living witnesses for the fitness of the Negro as voter and lawmaker.

95   Despite this the Negro governments were abolished in 1876 through violence and betrayal; and since then the Negro is still today robbed of his voting right, be it through physical force, through fraud at the elections or through clever lawmaking. The consequences of these concealed methods were so fatal that in about 1890 a movement arose in the South to rob the Negro of his voting right through a legal path. This has now actually happened in Mississippi, Louisiana, South and North Carolina, Alabama and Virginia and in other states a movement in this direction is making itself felt. The expressed purpose of these amendments to the [state] constitutions is (a) to rob no white voter of his vote, (b) to withdraw the vote from as many Negroes as possible. This has happened through the following voting qualifications.

1   Education. The voter must be able to read and write. (This is directed against Negroes, because the system of public schools in the South is much less developed for blacks than for whites.)

2   Property. The voter must possess taxable property in the value of not less than $300 and pay taxes on it. (This is naturally directed against the propertyless race of freedmen who before 1863 could have no private property and who today are disadvantaged because of their color and inadequate training in economic competition.)

3   Poll tax. A voter must have paid his poll tax. (This demand only has a disadvantageous effect when it is applied retroactively to a period of several years like in Virginia.)

4   Employment. A voter must have steady employment. (Herewith Negro workers are supposed to be excluded; it is a source of unequal treatment because the truth is difficult to ascertain here.)

5   Military service. Soldiers or their descendants may vote. (Guarantees the vote to all descendants of soldiers of the secession.)

6   Character. Persons of "good character," who "properly understand the duties of a citizen," may vote. (This is a source of great injustice and gives arbitrary power to those who register voters.)

7   The "Grandfather Clause." Persons who were able to vote on January 1, 1867—i.e., before Negroes received the right to vote—or their descendants may vote if they are enrolled within a specific time. (Admits ignorant white voters while the same class of blacks is denied.)

8 The Understanding Clause. Persons may vote who can "understand" a paragraph of the Constitution and explain it when it is read to them. (Gives great freedom of decision to the election officials.)

96   In the attitude of American public opinion to the Negro question one can recognize with astonishing precision the dominant views about the forms of government. In the 1860s we stood strongly enough under the influence of the reverberation of the French Revolution in order still to believe rather strongly in universal suffrage. We argued—rather logically, as we then believed—that no class is so good, honest and unselfish that it might be completely entrusted with the political destiny of the others, that in every state those directly concerned decide best about their own destiny and that, consequently, the greatest good for the greatest number is only to be attained when each is given the right to have his vote count in the politics of the state. Certainly, there were objections to our arguments, but we believed to have convincingly refuted them. If someone complained about the lack of education of the voters, we answered: "Teach them." If others complained about their venality, we replied: "Take the right to vote away from the venal or put them in prison." And if finally someone feared demagogues and the inborn baseness of many people, then we asserted: that time and bitter experience would teach even the most hardheaded. At that time the question of Negro suffrage was raised in the South. What should happen to this unprotected, suddenly freed people? How should it be protected from those who did not wish its freedom and who were determined to destroy it? "Not with violence" said the North, "not with preferential treatment from the government" said the South—"therefore through the vote, the only and legal weapon of a free people" said the healthy common sense of the nation. No one thought at that time that the former slaves would use the vote especially intelligently or very effectively. But it was believed that the possession of so great a power in the hands of a great class of the nation would force its fellow citizens to educate this class to a rational use of this power.

97   In the meantime the nation changed its thinking: the unavoidable period of the moral retrogression and the political swindles that always follow wars came over us too. The political scandals became so notorious that respectable people began to concern themselves no longer with politics, and thus politics became unrespectable. People began to pride themselves for having nothing to do with their own government, and thus they

made themselves guilty of tacit consent to those who saw public offices as a private source of enrichment. This view made it easy to close an eye to the suppression of Negro suffrage in the South and to advise the better Negroes to let politics take its own course. The respectable citizens of the North who neglected their own citizenship duties found the exaggerated importance that the Negroes attributed to voting rights laughable. Thus it easily came about that the better classes of Negroes followed the foreign advice and gave in to domestic pressure and no longer worried about politics; the exercise of the voting right was left to the simple-minded and venal of the race. The black voters who remained were not trained and educated, but corrupted still more through open and shameless bribery, through violence and fraud, until they were completely saturated with the thought that politics is a means to enrich oneself through dishonest means. But today, when Americans are beginning to understand that the persistence of republican institutions on their continent depends on the purity of the elections, on the education of the voters to the citizenship duties and on making voting itself a holy obligation which a patriotic citizen can neglect only to the ruin of himself and his children's children—in these days where we strive for a renaissance of citizen virtues—,what should we say to the black voters of the South? Do we still want to say to him that politics is an unrespectable and useless form of human activity? Do we want to cause the best class of Negroes to take less and less interest in government and to give up their right to such interest without protest? I do not say a word against the legal attempts to take the vote away from criminality, ignorance and pauperism. But few pretend that the current movement for the restriction of the suffrage in the South pursues this purpose; it is almost every time and in every case clearly and openly stated that the purpose of the laws is to drive blacks out of politics.

98   Today the Southern black has almost no part in determining how he should be taxed or how these taxes should be used; who should execute the laws and how they should be executed; how the laws should be made and who should make them. It is deplorable that in these critical times the greatest exertions must be made in order to bring the lawmakers of several states to the point during a controversy that they will even listen to a respectful presentation of the matter from the side of blacks as well. From day to day Negroes come more to viewing laws and jurisdiction not as protection, but as sources of humiliation and oppression. The laws are made by people who have little interest in them; they are executed by people who have absolutely no reason to treat the blacks with politeness

or consideration; and finally, the accused is not judged by his own kind, but often by people who would rather punish ten innocent Negroes than set a single guilty one free.

99   Until now I have attempted to clarify the physical, economic and political relations of Negroes and whites in the South as I see them, and to this purpose I have also included the questions of criminality and education. But after all that has been said about these more graspable aspects of human relations, for a correct description of the South an essential part remains that is difficult to fix in generally understandable terms: the atmosphere of the country, the thoughts and feelings, the thousands of small actions of which life consists. In every community or nation it is these small things that do not let themselves be grasped easily, but which are of the utmost importance for every clear picture of social life in its totality. What is thus true for all human communities is especially true for the American South where, beyond written history and beyond the printed laws, such storms and struggles have for a generation convulsed the hearts, where occurs such a fermentation of feelings and a struggle of spirits as have seldom been experienced by any people. Inside and outside the dark shadow of color powerful social forces were at work: striving for progress, next to which is destruction and despair; tragedies and comedies are being played out in social and economic life, and storms of destiny fling the hearts of people up and down so that in this land suffering and joy abide next to one another and change and commotion prevail.

100   The center of the spiritual struggle was always the millions of black freedmen and their sons whose destiny is so fatefully bound to that of the nation. And yet the occasional visitor to the South sees little of that: he notices the increasingly frequent recurrence of black faces during the journey southwards, but otherwise the days glide peacefully by, the sun laughs and this small world seems as happy and content as other worlds that he has visited. Indeed, he hears so little of the question of questions, of the Negro problem, that one could almost believe that it was intentionally kept secret. The newspapers seldom mention it, and when they do, it happens coolly and looking down from above, and it appears as though everyone forgets and ignores the dark half of the land until the astonished visitor is inclined to ask whether the problem exists at all. However, if he whiles away enough time, then comes the awakening: perhaps he is a witness of a sudden outbreak of passions that terrify him in their dark intensity, more probably through the gradual appearance of things that he did not notice at first. But little by little his eyes begin to notice the shadows of

the color line; he encounters crowds of Negroes and then again of whites; or he suddenly notices that he does not see a single dark face; another time he perhaps finds himself at the end of a walk in a strange assembly where all faces are colored dark or brown and the indeterminate, uncomfortable feeling of being a stranger comes over him. Finally he recognizes that the world around him has silently, without resistance, divided itself into two great streams. They run their course in the same sunshine, they nourish themselves and mingle their waters in apparent unconcern, they divide themselves again and flow widely separated. Everything happens quietly, no mistakes are made, or if one does occur, the law and public opinion stand on guard as, for example, recently when a Negro and a white woman were arrested because they spoke to one another on Whitehall Street in Atlanta.

101   With more exact observation one will see that despite all the physical points of contact and despite the daily interaction between these two worlds, there is almost no commonality of intellectual and spiritual life nor are there points of contact where the thoughts and feelings of the one race can come in direct contact with those of the other. Before and immediately after the war, as the best Negroes were house servants in the best white families, bonds of intimacy, of affection and sometimes of blood relations between the races existed. They lived in the same home, shared family life, often attended the same church and talked and amused themselves together. But since then the increasing civilization of the Negroes has naturally led to the development of higher classes: there is an increasing number of ministers, teachers, doctors, merchants, artisans, and independent farmers that from nature and through upbringing are the aristocracy and leaders of the blacks. Nevertheless, little or no intellectual and spiritual interaction exists between them and the best white elements. They attend different churches, they live in different parts of the city, they are strictly separated from one another in all public assemblies, they travel separately and begin to read different newspapers and books. The coloreds have either no access at all to most libraries, lectures, concerts and museums or only under conditions that must wound the self-esteem of those classes whose visits were to be expected. The daily newspapers report the incidents of the black world from above looking down, without great concern for accuracy and so it goes through all categories of intellectual means of communication: schools, assemblies, welfare endeavors and so on. The white is bound just like the Negro by the color line and many humane plans, many intentions of open-hearted empathy and generous brotherhood between the two must remain unrealized, because some busybody

pushed the color question into the foreground and called out the enormous power of the unwritten laws against the reformers.

102   It is hardly necessary for me to say still more about the social contact of the two races. Nothing has replaced that fine sympathy and love between many masters and servants which in the last years [of slavery] allowed the sharp emphasis on the color line almost completely to disappear. One can imagine what it means to a world that places so much value on extending a hand to a man and sitting next to him, on looking him straight in the eyes and thinking that he too has a feeling heart, a world in which a shared cigar or cup of tea means more than the House of Representatives and journal articles and speeches—one can imagine what it would mean to such a world when almost every social friendliness between the alienated races ceases and the separation is even expanded to hotels, parks and streetcars.[57]

103   There is no social interaction with the black population. On the other hand, the South is—as though driven by a guilty conscience—exaggeratedly generous where it is a matter of simple alms and the support of the old and sick and social contact does not come into question. Black beggars are never sent away with empty hands and an appeal to benevolent hearts always finds a response. I remember that one time in a cold winter in Atlanta I did not approach a welfare foundation because I feared that Negroes would be disadvantaged. When I later asked a friend: "Are blacks supported too?" he said: "Naturally, almost only blacks."

104   But the heart of the matter is not touched by this. Human progress is not promoted through alms, but through compassion and common work among those classes that would not accept alms. But in this land the color line separates at the heights of [social] life, those who should naturally be friends and comrades in the struggle for the good, the noble and the true, while it is effaced and disappears in the depths of social life, in the whiskey bars, in the gaming dens and in the bordello.

105   While this quiet struggle of the races rages in the South, the ideology [Ideenkreis] of the American people has shifted. The causes of this are (1) the growing inequality in the distribution of wealth, (2) the rise of imperialism and (3) the color line.

106   The doctrine of democratic equality as it was announced in America 60 years ago emanated from the obvious social equality of Americans at that time. They began life with little accumulated wealth, but rich sources of help stood open to them; the economic starting point was rather equal for all, mostly the end point too. Even if someone became

richer than his fellows through cleverness or thriftiness, the sons easily squandered the wealth so that the figure of speech "between shirtsleeves and shirtsleeves lie three generations," became a telling expression for economic rise and fall. The second half of the nineteenth century saw many indications of a change. The large corporations came into being; the millionaire followed soon after; and little by little the American nation became conscious of the fact that in the distribution of prosperity great and apparently lasting inequalities predominate. Private wealth of fabulous and almost incomprehensible proportions was accumulated next to which appeared the question of the poor, the lack of employment, homelessness and child misery. For a nation that is so individualistic as the United States, it was difficult to look these new problems in the face and to admit that in America too class differences have become visible.

107   But instead of turning its thoughts and mental powers to the solution of these steadily growing social problems, a new turn occurred and, despite all of its previous traditions, the United States became a "world power" in that it annexed several foreign territories in different parts of the world. How can one explain this peculiar development? Every growing nation naturally has its time where it is overcome with the sickness of imperialism, but in most cases predisposing causes can be determined—in England the adventurous seafarers prepared the ground, in France it was the Napoleonic epidemic and in Germany the boiling of the new national feeling. But in America this politic was ridiculed and not considered good; the brotherhood of nations was emphasized and not the tutelary relation. But this has changed—and did it not least occur because America discovered within its own borders a large class of citizens that it did not call brothers and did not want to treat justly, not to mention as equally entitled? This was naturally not the only cause of the annexation of the Philippines, Puerto Rico, Panama and Hawaii, but it contributed.

108   The indications of great changes cannot escape any candid observer. There was a time when personal achievement meant much more than today; the phrase "upper and lower classes" begins to mean something; strong and influential groups look with disapproval at every form of education that is not above all and exclusively intended to secure the perpetuation of the current social and economic situation. Americans begin to show not only open contempt for the "bastard races," but also a growing respect for snobbism and they gladly began to forget the color of their grandfathers' fingernails. Great contemporary forces, broad-

hearted philanthropy and a healthy democratic ideal are certainly not lacking, and yet all know that American democracy is very sick and that even large and growing efforts at social reform develop tendencies that make them just as often into contributing causes of social separation as of the promotion of the advance of classes.

109   That the mass of Americans notices and reflects upon the growth of class differences especially in economic relations is evident in the results of the last three presidential elections. This vote is in no way thought out or logical, but it gives expression to a widespread and deep feeling that might be expressed in the following words: "If in a land of unlimited opportunities a group of people works together for its livelihood and if a man accumulates more wealth from the fruits of this labor than he will ever be able to spend, while the others can hardly live somewhat respectably, then this is an unjust distribution of the profit. And if on the basis of this unjust distribution increasing class and racial privileges are built, then the injustice becomes a lasting one and a crime." I do not want to say that the quarter million who voted for Mr. Debs in 1904, or the million who voted for the silver-currency man in 1900 and 1896 had a clear picture of the evil of which I have spoken or rational suggestions for improvement.[58] I only want to express what the protest really was that guided them unclearly during the election, and to say that they were right.

110   As soon as the poison of the class mentality penetrates the life-spirit of a nation, then the standpoint of the privileged classes alone determines its judgment of good and evil. In the United States this can especially be seen in the school question. How should the children of the serving classes be raised? Earlier the Americans said: "as men"; now they whisper: "as servants, then we will have better servants." How should the children of the artisans be raised? "As carpenters," they begin to think, "so that we will get better houses." That seems to be a healthy logic and it is, too, when servants and comfortable houses are the final goals of national life. But are they? Class hierarchy grows today in America, in the land that was founded as a mighty protest against this folly that rules the world. It grows almost undisturbed, for its victims today are mostly blacks. But the Americans should not for that reason let themselves be lulled into a false security! The Negro question is only one indication of the increasing class and racial privileges and not, as many optimistically believe, its cause.

111   The only salvation from such a situation evidently lies in not placing all energy on the class standpoint.

112　We want to adopt the old national standpoint in the Negro question and shove aside on the one hand the demands of the plantation owners of the South and the capitalists of the North, on the other the purely personal wishes of the blacks; and here we must first establish certain axioms of the situation:

1　The Negro question is an inescapable legacy from which America cannot free itself without further ado. It is a debt that has been entered into to the advantage of the Americans living today. The contemporary industrial development of America is based on the blood and sweat of unpaid Negro labor in the seventeenth, eighteenth, and nineteenth centuries. The black race's right to exist is based on that. Men who 10 or 20 years ago came ragged and ruined across the ocean have no right to drive Negroes from the land that their ancestors trod upon before the pilgrim fathers.

2　Caste mentality produces caste mentality; the fact that there is in America a proscribed race also makes it easier to proscribe classes, and class privileges are responsible for the fact that Negroes find deaf ears for their wishes.

3　The political situation in the South where most Negroes live can only be temporary or the republican form of government is condemned to death. If the "rotten borough" system is naturalized in Louisiana, Alabama and South Carolina, if the payment of taxes without parliamentary representation becomes the norm south of the Ohio, then democracy will not only perish there, but the beginnings of a free government in the entire country will be nipped in the bud.[59]

4　The well-being of the American worker would be seriously threatened if the Negroes of the South are made into a proscribed, patronized class whose living conditions come close to serfdom and that enters into competition against the rest of the working class.

Keeping in mind these four points, we can thus formulate the more comprehensive question: can the white and black race live together in America in freedom and equality?

113　What does "living together" mean in a free, modern state? It means first of all economic cooperation—joint labor for a livelihood, further, political interests come into consideration, and finally it means complete social freedom for all, according to their personal needs, as long as the freedom of the one does not hinder that of the other.

114 Objections have been raised against all of these forms of common life and, indeed, by alluding to the ignorance, to the inability to perform and the immorality of the Negroes, and to the repugnance that many people have to personal interaction with them. For example, artisans, women workers, clerks did not want to have Negroes as fellow workers because they are supposedly unskilled. As a race Negroes are unskilled, but many Negroes are certainly capable people, and to refuse to accept a skilled worker because his brother or cousin or some still more distant family member is unskilled is more foolish than the proscription of a man because his father was a rag-picker [*Gassenkehrer*] or peasant. Many states refuse blacks the right to vote, officially because of a lack of education. Forty-five percent of the Negro race are illiterate; but many black men are not uneducated, and it is senseless to take the right to vote away from an educated Negro because there are members of his race who are not. Many people raise their objections against the Negro criminal; with justifiable indignation they point to the criminality, the immorality, the depravity of many Negroes. And that is correct—it is not to be regretted that the American people oppose crime, but only that they are often too mild in their judgment. But for that reason all the more justice should be accorded to the individual Negro who is not a criminal so that his fellows see that it is worthwhile to remain respectable.

115 But most objections that are made against blacks and whites living together are not at all clearly based on pointing out the lack of education, inability, or criminality of the Negroes. It is simply a matter of unconsidered antipathy toward blacks, not necessarily a matter of hate or ill will. One feels an antipathy, their physical characteristics are unpleasing, they alienate. This is characteristic for the behavior of the better classes of whites toward the Negroes in the North, and since they make no secret about it, the masses imitate them and, in so doing, exaggerate. And the shop girls and factory workers, the foreign immigrants—all who are conscious of their own precarious position on the border line see the shadow of caste and flee hurriedly so that they themselves will not be entwined in it.

116 Free human beings indeed have a right to their sympathies and antipathies. That is one of the cultural achievements. But when personal antipathies and moods are given into to the point that democracy is en-

dangered, that progress is derailed, that human souls are enchained and 9 million are forced into a life full of despair and humiliation, then it is time to limit somewhat the rule of sympathies and antipathies with healthy common sense and the most common respect. It is a prerogative of the American woman to choose her husband; but it is not her prerogative or her duty to choose husbands for all of her neighbors. It is a prerogative of the American citizen to buy those comforts that he can afford, in the train, theatres and other public institutions. But it is not his prerogative to insist that I do not have the same right. It is a holy prerogative of every American to decide who shall enjoy the hospitality of his home, but no man may presume to audit the guest lists of the nation or of an individual of the nation. It is the duty of every citizen to help govern his city and his country, but it is not his duty to want to tear this privilege from his neighbor simply because his neighbor has red hair. In other words: it is the prerogative of every American to give in to his personal antipathy toward certain races or individuals, but this personal antipathy may not be permitted to hinder other people at work, in the exercise of their political rights and obligations, and in the enjoyment of public institutions. If it is really permanently impossible for respectable white men and respectable blacks to work and vote together, to visit the same public events, to allow each other to go their own ways in their legitimate peculiarity, without it resulting in war, slavery, caste difference, lies, stealing and lynching, then American democracy is a dream. If human collaboration is made impossible through lack of education, then we have an education problem not a racial problem. If collaboration is hindered by inability, then it is a matter of training that is not exclusively a racial matter. Insofar as crime is a problem, it is just as much a problem for whites as for blacks.

117   The fact of racial antipathy is as old as the interaction of people with one another. But the history of the centuries is the history of the discovery of the human soul and in every age the curse of the average person was his own narrowness, his blindness toward the riches that surrounded him, the notion that his own narrow heart and his small mind are the measure and borders of the universe. Above all in our days we do not want to forget the trivial observation that even in the nooks and alleys, and under threadbare clothing, lay hidden riches and depths of human life that we will perhaps never experience in ourselves.

118   In the struggle for his human rights the American Negro relies above all on the feeling of justice in the civilized world. We are no barbarians

or heathen, we are educable and our education is increasing; our economic abilities have proven themselves. We too want to have our chance in life. Whoever wants to get acquainted with our living conditions, be welcome; we demand nothing other than that one gets acquainted with us honestly and face to face, and does not judge us according to hearsay or according to the verdict of our despisers.

119   And above all consider one thing: the day of the colored races dawns. It is insanity to delay this development; it is wisdom to promote what it promises us in light and hope for the future.[60]

NOTES

Editor's note: This essay originally appeared in German in the *Archiv für Sozialwissenschaft und Sozialpolitik* (Du Bois 1906a). The journal was jointly edited by Werner Sombart, Max Weber, and Edgar Jaffé in Heidelberg, Germany. Although a translator of Du Bois's original English text into German is not given in the publication, correspondence between Du Bois and Elisabeth Jaffé-von Richthofen (a friend and colleague of Weber's and Jaffé's spouse) indicates that she may have taken the main responsibility for a somewhat collective translation, along with at least two of the editors of the *Archiv*. The translation of this text into English was first published in *CR: New Centennial Review* in 2006 and was subsequently reprinted, with additional annotations, in *The Problem of the Color Line at the Turn of the Twentieth Century: The Essential Early Essays* (Du Bois 2015f).The translation is reproduced here by the kind permission of Joseph Fracchia, the editors of *CR*, and Michigan State University Press, and by courtesy of Fordham University Press. All table titles are provided by the translator and editor. All editor's notes in this appendix (marked EN) are mine; translator's notes (TN) are Fracchia's; and the author's notes (AN) at n. 18 and n. 60 are Du Bois's.

The original German publication of the essay carried this editor's note: "The following, and also a series of other new publications by Negroes and about Negroes in the United States, will be reviewed by one of the editors in one of the next few volumes. This will provide the occasion to address several of the contentual [*sachliche*] dimensions of the problem. In the meantime, we are pleased to be able to provide one of the most outstanding intellectual representatives of the American Negroes the opportunity to express his views."

1   [EN] This phrase is in Latin in the original essay. Du Bois refers here to the doctrine of "mental reservation" that developed from the inception of the early modern period in Christian theology in Western Europe. It is a form of deception understood by the holder of the reservation as something other than an outright lie. Such deception would occur in two general forms: either the implication of an untruth that is not

actually stated or the qualification of spoken words by an unspoken mental addition. The latter would be addressed to, or known by, only the speaker and God. It has remained controversial.

2 [EN] Du Bois often indexes the historical meaning of the French Revolution, perhaps the signal transformative moment of modern European political historicity, which had worldwide implications (Baker 1987). Yet he is also indexing the beginning of the legal suppression of the slave trade (e.g., the act passed by the UK Parliament on 25 March 1807 and the legally equivalent act passed by the US Congress in early March 1807, neither of which stopped the trade in actual fact or abolished slavery in their respective domains of sovereignty, noting especially the context of the new United States). Du Bois's doctoral dissertation on the history of the suppression of this trade remains useful today for scholarship (Du Bois 1896).

3 [EN] John Quincy Adams (1767–1848) was the sixth president of the United States (1825–1829). In 1828, he was defeated by Andrew Jackson (1767–1845), who then served two terms as the seventh president of the republic (1829–1837). Adams was the son of the second president, John Adams (1735–1826; served 1797–1801). He was highly educated (including wide study in Europe, then training at Harvard University); served as a lawyer and university professor; and held national public office as a diplomat (including the position of secretary of state) and senator before his elevation to the presidency. By contrast, Jackson, born of Scots Irish colonists, was raised on the frontier in the Carolinas and Tennessee. He received sporadic formal education but eventually achieved financial success as a lawyer, land speculator, and large-scale slave-owning planter. Having joined the state militia early in life, Jackson was catapulted into national prominence by his command of successful military campaigns during the War of 1812, against the Creek in 1814, and against the British at New Orleans in 1815, which eventually promoted his election to the presidency.

4 [TN] Misspellings of English words, names, and place names used in the German original have been simply corrected without comment. Brackets either indicate English words added for the sake of clarity or contain the original German word(s) if not easily and clearly translatable.

5 [EN] Du Bois's doctoral dissertation was an account of the history of the efforts from the seventeenth century to the nineteenth century to end the slave trade to the United States (Du Bois 1896).

6 [EN] Du Bois is indicating two post–Civil War systems of labor pertaining to African Americans in the United States to which he persistently and systematically called attention, in particular in his work from the late 1890s to the start of World War I. On the former, peonage, he draws in paragraphs 12–43 of this essay on the extensive research on Southern rural agriculture among African Americans that he conducted in several settings—southern Virginia, eastern and southern Georgia, and central Alabama, in particular—from 1897 to 1907 (see Du Bois 1898a, 1901a, 1901d, 1911). On the latter, "convict lease" labor, in paragraphs 44–51, Du Bois essentially draws from,

and revises, the essay "The Spawn of Slavery: The Convict-Lease System in the South" (Du Bois 1901f; see also Du Bois 1899a).

7 [EN] In paragraphs 12–24, Du Bois draws more or less verbatim from "The Negro Farmer," the report he prepared for the US Census Bureau based on the twelfth national census data (Du Bois 1904a). This report was supplemented and republished in 1906 (see Du Bois 1906b). Given the general difficulty of obtaining either of these early publications, citations here are to the report as it was reprinted in Du Bois 1980c, esp. 254–56.

8 [TN] In the discussion of the various nuances of the sharecropping system throughout this section, Du Bois's translators (from the original English into the German) use variations on the term *Pächter* to capture the nuances of the system, and even then in the German text resort is taken in one case to the English term *croppers* (para. 33). In the translations of these terms into English from the German, the following criteria has been used. The term *Pächter* itself appears in two ways: in a generic sense, which has been translated here as "tenant," and in a specific sense, referring to a tenant who pays money rent, which is translated as "renter." Since the *Halbpächter* is defined in the text as one whose rent consists of a share of the harvest, it is translated here as "sharecropper." The English term *croppers* appears also to denote those who are essentially wage laborers but who receive their wages not in cash but as a share of the harvest. In one of the best recent works on tenant taxonomy in the post–Civil War South, the authors Roger L. Ransom and Richard Sutch (1977) divide into two categories what is described in Du Bois's essay under one term. They define sharecropping as a system in which all but board and clothing was provided by the landlord, who then took in return 50 percent of the harvest. They add, however, the category of "share tenancy" to describe the system in which the landlord provided only land, housing, and sometimes fuel, while the tenant provided tools, seed, wagons, etc. In this case, the landlord took only one-fourth to one-third of the harvest. Ransom and Sutch (1977, 92) add that this form was relatively rare since it required an amount of initial capital that few freedmen possessed. Du Bois, however, refers specifically to this system of working on "thirds or fourths" as a system of sharecropping, only quantitatively different from a situation in which the landlord took half of the crop.

[EN] In "The Negro as He Really Is" (Du Bois 1901b), later slightly revised and divided to form chapters 7–8 of *The Souls of Black Folk: Essays and Sketches* (Du Bois 1903f, 110–62), Du Bois most often uses the French word *métayer* (and thus, notably, in that eighth chapter), yet as he several times also refers to Italy, he may thus be understood to likewise index the whole historical complex known as *mezzadria* in the Italian. The term *métayer* was used throughout Europe in the nineteenth century, referring there in particular to a system of partial payment from harvest for the use of land, capital, and other forms of outlay, alternatively speaking of the whole as "debt peonage" (Du Bois 1901b, 1903b, 1903c). Notably, in both of his presentations of this formulation at the turn of the twentieth century, Du Bois references Arthur Young (1792), the well-known English critic of such systems during the late eighteenth century, especially with regard to England, France, and Italy, with Du Bois comparing the post–Civil

War order in the southern region of the United States at the end of the nineteenth century to those late eighteenth-century formations in historical Europe.

9 [EN] As a graduate student at the University of Berlin from September 1892 to March 1894, Du Bois worked in the famous "Nationalökonomie" seminar at that institution with Gustav Schmoller and Adolph Wagner over the course of some fifteen months, from October 1892 until December 1893. There he completed a study that could have served as an inaugural doctoral thesis in the German university system of the time, making a presentation of his work in early December 1893. According to Du Bois's report to the Slater Fund of 29 March 1894 (Du Bois 1973c, 27), the study was eventually titled "Die landwirtschaftliche Entwickelung in den Südstaaten der Vereinigten Staaten." It is well known that, despite support from Schmoller and Wagner, Du Bois was unable to receive the degree. Du Bois recounts his understanding at the time of the decision by the Berlin faculty in the report to the Slater Fund. Du Bois sent three reports to the Slater Fund. The title of the project is given as "Der Gross- und Klein Betrieb des Ackerbaus, in der Südstaaten der Vereinigten Staaten, 1840–1890" (The large- and small-scale management of agriculture in the Southern United States, 1840–1890) in the report dated 10 March 1893, as "Der landwirtschaftliche Gross- und Kleinbetrieb in den Vereinigten Staaten" (A comparison of large- and small-scale agriculture in the United States [a very loose translation]) in the report dated 6 December 1893, and as "Die landwirtschaftliche Entwickelung in den Südstaaten der Vereinigten Staaten" (Agricultural Development in the Southern States of the United States) in the report dated 29 March 1894 (Du Bois 1973c, 23, 26–27). In this essay, it is quite possible that Du Bois is referencing assessments that he had begun to develop in that study. However, the proposed doctoral thesis remains unavailable at the present time, for all appearances now lost in its original form. Also, the scale of agricultural enterprises in the American South would have been of interest to both Schmoller and Wagner, as well as to Max Weber (the first addressee of this essay), for the "eastern question" in Germany from the 1870s onward was very much concerned with the decline of large-scale estate or manorial production in that region during the last quarter of the nineteenth century, with implications for the whole of the economy of the new (post-1870s) German Reich.

10 [EN] Paragraphs 25–28 are in a form that is taken almost verbatim from Du Bois 1906b; 1980c, 256–58. An earlier version of the same passages can be found in "The Negro Landholder of Georgia" (Du Bois 1901d, 1980d, 117–18).

11 [EN] Whereas Du Bois's 1904 report on the Negro farmer and its 1906 supplementary revision were based on the US Census of 1900, Du Bois can be understood here to refer in particular to "The Negro Landholder of Georgia" (Du Bois 1901d; 1980d, 117–18). That report addresses the change in such holdings from the inception of the US Civil War to the 1890s based on both the national census data of 1880 and correspondence with county-level tax administration offices throughout that Southern state.

12 [EN] Paragraphs 30–34 reproduce Du Bois's formulations from "The Negro Farmer" (Du Bois 1906b; 1980c, 258), which, in turn can be found in Du Bois 1904a. This

conceptualization also appears in Du Bois's testimony to the US Industrial Commission of 1901 (Du Bois 1980h, 72–73). However, most notably, Du Bois presented this same phrasing in "The Negro as He Really Is," his 1901 essay focused on Dougherty County in southeastern Georgia, which, as previously noted, was reprised and somewhat remarked in its publication as the seventh and eighth chapters of *The Souls of Black Folk: Essays and Sketches*, with phrasing akin to paragraphs 30–34 of the present essay (see Du Bois 1901b, 864–65; 1903c, chap. 8, 156–60, paras. 35–39).

13 [TN] "Croppers" is in English in the original.

14 [TN] In this and the following three paragraphs, Du Bois seemingly uses the term *Pächter* in its generic sense as "tenant," which can refer both to renters (*Pächter*) and sharecroppers (*Halbpächter*). Since the scenario he describes in these paragraphs could befall both the renter and the sharecropper, I have translated *Pächter* throughout as "tenant."

15 [EN] Paragraphs 35–37 are parallel in both concept and phrasing, more or less verbatim, to paragraphs 16–18 in chapter 8 of *The Souls of Black Folk: Essays and Sketches* (Du Bois 1903c). In turn, this specific descriptive phrasing seems to first appear in Du Bois's discourse "The Negro as He Really Is" (Du Bois 1901b, 861).

16 [EN] Paragraphs 38–43 are in essence a rephrasing of paragraphs 26–30 of chapter 8 in *The Souls of Black Folk: Essays and Sketches* (Du Bois 1903f); in turn, the same phrasing had already been offered in "The Negro as He Really Is" (Du Bois 1901b, 861–64). In the German-language text from 1906, the year referenced in the first sentence of this paragraph is given as "1889." However, that is most certainly a typographical error, for the year is given as "1898" in *The Souls of Black Folk: Essays and Sketches* (Du Bois 1903c, chap. 8, 149–50, para. 26), of which the paragraph here, including the first sentence, is in essence a replication. Likewise, as is commonly understood, cotton prices for US production fell dramatically, in some cases below the cost of production, in 1898. It is notable that this paragraph as it appears in *The Souls of Black Folk: Essays and Sketches* is an addition rendered during the revision of "The Negro as He Really Is," the essay from which it derives, for inclusion in the book; it does not appear in that essay from 1901.

17 [EN] The phrase given in the German text as published is "Es ist nicht recht." In the English, as given in chapter 8 of *The Souls of Black Folk* (as well as the 1901 essay from which it derives), the concluding statement is given as "*It's wrong*," with this punctuation and emphasis found only in the book version of the English original (see Du Bois 1901b, 863; 1903c, chap. 8, 151, para. 27).

18 [AN] Amendment to the constitution of the United States that forbids slavery.

19 [EN] The sentence in English reads: "A black stranger in Baker County, Georgia, for instance, is liable to be stopped anywhere on the public highway and made to state his business to the satisfaction of any white interrogator. If he fails to give a suitable answer, or seems too independent or 'sassy,' he may be arrested or summarily driven away" (Du Bois 1901b, 863; 1903c, chap. 8, 153, para. 29). In German, it reads: "So kann z. B. ein fremder Schwarzer in Baker County, Georgia, überall auf der Landstraße angehalten werden, um irgend einem neugierigen Weißen Rede und Anwort über sein Vorhaben zu

stehen. Wenn er keine befriedigende Antwort gibt, oder zu selbstbewußt erscheint, kann er festgehalten oder einfach über die Grenze gebracht werden" (Du Bois 1906a, 43).

20 [EN] The word *villeinage* translates here as the German noun *Frohndienst*. The full sentence in the German text is: "So kommt es, daß in den ländlichen Distrikten des Südens geschriebene und ungeschriebene Gesetze über weite Strecken ein System von Frohndienst, Bindung an die Scholle, Patronatsherrschaft verhängt haben" (Du Bois 1906a, 43). In *The Souls of Black Folk: Essays and Sketches*, Du Bois uses the English word *peonage* (Du Bois 1903c, chap. 8, 153, para. 30). This passage, as rendered in English in *The Souls of Black Folk: Essays and Sketches*, does not appear in the "The Negro as He Really Is" (Du Bois 1901b).

21 [EN] Du Bois often uses the term *black belt*, sometimes with initial capitalization (Du Bois 1898a, 1899b). "The Negro as He Really Is" and its revised and reprinted version in *The Souls of Black Folk: Essays and Sketches* most especially indicate the status of this reference in his discourse. Indeed, chapter 7 of the book is titled simply "Of the Black Belt" (Du Bois 1903b). While common in colloquial terms and political discourse at the time of his writing at the turn to the twentieth century, *black belt* referred in a somewhat variably defined manner to a band of counties with majority–African American populations that ran through the center of the Deep South, from southern Virginia and the eastern and southern Carolinas through Georgia, Alabama, Mississippi, and Louisiana and into eastern Texas. While incipient forms of this concentration might be noticeable historically from the early decades of the nineteenth century, parallel to the industrialization of cotton agriculture in particular, Du Bois here proposes to re-mark this demographic movement among African Americans as it pertains specifically to the post–Civil War, and especially the post-Reconstruction, economic and political topography across the Deep South (see Du Bois 1980c, 295; 1980h, 68).

22 [EN] From this sentence to the end of this section of the essay, at paragraph 51, Du Bois in essence presents a revision of the first half of "The Spawn of Slavery: The Convict-Lease System in the South" (Du Bois 1901f).

23 [EN] See the essay "The Freedmen's Bureau" (Du Bois 1901a). See also Du Bois 2015d.

24 [EN] David Walker (1785–1830) published his famous seventy-six-page antislavery challenge, *Appeal . . . to the Colored Citizens of the World*, in 1829, with the text going through three editions in less than a year. Frederick Douglass (1818–95) published a narrative of his experience as a slave in 1845, the best known and most celebrated of such narratives of slavery (Douglass 1979, 1994). George Washington Williams (1849–91) published his six hundred-page pioneering *History of the Negro Race in America from 1619 to 1880* in 1883. Booker T. Washington (1856–1915), born into slavery, became one of the most powerful people in America at the turn of the twentieth century (see Washington 1901). Paul Laurence Dunbar (1872–1906) was the author of a dozen books of poetry, five novels, four short-story collections, and a play, publishing his last collection of poetry in the year prior to his death at thirty-three, which occurred in Feb-ruary 1906, as Du Bois was preparing this essay (see, e.g., Dunbar 1905). Charles Wad-dell Chesnutt (1858–1932), a correspondent and interlocutor of Du Bois's, published

several of his most important works around the turn of the twentieth century (see, e.g., Chesnutt 1901).

25 [EN] The closing chapter of *The Souls of Black Folk: Essays and Sketches* proposed an influential interpretation of African American "spirituals" (Du Bois 1903e).

26 [EN] In 1905, four million marks (understood as Goldmarks, the gold-based currency of the German empire from 1863 to 1914) would have had an exchange value of approximately $1 million USD based on the most reliable recent scholarly handbooks on the history of modern world currency exchange rates (Denzel 2010). While extrapolation to twenty-first-century values is uncertain, it would not be unreasonable to calculate that value to roughly $25 million in 2010 and perhaps more in 2025 (but for a much smaller population).

27 [EN] This section of the essay draws from three previous texts by Du Bois. The first third reproduces, with emendations, the central paragraphs of chapter 9 of *The Souls of Black Folk: Essays and Sketches* (Du Bois 1903f). The middle third is drawn from *The Negro Artisan*, the report of the seventh Atlanta University study (Du Bois 1902). And the closing third draws from a brief text that, as noted earlier in the volume, Du Bois prepared and used often during 1904 as a kind of stump speech during his prolific lecture tours (see Du Bois 1980a, 1982c).

28 [EN] Edmund Asa Ware (1837–85) was born in North Wrenham (Norfolk), Massachusetts, and graduated in Yale University's class of 1863. After arriving in Atlanta in 1866 as the American Missionary Association's (AMA) superintendent of schools in that city, he took up the same position in 1867 under the Freedmen's Bureau, but for all of Georgia. He was one of the eleven signers of the charter to establish Atlanta University; served as the president of its Board of Trustees; and was appointed its first president in 1869, a position he retained until his death in 1885. Du Bois was a professor at this institution, the most significant academic appointment of his career, at the time that he composed this essay on "the talented tenth" (see Du Bois 2015f, 209–42).

29 [EN] Erastus Milo Cravath (1833–1900), born in Homer, New York, of French Huguenot ancestry, earned two degrees at Oberlin College, followed by a doctorate in divinity from Grinnell College. As a field secretary with the AMA after the Civil War, he helped found Fisk University in Nashville, Tennessee, serving as its first president from 1875 to 1900. There, he was a teacher of Du Bois as Du Bois pursued his first bachelor of arts degree from 1885 to 1888.

30 [EN] Samuel Chapman Armstrong (1839–93) was born on the island of Maui, in Hawai'i, into a missionary family. After an initial education in the islands—notably, at Punahou School in Honolulu (founded in 1841 for the children of Christian missionaries from across the Pacific region; among its twentieth-century graduates was Barack Hussein Obama, the forty-fourth President of the United States)—he graduated from Williams College in Massachusetss. During the US Civil War, he volunteered for the Union Army, eventually rising to the rank of colonel in the command of the 8th Regiment of the United States Colored Troops in late 1864, in particular during the siege of Petersburg, Virginia. At the end of the war, he joined the Freedmen's Bureau and in

1868, with the support of the AMA, helped to found the Hampton Normal and Agricultural Institute (now Hampton University) in Hampton, Virginia, for the education of freedmen. Booker T. Washington remains the school's most famous alumnus.

31 [EN] As noted earlier in this volume, due to its importance to the argument of this part of the essay that Du Bois sent to Weber—who should be understood to have doubtless immediately recognized its direct bearing on what he had asked of Du Bois in November 1904 and on his own consideration of the organization of social economic relationships in Eastern Prussia—it should be underlined here that chapter 9 of *The Souls of Black Folk: Essays and Sketches* is the source of the first half of this section of "Die Negerfrage." It is also a slight revision and reprinting of the essay "The Relation of the Negroes to the Whites in the South" (Du Bois 1901e; 2015f, 189–208).

32 [EN] The Latin phrase expresses the sense of something intermediate between two things. Translated literally, it reads as "a third something."

33 [EN] Thomas Carlyle (1795–1881), was a Scottish writer, historian and social critic who became especially prominent during the Victorian era, across the second half of the nineteenth century. An acute critic of the conditions of the poor in England, especially during the middle decades of the nineteenth century, he produced as his first major work a widely read, three-volume history of the French Revolution, underscoring the conditions that motivated the revolutionaries (Carlyle 1888). On this question, in several contexts, he argued that the conditions of living for the poor in the United Kingdom, especially in a city such as London—as indicated, for example by mortality rates for children (e.g., under five years of age)—were worse than the conditions for Negro slaves in the US South. He is also infamous for an 1849 essay criticizing the abolition of slavery in the Caribbean and expressing a categorical denegation (i.e., a racist disposition) toward Negroes or people of African descent or background as a group.

34 [EN] This phrasing is also in "The Relations of the Negroes to the Whites in the South" (Du Bois 1901e), reprinted with slight revisions as the chapter 9 of *The Souls of Black Folk: Essays and Sketches* (Du Bois 1903d). While the fifth edition of that book, issued in 1904, retains the original phrasing, by the ninth edition, issued in 1911, the phrase "unscrupulous Jews" had been changed to "unscrupulous foreigners," with the latter phrase remaining in all of the subsequent editions published by McClurg and Company. (I have not yet been able to review the sixth, seventh, and eighth editions of the book.) In the jubilee edition of 1953, published by Blue Heron Press, that phrase was further changed to read "unscrupulous immigrants" (Du Bois 1953, 169). Herbert Aptheker has remarked on this and other similar phrases in Du Bois's early writings (see Aptheker 1971).

35 [EN] The full reference for this quotation is in *The Negro Artisan* (Du Bois 1902, 153; Ely 1890, 42).

36 [EN] The full reference for this quotation is in *The Negro Artisan* (Du Bois 1902, 153; McNeill 1887, 113).

37 [EN] The full reference for this quotation is in *The Negro Artisan* (Du Bois 1902, 153; Powderly 1889, 51).

38 [EN] The full reference for this quotation is in *The Negro Artisan* (Du Bois 1902, 153–54; McNeill 1887, 126).

39 [EN] The full reference for this quotation is in Du Bois 1902, 154; McNeill 1887, 162.

40 [EN] The full reference for this quotation is in Du Bois 1902, 154; McNeill 1887, 136.

41 [EN] The full reference for this quotation is *not* given in *The Negro Artisan*, but it can be located by way of Du Bois's references there to a speech by Terence V. Powderly (1849–1924), the leader of the Knights of Labor during this time (Powderly 1889, 429).

42 [EN] The full reference for this quotation is given in *The Negro Artisan* (Du Bois 1902, 155; Ely 1890, 83)

43 [EN] The full reference for this quotation is given in *The Negro Artisan* (Ely 1890, 155; McNeill 1887, 171).

44 [EN] This quotation refers to the "Manifesto of the International Working People's Association, Anarchists Blacks." The full reference is given in *The Negro Artisan* (Du Bois 1902, 155; Powderly 1889, 693).

45 [EN] The following words are in quotes in the English text of *The Negro Artisan*: "the color line had been broken, and black and white were found working together in the same cause" (Du Bois 1902, 155; McNeill 1887, 360).

46 [EN] The full reference for this quotation is given in *The Negro Artisan* (Du Bois 1902, 155).

47 [EN] The full reference for this passage is given in *The Negro Artisan* (Du Bois 1902, 155–56; Powderly 1889, 651–62).

48 [TN] "Grand-Master Workman" was the organizational title of the leader of the Knights of Labor, Terence V. Powderly.

49 [EN] The full reference for this quotation is given in *The Negro Artisan* (Du Bois 1902, 155–56; Powderly 1889, 651–62). There, for this specific sentence, Du Bois refers to the US Industrial Commission Reports (Du Bois 1902, 156; Egerton and Durand 1901, 19).

50 [EN] In *The Negro Artisan*, Du Bois places within this quotation his own following notation: "As a matter of fact it practically excludes Negroes still" (Du Bois 1902, 156).

51 [EN] In *The Negro Artisan*, Du Bois specifically cites the source of his quotation in paragraphs 89 and 90 as the report prepared by Charles E. Edgerton and Edward Dana Durand for the US Industrial Commission (Du Bois 1902; Edgerton and Durand 1901, 36–37).

52 [EN] In *The Negro Artisan*, Du Bois includes the following note to this summary (as given here in paragraph 91: "The above statement has been submitted to the President of the American Federation of Labor for criticism. Up to the time of printing this page no reply has been received. If one is received later it will be printed as an appendix" (Du Bois 1902, 157).

53 [EN] Samuel Gompers (1850–1924), although born in England, became a key leader in the history of the labor movement in America, specifically as a founder of the American Federation of Labor (AFL), of which he was a long-serving president. He

was especially known for his promotion of harmony among the different craft unions that made up the membership organizations of the AFL.

54 [EN] The full reference for this quotation is given in *The Negro Artisan* (Du Bois 1902, 158).

55 [EN] This quotation is attributed to Albion Tourgée (1838–1905) in 1890, as reported in an essay on the disfranchisement of African Americans published by John L. Love (ca. 1865 or 1877–1931) in 1899 as a member of the American Negro Academy (Love 1899, 10). It was often quoted by Du Bois.

56 [EN] These words are from a speech given by Thomas E. Miller (1849–1938), one of six members of the South Carolina Constitutional Convention of 1895. Du Bois is citing the speech as it is reported in Love (1899, 11–13). This statement also was often quoted by Du Bois.

57 [TN] Here there is either a grammatical or typographical mistake or the German is using a formulation that is no longer current. Whatever the case, the meaning is unmistakable. The German reads: "Man kann sich vorstellen, was einer Welt, wo es so viel bedeutet, einem Mann die Hand zu reichen und sich neben ihm zu setzen, ihm offen in die Augen zu schauen und daran zu denken, dass auch er ein fühlendes Herz hat, wo eine gemeinsame Zigarre oder Tasse Tee mehr bedeuten als die Abgeordnetenhäuser und Zietschriftenartikel und Reden, es heisst, wenn fast jede soziale Freundlichkeit zwischen den entfremdeten Rassen aufhört und die Trennung sich sogar auf die Hotels, Parks und Strassenbahnwagen ausdehnt."

58 [EN] Eugene V. Debs (1855–1926) was a major American labor leader of the turn of the twentieth century and a founding member of the Industrial Workers of the World. He was also several times the Socialist Party's candidate for the Presidency of the United States. William Jennings Bryan (1860–1925) was a candidate for the US Presidency in the intensely fought elections of 1896 and 1900 and in the election of 1908, in which he was defeated by William McKinley (1843–1901). In 1896, Bryan campaigned in favor of "free silver," a policy that proposed using an inflationary money policy rather than the "gold standard" policy in which the standard economic unit would be based on a determined weight in gold. The issue pitted a Northeastern economic establishment against farmers, in particular, and others who sought higher prices for their products during the depression years of the early 1890s.

59 [TN] "Rotten borough system" is in English in the original.

60 [AN] In the following publications the author [W. E. B. Du Bois] addressed in greater detail the questions raised above: *Atlanta University Publications,* nos. 1–9 [(Conference for the Study of the Negro Problems 1896; Conference for the Study of the Negro Problems 1897; Du Bois 1898b; Du Bois 1899c; Du Bois 1900a; Du Bois 1901c; Du Bois 1902; Du Bois 1903a; Du Bois 1904b)]. *The Souls of Black Folk,* 1903, 265p [(Du Bois 1903f)]. *Philadelphia Negro,* 1899, 520p [(Du Bois and Eaton 1899)]. *Bulletin of the U.S. Census,* No. 8 [(Du Bois 1904a)].

NOTES

....

An early version of parts of this work was published in two essays in *CR: The New Centennial Review* (6, no. 3, and 7, no. 1). I thank Michigan State University Press and the editors of *CR*, Scott Michaelsen and David E. Johnson, for their permission to reinscribe that presentation as the basis for this book-length publication.

1 The Du Bois–Weber correspondence can be found in the microfilm edition of *The Papers of W. E. B. Du Bois* (Du Bois 1980f, reel 3, frames 663–75). The reference is to the Congress of Arts and Sciences held in conjunction with the Universal Exposition of 1904 in St. Louis, Missouri, as a celebration of the centenary of the Louisiana Purchase (Rogers 1905–7). Weber gave his first public lecture in more than half a dozen years at the congress, after having suffered a breakdown in 1897 and persisting incapacitation for the next five and a half years. His attendance and presentation at the congress were the precipitant occasion for Weber's trip to the United States. He had been invited by Hugo Münsterberg, a professor of psychology at Harvard University, whom Weber had come to know at the University of Freiburg, and who was one of the organizers of the congress. Some five years after the conclusion of the correspondence recorded here, in the context of a heated dialogue about race at the founding sessions of the Deutsche Gesellschaft für Soziologie (German Sociological Society) in October 1910, Weber spoke affirmatively of meeting Du Bois in St. Louis, indicating that they shared the occasion of a breakfast together (Weber 1911, 164; 1971; 1973, 312).

2 The mention of Werner Sombart, who also lectured at the Congress of Arts and Sciences, may indicate that Du Bois met him in St. Louis in the company of Weber. Sombart, whom Weber and Jaffé invited to join them as an editor of the *Archiv*, earned his doctorate in Berlin under Gustav Schmoller and Adolph Wagner just two years before Weber earned his own degree there under the same scholars, along with Levin Goldschmidt as his key adviser. During the 1890s, Sombart developed a close engagement with the thought of Karl Marx, and although he was never a Marxist as such, he was thus viewed as a radical in the early years of his career. Hence, he received only an out-of-the-way appointment at the University of Breslau, appointments at the University of Heidelberg and the University of Freiburg being vetoed by the respective provincial-level ministries. He later came to repudiate his 1890s position and eventually received an appointment at the University of Berlin in 1917. During the 1920s and 1930s, he moved to the right and was sympathetic early on to the tenets of National

Socialism even as he later offered some criticism of the movement. Already moving away from his early sympathetic interpretation of Marx around the time of the founding of the *Archiv* in 1904, he became a central theoretical sparring partner for Weber throughout the remainder of Weber's life. Sombart's magnum opus on the history of capitalism had just been published in three volumes in 1902 (Backhaus 1996; Sombart 1924).

3 Houston Stewart Chamberlain was a British-born Germanophile whose ideas of racial hierarchy—in particular, an anti-Semitism of a culturalist kind—came to play a substantive part in the devolution of nationalist and anti-Semitic thought in Germany, especially in the thought of Adolf Hitler and the policies of the National Socialist Party. His main work, translated into English as *The Foundations of the Nineteenth Century*, was first published in 1899 (Chamberlain 1911). In 1903 it was reissued in a fourth edition, for which Chamberlain wrote a new foreword, "Dilletantismus, Rasse, Monotheismus, Rom." It is perhaps this text—and if so, especially, this reissue of it—that Weber has in mind here.

4 In the extant manuscript, this word is virtually illegible. However, its importance in the text compels an attempt at decipherment. Even after consultation with several other readers, I remain uncertain in my own judgment as to the English word that Weber intended to inscribe here. As was common at the turn of the twentieth century, *anthropology* in this sentence refers to what is commonly understood as physical anthropology today.

5 Most likely the speech mentioned here was a version of one given by Du Bois on some half-dozen occasions, at least, throughout 1904, on the theme of a "rising caste mentality" in America. The occasions were part of a series of short lecture tours that were more or less related to Du Bois's increasing prominence following the tremendous reception of *The Souls of Black Folk: Essays and Sketches* upon its publication the previous year. But the lectures were also undertaken in support of Atlanta University's efforts to maintain or secure financial support from Northern philanthropists. A version of a text exists that was apparently associated with these occasions throughout 1904. As the scholastic aspect of this matter entails a small bibliographic conundrum, I simply note here two points of information. First, a typescript titled "Caste in America," consisting of fifteen half-sheets that are each approximately four by six inches in size, with marginal emendations in hand script, is in *The Papers of W. E. B. Du Bois*; it is most likely the original "hard-copy" text for the speech that Du Bois presented throughout the United States from at least February through December 1904. There it has a typescript document title placed by the curator, "Caste in America," with the words "New York Twentieth Century Club, 1904" below it (Du Bois 1980b). While the title is also on the document itself, I have not yet been able to ascertain the basis for the curator's attribution of the occasion of its presentation in New York. Second, Du Bois presented a lecture on 18 October 1904 in Des Moines, Iowa, before a convention held under the auspices of what is now known as the National Council of the Congregational Churches of the United States. This speech was reported in the Des Moines *Register-Leader* on 19 October; simultaneously, the story of the lecture was picked

up by the wire services and widely reported throughout the United States, at times in contradictory and confused terms. Aptheker presented the *Register-Leader* reportage of the speech in question in his collection of Du Bois's published *essays*, even as the head-note that he supplied suggests that it is a journalistic *account* (Du Bois 1982c). Yet it is essentially the same text as the typescript in the Du Bois papers, although there are some differences in wording, paragraph breaks, and punctuation. At this juncture, my best supposition is that Weber read an account of a lecture by Du Bois from late October—perhaps a wire service report based on, or reproducing in some sense, the text printed in the *Register-Leader*—on the theme in question.

6   And by way of this judgment, we can then propose a specific point of correction to the scholarship concerning Du Bois's life. Aptheker proposed in his 1973 introduction to *The Souls of Black Folk: Essays and Sketches* that Weber had attended the annual Atlanta Conference for the Study of the Negro Problems in 1904, the year that he came to the United States (Aptheker 1989, 75). However, we are able to confirm from the first paragraph of Weber's letter included here that he did not visit Atlanta University. This is also confirmed circumstantially by the fact that the conference took place in May, and the Webers departed Germany only during the last two weeks of August and arrived in the United States, in New York, proximate to the end of that month. I adduce a further correction of this order pertaining to *The Souls of Black Folk: Essays and Sketches* a bit later in the commentary. During the 1920s, Weber's wife, Marianne, prepared the biographical narrative of his life that has remained authoritative for the past eight decades, although contemporary scholarship is transforming its position. She indicates the dates that I have generally adduced here in the biography (Marianne Weber 1988, 280). Marianne Weber was an intellectual in her own right and an intellectual and political leader of the middle-class women's movement in Germany during the first half of the twentieth century. Most of her work remains only in the German, with the notable exception of the biography. The collection of her essays published at the end of World War I conveys the character of her work (Marianne Weber 1919). Indeed, she would go on to become politically active in the 1920s, after her husband's death. Although it must be noted, the massive biography of Weber by Joachim Radkau adds little elucidation to the principal concerns of this volume (Radkau 2005, 2009). On contemporary literature, see the work of Guenther Roth in this line (Roth 2001, 2002, 2005). The more recent work by Peter Ghosh is noted in the coda of this book (Ghosh 2014).

7   Additional related correspondence from the autumn of 1905, of which we know at present that there are two extant texts, are indicated and considered later in the chapter.

8   At this time, the letters from Du Bois to Weber do not appear to have survived. This judgment is based on two circumstances. First, they do not appear to be among the curated material of the Du Bois papers or among the papers of Max Weber. The first assessment is based on my own search and several conversations over the years, first with Linda Seidman, now retired, and more recently with Danielle Kovacs, both curators of the W. E. B. Du Bois Collection in the Special Collections Department at the

W. E. B. Du Bois Library, University of Massachusetts, Amherst. The latter conclusion is based on my correspondence with Dr. M. Rainer Lepsius, a principal editor focusing especially on the correspondence of the *Max Weber–Gesamtausgabe* (Complete works of Max Weber), which has been published in an ongoing series by Mohr Siebeck of Heidelberg since 1984 (Weber 1984a). He wrote to me that, as of early September 2006, the editors did not have any letters to Weber from Du Bois or letters other than those noted earlier to Du Bois from Weber.

9 Of the letters exchanged between Du Bois and Weber during November 1904, responses are each dated within seven to ten days after the date given in the initiating letter. From this thumbnail generalization I have roughly calculated the likely time frame for the posting of Weber's initial letter. Marianne Weber gives an account of the couple's US sojourn in the chapter of her biography titled "The New Phase," which describes Weber's halting and never finally stable recovery from the major illness of his life that had lasted for some six years. In her story, America appears as a revitalizing breath of fresh air to the scholar (see Marianne Weber 1988, 279–304, esp. 301–3). Her description of the timeline of their travel in the United States is ambiguous in terms of our interest here. Future scholarship may clarify these matters.

10 There is one exception. A photograph of the letter from Weber to Du Bois of 17 April 1905 has been published, but it is barely legible for scholastic purposes in that form (Scaff 1998b, 95).

11 The manuscript of this letter has the date "4/11" inscribed just below this date "30/III 05." It seems likely that it is in Du Bois's hand, or that of his secretary. It is perhaps the date on which Du Bois received the letter. Or it is the date of a possible reply by Du Bois. If the latter, it would be an additional letter to those we have enumerated, making the total number ten.

12 Elisabeth Helene Amalie Sophie Freiin (Baroness) Jaffé-von Richthofen, commonly known in this context as Else Jaffé, began her doctoral study with Max Weber in the late 1890s as one of only four students at the University of Heidelberg who were women. She completed her degree in 1901 with Otto Wagner as a supervisor. Through a mutual friend, Frieda Schloffer (later known by her married name, Frieda Gross), she became a lifelong friend of Marianne Weber, beginning in the years 1894–95 in Freiburg. Else was also the sister of Frieda von Richthofen, who would later become the companion, then wife, of D. H. Lawrence. (She was known to the world as Frieda Lawrence.) In 1902, Else von Richthofen married Edgar Jaffé. She corresponded with Du Bois about the idea for this translation in late 1905; that correspondence is noted later in part I. Edgar Jaffé, from a wealthy transnational family in the textile business by which he had already made his own substantial fortune by 1902, studied with Gustav Schmöller at the University of Berlin but finished with Weber at the University of Heidelberg in 1904. He and Else became principal figures in the intellectual and social circle around Max and Marianne Weber. In part through Weber's urging, Edgar purchased the *Archiv* in 1903. He taught the sociology of business organizations first at his alma mater and then in Munich until his death just after World War I.

13 William Ewart Gladstone was a British Liberal Party statesman and prime minster for multiple terms between 1868 and 1894. Known as a political reformer and famous for his populist speeches, he initially opposed abolition, giving an infamous speech in 1862 supporting the Confederacy in the US Civil War. He was initially an opponent of factory legislation in England. He was the fourth son of Sir John Gladstone, a Scottish-born owner of plantations and slaves in the Caribbean during the first half of the nineteenth century, who made a fortune trading in corn with the United States and cotton with Brazil. Liverpool was a key depot in his operations; his son, the future prime minister, was born there in 1830.

14 The people to whom and texts to which Weber refers here are most likely: Booker T. Washington's second autobiography on industrial training (Washington 1904), perhaps given to Weber upon his visit to Tuskegee in October 1904 (it should be noted that Washington's first and most famous autobiography had already been rendered in German [Washington 1902], and others followed over the next decade); Thomas Nelson Page (1904), of whose recently published book Du Bois would publish a review just two months later, in the 1 May 1905 issue of *The Dial* magazine (which would also review a small book by Edward A. Johnson that Du Bois would cite later in this correspondence on 18 April [Du Bois 1977, 9–13; Johnson 1904]); the American Negro Academy Occasional Papers, which up to that time could have been drawn from among the first eleven numbers and may have included Du Bois's essay in the series "The Conservation of Races," as well as texts by Kelly Miller, Alexander Crummell, John L. Love, Archibald H. Grimké, William S. Scarborough, John W. Cromwell, and John Hope, among others (American Negro Academy 1969; Du Bois 1897a; Moss 1981); Walter F. Wilcox, a professor of economics and statistics at Cornell University and a special agent for the US Census Bureau, whose essay on the twelfth census and the Negro had recently been published (Wilcox 1904) and with whom Du Bois was in collaboration and correspondence for several years, perhaps beginning in 1904. Du Bois worked with Wilcox in 1905 on statistical matters for a republication of the Du Bois's Census Bureau report "The Negro Farmer," and he is listed as a speaker in the annual report published from the Atlanta Conference in May 1905. This is so, even as it is also clear from their correspondence, in an exchange of letters dated 13 and 29 March 1904, respectively, for example, that Du Bois was profoundly critical of the presuppositions of Wilcox's approach to the question (Du Bois 1973c, 74–75). The review in question does not appear, even though the editors of the *Archiv* (most likely Weber) placed a note at the head of Du Bois's "Die Negerfrage" that such would be forthcoming, along with additional work on the so-called Negro question (Du Bois 1906a, 31; 2006, 288; 2015d, 330). However, in 1905, Sombart published a survey of the US government publications issuing from the twelfth census, especially concerning the matter of labor (Sombart 1905). His review was probably prepared on the basis of material that he collected while he was in the United States, with Weber, for the Congress of Arts and Sciences in 1904. In fact, as it turns out, Du Bois was a contributor to several of the publications reviewed by Sombart. The most important are a substantial

testimony that Du Bois gave in February 1901 before the US Industrial Commission in Washington, DC—the transcript of which, included in the report of the commission, is a virtually neglected text that provides a root-level and clarifying summary account of Du Bois's formulation of his project of the study of the Negro at the turn of the century (Du Bois 1980h)—and his report "The Negro Farmer" in the special volume from the US Census Bureau on the twelfth census focusing on the American Negro (Du Bois 1904a, 1906b). Du Bois himself would draw directly on this work in the opening section of his contribution to the *Archiv*. Indeed, the report is cited in the bibliography placed by Du Bois at the end of "Die Negerfrage."

15 At present, I have been unable to determine which publication is the "official" one to which Weber refers. It is likewise uncertain who the "Viereck" in question is, although it is possible that Weber is referring to Louis Viereck, a founder of the German Socialist Party and a prominent figure in German American discourse at the turn of the century. He came to the United States in the early 1890s and, among other writings, published a description of his travel around the United States in 1903 through the Deutsche Gesellschaft der Stadt New York (German Society of the City of New York) (see Viereck 1903). It is possible that Du Bois had mentioned the person in question in his March letter to Weber.

16 Emphases are marked on the manuscript of the letter as extant. The originator of those marks (Du Bois or Weber) is not always clear. For example, the emphasis on "November 1st" and the surname "Jaffé" appear to be by Du Bois, noting pertinent information. However, the emphasis on the phrase "to be translated in German" could be by either Weber or Du Bois. The emphasis on the phrase "if you give" perhaps makes most sense as Weber's.

17 Two different orders of notation must be given here. First, in January 1905, in Heidelberg, following scheduled speeches by Marianne Weber and Ernst Troeltsch, Max Weber spoke impromptu for more than an hour at a public discussion on America. While the essential thought of his later text on "religious sects" in America was given its first public airing on that occasion, of equal importance for our considerations here is that he also spoke about "the Negro question" as apparently the most intractable and "serious" problem confronting the United States as a whole (see "America-Abend des Nationalsozialen Vereins," *Heidelberger Zeitung*, 21 January 1905, 47, cited in Scaff 1998b, 79n1). Should we surmise, then, that Weber was already reading *The Souls of Black Folk: Essays and Sketches* during the winter months of December 1904 and January 1905? This would be at the time Weber was beginning the second part of his essay on "the Protestant ethic." The question is not at all unreasonable. Second, this is in contradistinction to Aptheker's statement that "Weber had already read *Souls*" at the time of his visit to the United States in the autumn of 1904 or, at least, before his return to Germany in late November of that year (Aptheker 1989, 75). That dating seems unlikely for the reasons adduced earlier and because of the pace of the Webers' visit to the United States, especially during their extended stay in New York in November after their tour (Marianne Weber 1988, 302).

18 The texts cited are Sinclair 1905; Johnson 1904; and Collins 1904.

19 In his milestone bibliography, *Black Access: A Bibliography of Afro-American Biblio-graphies*, Richard Newman writes: "The first bibliography of black bibliographies was compiled by W. E. B. Du Bois as part of *A Selected Bibliography of the Negro American: A compilation made under the direction of Atlanta University; together with the Proceedings of the Tenth Conference for the Study of the Negro Problems, held at Atlanta University, on May 30, 1905.* This bibliography of bibliographies consisted of twenty-six items and served as an introduction to a major Afro-American bibliography, a booklet of seventy-one pages, the largest ever compiled up to that time. Five of the bibliographies listed had appeared in previous Atlanta University conference publications, four were bibliographies in the Johns Hopkins University series of studies of slavery in the vari-ous states; in fact, all but four were appendices to monographs" (Newman 1984, ix). Newman's finding illustrates, in one specific area of scholarship, the fundamental and innovative character of the role that Du Bois played in formulating and constructing scholarship in the study of African Americans in the United States in general. Du Bois as a "first" is almost a defining trope in scholarship on his work and his writings. Yet in several odd and decisive ways, the very ubiquity of this fact in Du Bois's biography seems often to shield such apparent facts from any careful and sustained thought.

20 Therein, Du Bois cites the *texts* of Johnson (1904, 28) and Sinclair (1905, 39), respec-tively, but cites only the *bibliography* of Collins (1904, 9).

21 My deciphering of the script as "And so then" is uncertain. Also, the word *perhaps* is written after this script and then struck through. Weber did *not* succeed in returning to the United States. After the signature "Prof. Max Weber" the name "Max Weber" is written in capital letters in a different hand.

22 Emphases (doubled in the first instance here in the form of underlining) are marked on the manuscript of the letter as extant. It is not clear whether the marks were made by Weber or Du Bois; it is possible they were made by both. A second version of this letter that is essentially the same is in the Du Bois papers. The latter version appears to be a kind of deciphering transcription of the original. The handwriting is different from that which we have come to recognize as Weber's. It is perhaps Du Bois's hand script or that of an assistant. Several spelling changes in the names are either misspell-ings or coincide with the English spelling of German names. Also, certain words are simply dropped from one version to the other—for example, the virtually indecipher-able words of the original are simply left aside. This is the transcribed version:

Heidelburg [*sic*], May 1, 05

My Dear Colleague:

I thank you very much for your kind letter. We have engaged a pub-lisher—Dr. P. Siebeck (firm of F. C. B. Mohr) Tübingen, the publisher of the "Ar-chiv für Socialpolitick" [*sic*], of *course* with reservation of your previous consent to the making of the translation. I beg you to inform your publisher, and hope there will be no difficulties [*sic*]

The library of our University will certainly, be very glad to have your univer-sity publications [*sic*] I thank you very much for your useful information [*sic*]

Will you not have your "Sabbath-year" of the next years? I hope you will come to Germany then & visit us. I shall come to the United States I think, 1907 or 8.

Yours very [illegible], Prof. Max Weber

Address of the before mentioned publisher:
Herr F. C. B. Mohr's Verlag, Herr Dr. Paul Siebeck Tübingen
Wurtemberg [*sic*], Germany

23 As stated in n. 3, Weber referred to Du Bois in October 1910 in the midst of a heated polemic on race at the founding meetings of the Deutsche Gesellschaft für Soziologie.

24 In October 1910, five months after Du Bois had packed up his academic office and moved from Atlanta to New York, Weber would characterize Du Bois in a debate about "race and society" as "the most important sociological scholar anywhere in the Southern States in America, with whom no white scholar can compare" at the founding meeting of the Deutsche Gesellschaft für Soziologie in Frankfurt. It almost goes without saying that due to the practices of the "color line" in the United States, and despite his rather remarkable credentials and record of scholarship, Du Bois at that time could not have been hired, for example, at the University of Chicago, Columbia University, Harvard University, Johns Hopkins University, or the University of Pennsylvania. A century later, perhaps, they might have competed for his talent and dedication.

25 Three pertinent texts are in the collection of pamphlets by Du Bois edited and published by Aptheker in the series The Complete Published Works of W. E. B. Du Bois: a confidential circular announcing the proposed meeting at Niagara, issued perhaps in the late winter of 1905, and two documents—a "declaration of principles" and a "constitution and by-laws"—issuing from the occasion of the first meeting of the group in July 1905. All were ostensibly prepared by Du Bois as "provisional secretary" for the group (Du Bois 1986b, 53–65). These texts, along with others of the moment, record the rhythm according to which one motif of Du Bois's practice up to this time—the attempt to institutionalize a new leadership for the African American—becomes the most prominent and his practice undergoes a shift in its internal organization, even as the composition and fundamental commitments therein arguably remain the same. Whereas in the 1890s, Du Bois proposed an epistemological leadership conceptualizing the American Negro Academy as "an intellectual clearing house" (Du Bois 1897a, 12, para. 18; 2015b, 58, para 18) that would make possible the best judgments and interventions of policy, by the middle of the first decade of the twentieth century, the proposition of a political form of leadership had begun to move to the forefront of his practice, even as the former remained his most fundamental vocational commitment.

26 Marianne Weber gives the following account in her biography: "The treatise about the spirit of capitalism now quickly approached completion. At the end of March, after scarcely three months of work, the second part was finished. Weber wrote to [Heinrich] Rickert [Jr.]: 'I am working—amidst horrible torments, to be sure, but I do manage to work a few hours each day. In June or July you will receive an essay on cultural history that may be of interest to you: Protestant asceticism as the foundation

of modern *vocational civilization* [*Berufskultur*]—a sort of 'spiritualistic' construction of the modern economy' (April 2, 1905)" (Marianne Weber 1988, 356). Rickert was a neo-Kantian philosopher of Weber's generation at the University of Freiburg and then the University of Heidelberg whose 1902 study on concepts in the human sciences was a key point of interlocution for Weber (Rickert 1902, 1986).

27 It can be shown that the gradual formulation of the character of Weber's global problematic at the level of this specific text becomes legible only as one reads the initial two-part essay on "the Protestant ethic" (Weber 1905a, 1905b) in relation to the text as Weber prepared it for republication in 1919, along with other texts of this latter time. Notably, these texts include the famous "prefatory remarks" to his collected essays on the sociology of religion (Weber 2002a). This relationship is best understood in light of the rich debate that the original essay set in motion during the intervening years, in which Weber was a principal interlocutor (Chalcraft and Harrington 2001; Ghosh 2014; Lehmann and Roth 1993; Seyfarth and Sprondel 1973; Swatos and Kaelber 2005; Marianne Weber 1988). For the Anglophone reader, this relation is now available for understanding by way of the translation into English of the 1904–5 essays (see Weber 2002d). The editors and translators of the 2002 edition proposed this thought in their remarks on the two versions of the essay (Baehr and Wells 2002, xxxiv–xxxv). But this thought is not new. While the editors cite Marianne Weber's biography (1988, 331–34), even Wilhelm Hennis can be understood to have made a similar proposition more than two generations earlier, if in a more qualified *and* more assertive formulation (Hennis 1988, 26–28). Note also Schluchter 1981. Herbert Marcuse, however, proposed the farthest-reaching perspective at the famous Weber centennial conference held at Heidelberg in 1964 (see Marcuse 1971), and from an almost opposite position, Benjamin Nelson acknowledged the same in his commentary thereon (see Stammer 1971, 167–68). It is perhaps from this perspective, too, that Weber's thought of America as a historical entity should be understood. It is along this track—the formulation of a general concept of modern historicity—that Weber's lecture at the Congress of Arts and Sciences in St. Louis in September 1904 (Weber 1906, 1998) and the essay on the forms of religious association with the United States as an example that he prepared some six months after his return to Germany should be understood (Weber 2002b; 2021, 180–90). They each presume his conception of Europe's historicity and pose the question of America as a comparison under the heading of this conception. Then, likewise, consider Weber's question about "the relations between the (so called) 'race-problem' and the (so called) 'class-problem'" in America as posed in his initial letter to Du Bois.

28 The remarkable intervention of Karen E. Fields in this domain must be noted, including her translation and trenchant introduction of Durkheim's *Formes élémentaires de la vie religieuse* (1995). But especially deserving of wider engagement is her "imaginary conversation between W. E. B. Du Bois and Émile Durkheim" (Fields 2002). The pioneering audacity of the latter should stand as all the more compelling in light of the interlocution being adduced in this volume. Fields's thought project, for me, is exemplary.

29 The kind of "circle" of which the Webers were the center at Heidelberg, along with the Jaffés, was well known in its time. Werner Sombart, Emil Lask, Mina Tobler, Karl and Gertrud Jaspers, Georg Simmel, Gertrud Bäumer, and György Lukács, for example, were key players at various moments in this ongoing "salon" conversation before World War I (Marianne Weber 1988, cf. 368–70).

30 The text was translated from German by Joseph Fracchia (see the appendix). The German text, along with a draft of Du Bois's reply, are in Du Bois 1980f, reel 2, frames 265–67.

31 The journal was founded under this name (perhaps translated as "journal for social legislation and statistics") in 1888 by Heinrich Braun, from whom Edgar Jaffé purchased it in 1903 (Factor 1988, 1–8). The new editors changed the name to *Archiv für Sozialwissenschaft und Sozialpolitik* (perhaps "Journal for social science and social policy") but apparently had not yet updated the stationery. Also, an older postal address appears to have been Rohnbacherstrasse 21, for Uferstrasse 8A, the new or current address, is stamped over it almost illegibly.

32 The word *Einfachheit* used here is translated literally as "simplicity". But also, and especially in this context, it connotes straightforwardness and clarity.

33 I added the punctuation marks and comment in brackets to this presentation of this letter to enhance legibility, as this seems to be a quick draft sketched in one breath, as it were.

34 The word *reservation* is written here in the manuscript and then crossed out with the German word given below it in quotation marks.

35 A letter to Du Bois dated 13 March 1905 from Francis Fisher Browne, his editor at McClurg and Company, indicates that the London publisher Archibald Constable and Company had ordered one thousand copies of *The Souls of Black Folk: Essays and Sketches*. Another letter, dated 31 May 1905, indicates that, along with the possible German translation, Browne had already solicited and received a translation of several chapters of *The Souls of Black Folk: Essays and Sketches* into French in preparation for a trip to Europe during the summer of 1905 and that he hoped to interest a French publisher—in particular, Hachette—in issuing a translated edition. Browne was unable to make the trip for reasons of his health. And as a letter from Browne to Du Bois dated 7 September 1905 makes clear, no French publisher at that time had an interest in bringing forth a translation (Du Bois 1980f, reel 2, frames 433–518).

36 The unification of the German states was historically coextensive with the promulgation of Reconstruction in America and its aftermath. Thus, the question of historicity in general, and its specific formulation as the project of the human sciences. was profoundly rooted in nineteenth-century German discourse. It can be shown that Du Bois understood the African American situation in relation to both of these legacies.

37 Indeed, a translation into German would be realized only in 2003, after the work had already been translated into French, Chinese, Japanese, and Spanish (see Du Bois 1959 [1903]a, 1959[1903]b, 1965[1903], 2001, 2003).

38 While the course of events during the winter of 1905 and the year of 1906 remains unclear, by the early months of 1907, Else Jaffé had become involved in an intimate

relationship with the libertine psychoanalyst and writer Otto Hans Adolf Gross; she gave birth to his child in December 1907. Among other strains, it had a direct impact on her relationship with Marianne and Max Weber (Green 1988, 3–175, esp. 24–27, 33, 54–55, 105, 366ff; 1999; Mitzman 1970, 277–96; Schwenker 1987; Marianne Weber 1988, cf. 370–80; Weber and Baumgarten 1964; Whimster and Heuer 1998). In the context of our discussion here, and given the specific dynamics of her relationship with Max Weber over many years, it is reasonable to believe that such a complication might have slowed attention on her part to a somewhat difficult project that had been directly suggested by him. Scaff also notes this possibility (see Scaff 1998a, 80n7).

39   Proximate to the middle of the first decade of this century, Rebecka Rutledge Fisher completed a study and translation of this text from French, during which she determined that it is drawn essentially verbatim from Du Bois's 1902 Atlanta University study on the Negro worker—or "artisan," as he preferred to nominalize it at the turn of the century. I was able to confirm this in direct correspondence (see Du Bois 1902, 1906c).

40   Chapter 9 of *The Souls of Black Folk: Essays and Sketches*, which is the source of the first half of this specific section of "Die Negerfrage," is, in turn, a slight revision and reprinting of the 1901 essay "The Relations of the Negroes to the Whites in the South" (see Du Bois 1901c; 1903d; 2015f, 189–208). The first systematic exemplification in Du Bois's work of the mode of description that he outlines here—indeed, the exact categories that he uses—is his study of African Americans in the rural community of Farmville. the research was undertaken during July and August of 1897, and the writing followed over the course of the early autumn of the same year (Du Bois 1898a, 1899b, 1980e). Du Bois undertook similar research during the summer of 1898 in the southern Georgia county of Dougherty (Du Bois 1903f, 110–63; 1980d). Both examples thus stand as the references for the description of social relations in the South that Du Bois proposes in this section. The Georgia example stands as the perennial one for Du Bois during this time, appearing not only as the background reference throughout *The Souls of Black Folk: Essays and Sketches* but also, especially, in chapters 7–9 (Du Bois 1903f, 110–88).

41   The deployment of the term *caste* in Du Bois's discourse, from the turn of the century through World War I—for example, in the closing two chapters of his study of John Brown (Du Bois 1909, 1973b)—must be especially remarked. It was a lexical appropriation of a term that had been rendered colloquial even as its incipiting formal organization took shape as a general order of demographic term—that was also at once legal, political, and economic—in the colonial discourse of the British in India during the eighteenth and nineteenth centuries (Cohn 1984; Dirks 2001, 1–123). Here it seems that Du Bois wished to give the term a critical sense. That is, he was not proposing that castes as such had ever existed up to, say, the turn of the twentieth century, even as a fully accomplished ideological project in India or elsewhere. This might well be understood in contradistinction to the use of the term *caste* in the work of both Marx and Weber. For Du Bois, the matter is a profound millennial historicity

that nonetheless is the scene and expression of a fundamental contestation of force in matters of supposed difference among groups of humans. That is thus to say, rather, in the phrase "caste spirit," he is nominalizing what he claims is a tendential projection in a "new" or renewed disposition among privileged groups of Americans (both "classes" and "races") at the turn of the century. For Du Bois, this was a contemporary appropriation of premises that had first been announced in a different historical era. In his argument, Du Bois is attempting to historicize this unfolding disposition in his historical present. His use of the term certainly carries all the ambivalent theoretical burdens of irony. Yet his general critical disposition to what he calls a "new caste spirit" is focused on the effects of systems of exploitation and the concomitant restrictions on opportunity. It sustains no claim that it can simply be taken as an account of the general possibility of such an order of system itself. In this sense, too, Du Bois's discursive practice here should not be simply submitted to the mid-century criticism by Oliver Cox (1948, 509–38) of the misplaced deployment of the concept of caste to explain the American situation by Gunnar Myrdal (1944), among others, that is for an interpretation of the question of the practices of distinction in the United States according to attributions of so-called race. What Cox rightly criticizes in Myrdal is a limit in acknowledging the economic and material organization of interest in the production of distinctions of race. Doubtless, Cox's engagement is on point with the question posed to Du Bois by Weber. Du Bois, it should be emphasized, had sought to attend to the premise of an ultimate limit to capacity or possibility of those less privileged in his deployment of the term *caste*; however, he just as resolutely named in his own way an understanding of the relation of historical systems of exploitation to the development of this tendential disposition. This he had already proposed over the course of the first decade of the twentieth century (e.g., in the reflection on John Brown), and it is a thought that he had already been led to summarize with regard to a global horizon by the inception of World War I (Du Bois 1915).

42 Farmville is about two hundred miles from the home of the relatives that Max and Marianne Weber visited outside Mt. Airy, North Carolina. The account of their trip to the area in October 1904, which is given in their letters, records that on the hill opposite and facing the house of James Miller, in whose home they lodged during their visit, stood the house of James's brother, Jeff Miller. Contemporary scholarship indicates that Jeff Miller's house, "with walls six feet thick, was constructed by slave labor" (Keeter 1981, 113; Wise 2006). Weber also recorded in a letter to his mother during or shortly after the visit that he and his wife had supper there on one occasion. The Millers had taken that name, changing the family name from Fallenstein (the name of Weber's maternal grandfather), sometime in the mid-nineteenth century. This history of immigration and integration, even marked by its particularity in the instance of the (Fallenstein) Millers, is a central ore line of the sedimentation that is at issue here (Roth 2001). Weber himself describes in his letter that their host's household included a "Negro" who ate alone and after everyone else. ("Finally the Negro ate by himself (he lives in a shack with some land, both of which he received from James)," Max Weber wrote in the letter to his mother [see Marianne Weber 1988, 297]). In another letter

of the same moment, referring to their visit to the Tuskegee Institute a week or so earlier and their travels by train through Georgia into western North Carolina, Weber makes a distinction between "the numerous half-Negroes, quarter Negroes, and one hundredth part Negroes whom no non-American can distinguish from whites" at the institute, on the one hand, and "the semi-apes one encounters on the plantations and in the Negro huts of the 'Cotton Belt, [who] afford a horrid contrast," on the other (Marianne Weber 1988, 296). An attempt to excavate and record the sedimented historical social and economic conditions in the South that made possible the circumstances of Weber's visible tableau, and that he experienced in the countryside outside Mt. Airy, was a central motif of Du Bois's work from 1897 to 1907. While the conditions of a "Negro with a shack and some land" given by a white landowner, is the exact thematic line of description in the opening section of "Die Negerfrage," it is most dramatically and poignantly exposed in the two chapters on the "Black Belt" in *The Souls of Black Folk: Essays and Sketches* (Du Bois 1903b, 1903c). Therein, Du Bois's account of the Negroes of "the plantations" and "the Negro huts of the 'Cotton Belt'" marks a powerful contradistinction to Weber's apprehension.

43 See W. E. B. Du Bois to Carroll D. Wright, Commissioner of the Bureau of Labor, letters dated 5 May and 14 June 1897, in Du Bois 1897b; 1897c, 1973c; 41–42.

44 A copy of the manuscript titled "Sociology Hesitant" is in Du Bois 1980g (see also Du Bois 2015d). This text was likely prepared by Du Bois sometime during the winter months of 1904 and 1905. Along with "Die Negerfrage," which should perhaps be understood in this context as in critical dialogue with Weber's contribution to the occasion (Weber 1906), this essay is a response to and interlocution with the Congress of Arts and Sciences of 1904 (see Rogers 1905–7). I simply note here that I brought the fact that this essay was available in the Du Bois papers to the attention of my close friend and colleague Ronald A. T. Judy in the spring of 1996, subsequently held several conversations with him by telephone regarding the essay after his retrieval of the text from the archive, and, in the spring of 1999, agreed to forgo my planned publication and introduction of the essay out of respect for his desire to do so. The occasion was the panel "W. E. B. Du Bois and the Turn of the Millennium" at the Collegium for African American Research, held at Westphalia University in Münster, Germany, on 20 March, 1999. Organized by Kevin Thomas Miles and me, the panel also included Robert Bernasconi and David Farrell Krell. As I recall, David Levering Lewis's listing of "Sociology Hesitant" as "since lost" in the first volume of his two-volume biography of Du Bois had led Judy to understand that the text was no longer available (Lewis 1993a, 202; 1993b; but see also Judy 2000). It seems likely to me, however, that the preparation of "Sociology Hesitant" should *not* be understood as related to the issue of the volumes of the proceedings of the Congress of Arts and Sciences, as Judy proposes in his commentary (Judy 2000), for the first volumes were not printed until December 1905. If anything, it might more usefully be regarded as related to Du Bois's audition of the discourse at the sessions of the congress in St. Louis and to the sedimented strata of an interlocution with Weber (along with other presenters on the social sciences at the event). Thereby, it might be considered part of Du Bois's response

to his whole exclusion from the formal and official discourse of the congress, as well as to his relation to the nascent institutionalization of a discipline of sociology that was evidenced in long preparation and organization and voluminous proceedings of the congress. In such a context, others with training similar to his (e.g., Albion Small of Chicago) were at that very time succeeding in establishing themselves as central figures in a new discipline, whereas such a possibility was foreclosed for Du Bois.

PART II. THE TERMS OF THE DISCUSSION

1 Although I give a further annotation of the formulation "the problem of the color line" in Du Bois's thought later in this volume, in other work I give a brief general summary of this thought in the context of a discussion of the historical example in Du Bois's work (see Chandler 2021). Notably, I refer to the question of Africa in modern historicity and propose more scholarly elaboration of the emergence of this conceptualization within Du Bois's early thought and its theoretical implications and epistemological bearing (Chandler 2022b).

2 Yet it should be noted that an objection to its virtuality is not fundamental for our hesitation, since virtuality has its virtues—for example, those that this essay attempts to respect. Lewis's virtuality is an operation of the "as if" of its status in relation to the problem of truth, *whatever truth is*, as if it were simply a presentation of a given. Rather than taking the demand for the traversal of such a problematic—how to think the limits of the archive in certain domains—as *part of the object of his account*, Lewis proceeds as if he could start from or remain outside the epistemic horizon according to which the archive itself was produced. Hence, he covers over the difficulty. It is for this reason, perhaps, that he cannot address, for example, the dynamics of the dimension in which the engagement between Du Bois and Weber would announce itself, even if under the figure of a historical limitation, as open to the risk or possibility of the eventual, including interventions such as our own. If Lewis had accepted this as a problem in any engagement with Du Bois—as a thinker—he might not have presumptively *decided* the meaning of the possible relation of these two figures. He would, rather, have tried to announce some terms—archival, narratological, or theoretical—for working through it. The license that is practiced here instead belies almost any epistemological justification.

3 Lewis's account is most likely derived entirely from Aptheker's comments on the matter in his introductory essay in the reissue of *The Souls of Black Folk: Essays and Sketches* (Du Bois 1973e) and in his headnote for the publication of one of the letters from Weber to Du Bois in his selection from Du Bois's correspondence (Du Bois 1973c, 106–7). Aptheker's introductory essay was later reprinted in a collection of his introductions to Du Bois's writings and is generally more accessible than the 1973 edition of *The Souls of Black Folk: Essays and Sketches*. Also, it was published at the time of Lewis's preparation of the first volume of his biography of Du Bois. Thus, I refer to this later text for the direct citation (see Aptheker 1989, 75).

4 It appears circumstantially (though it remains uncertain) that the Webers traveled through Atlanta by train sometime in early to mid-October on their way from Tuskegee, Alabama, to Mt. Airy, North Carolina (though they could have taken another route from southern Alabama to western North Carolina) as part of their return leg to New York City. For various reasons—perhaps including the logistics of timing, for Du Bois himself may have still been traveling in the Midwest, perhaps lecturing in Iowa, among other activities in his own slow return to Atlanta after his attendance at the Congress of Arts and Sciences at St., Louis where he had met Weber—they did not meet with Du Bois, even if such a stop occurred in their travels. The details of the Webers' travels during this part of their visit to the United States remain ambiguous, at best, according to current scholarship (Scaff 2011a, 103; 2011b).

5 Karl Gustav Adolf von Harnack was a professor of "sacred" history at Berlin and a friend of the Webers. At the time of the Congress of Arts and Sciences, at which he was a speaker, his seven-volume history of Christian doctrine was being rendered into English by multiple hands and published in the United States (Harnack 1898–1912). With the exception of the reference to Harnack, the Weber scholar Lawrence Scaff adduces the modifications of the English translation from the original letter that are included in brackets here (Scaff 2005, 88).

6 These texts on the Protestant ethic and on methodology in the social and cultural sciences would be among the first translations of Weber's writing into English, commencing some twenty years later. From the 1940s to the 1990s they defined his reception in the Anglophone context (Weber 1946, 1949, 1958a). In the sense of its pertinence to contemporary theoretical discussion, the earlier work on agrarian history is still to be rendered for the English-speaking audience, not only in translation, but, to some extent, in commentary (Käsler 1988; Riesebrodt 1989; Tribe 1989). Weber's visit to the United States in 1904 was facilitated by a network of transnational family relations (Roth 2005) and German expatriate professors. The latter included Hugo Münsterberg of Harvard University, a psychologist whom Weber had come to know at the University of Freiburg and who had invited him to address the congress in St. Louis (Marianne Weber 1988, 279–303), and Edwin R. A. Seligman of Columbia University, an economist and head of the Society for Ethical Culture, who was Weber's main host in New York City (Roth 2002, 519n11). Seligman would later write to Du Bois commending his poem "A Litany of Atlanta," which was written in the aftermath of the 1906 "race riots" in that city (Du Bois 1973c, 123; 1975a, 25–28). I have not been able establish whether Seligman knew Du Bois prior to Weber's visit.

7 Here I would note two essays by Scaff that reposition these matters somewhat (see Scaff 1998a, 1998b). These essays were incorporated into the book-length study *Max Weber in America* (Scaff 2011b). Scaff's work offers a certain kind of documentation and account of Weber's order of attention in the US situation. I have been proposing here the status of the question of relation: that what is entailed here is a double-layered and interwoven problematic. I also propose that a question of the thinkers in relation *and* of the general question of social relation (notably, matters of supposed categorical difference, at once questions of economic class and of the tendentious development

of differences in the social and historical formation of social groups among humans) that is the very theme or topic of their interlocution of 1904 and 1905 is a necessary and fundamental consideration for any engagement by practitioners in contemporary social thought with this example (exemplary example) of thinkers in relation to, and in this horizon of, historical problematization for thought in our time.

8 According to a note by Aptheker at the head of his 1976 publication of the two 1945 letters, "Manasse was born in Germany in 1908 and educated at the University of Heidelberg; he taught in the 1930s in Italy and England and from 1939 to 1973 was on the faculty at North Carolina Central University in Durham [North Carolina], where he is now professor emeritus" (Du Bois 1973d, 44). To the extent that Manasse studied at Heidelberg, completing an inaugural dissertation there in 1933 on Plato, his intellectual formation would have occurred in a context still powerfully marked by Weber's legacy. Indeed, as indicated in the *Vorbemerkung* of his dissertation, a principal mentor was Karl Jaspers, a devoted former student and associate of Weber (Manasse 1937). I had occasion to review an original edition of this study, donated to the Columbia University Libraries by the author upon his arrival in New York as a refugee in January 1939. See also the biographical sketch of Manasse in Schweitzer 1996.

9 The essay was published in *Social Research*. The journal issued from the New School for Social Research in New York City, an institution, as is well known, that was founded during World War I by pacifist professors seeking an arena of free discussion. In the 1930s it responded to the threat of fascism in Europe with alacrity and sponsored the immigration of many European expatriate intellectuals to the United States. The author listed his affiliation as the "North Carolina College for Negroes" (which was subsequently renamed North Carolina Central University).

10 The phrase is actually, "I heard Sering and Weber." Max Sering was a political economist in Berlin and a member of the Verein für Sozialpolitik. He was one of the prime organizers, beginning in 1890, of the major survey of agricultural labor conditions conducted by the association. Weber would be given the responsibility for interpreting and reporting on the most important part of this survey. Seven years older than Weber, Sering was in close intellectual discussion and dialogue with Weber during the early 1890s. In addition, the work and policy activity of Sering, who had already written a study of American agriculture, had real bearing on public policy and scholarship on rural sociology and agricultural economics globally well into the twentieth century, not only in Europe, but also the United States and Japan (Barkin 1970, 147, 171, 179; Riesebrodt 1989, 147–48).

11 The publication of the translation of *The Protestant Ethic and the Spirit of Capitalism* into English by Talcott Parsons in 1930 truly launched Weber's star in America. It is thus perhaps no surprise that his name appears for the first time in an autobiographical reflection by Du Bois during that decade, for the first draft of the narrative that became *Dusk of Dawn: An Essay Toward an Autobiography of a Race Concept* was most likely written sometime in 1938 (see Du Bois 1986a). In the extended version of the narrative of 1940, Du Bois also mentions that he corresponded with Weber, among others, at the turn of the century (Du Bois 1975b, 67). At a later moment—the last

years of the 1950s and the first years of the 1960s to his death, the time during which Du Bois was most involved with and devoted to his late autobiographical work—there was a general upsurge in the scholarly engagement with Weber in the approach to the centenary of his birth. This included the publication of translations into English of several of Weber's major studies of religion (see, e.g., Weber 1951, 1952, 1958b) and the republication of previous translations of several of his key texts, including *The Protestant Ethic and the Spirit of Capitalism* (Weber 1958a). All this had been preceded in the 1940s by the translation of several of Weber's turn-of-the-century methodological reflections (Weber 1949) and the still signal anthology edited by H. H. Gerth and C. Wright Mills (Weber 1946), as well as the first systematic English-language intellectual biography (Bendix 1960). It is my supposition that this context accounts for Du Bois's attentive notation in his last autobiographical text.

12   Existing biographical scholarship on both figures pertaining to this event is not so helpful here. Marianne Weber's account of Max Weber's life is famous for its vagueness with dates (Marianne Weber 1988, 279–303). The most comprehensive and widely known biographical account of Du Bois's life, by David Levering Lewis, hardly notices the occasion and certainly not in a manner relevant to the context we are attempting to adduce (Lewis 1993a). The two accounts of Weber's time in St. Louis that come the closest to these matters either do not mention Du Bois or mention his presence there only as a nominal possibility, effectively dismissed by a perfunctory or appropriative acknowledgment (see Rollmann 1993; Scaff 2005; Scaff 2011b, 100–108). Perhaps as the research concerning Weber's *Gesamtausgabe* proceeds fully into the correspondence of the difficult years of 1898 to 1903 and beyond, especially into the time surrounding his visit to the United States in late 1904, we will attain further clarification. The published correspondence in the ongoing preparation of the *Gesamtausgabe* began with the later years and proceeded back in time; by 2005, it made accessible correspondence only back to the end of 1905. Since then, a biography of Weber by Joachim Radkau has provided some specific assistance here (Radkau 2005, 2009). As I note in part III, a meticulous recent intellectual biography of Weber that works through much of the minutiae of the difficult half-dozen years that preceded Weber's beginning the preparation of the texts that became *The Protestant Ethic and the Spirit of Capitalism* appears to overlook the pertinence of the question I am posing here, even amid legible evidence otherwise that is included in its own text (Ghosh 2014).

13   The complete Du Bois–Weber correspondence can be found in the microfilm edition of *The Papers of W. E. B. Du Bois* (Du Bois 1980f, reel 3, frames 663–75).

14   I annotate this dimension of Du Bois's work more directly in an ongoing study; some initial or preparatory efforts from this work has been released (see Chandler 2014, 2022b).

15   This occurred some six months before the now celebrated appearance of this statement in the manifesto written by Du Bois as the secretary of the gathering in London in July 1900 that was the first grouping to be called "Pan-African" (Du Bois 1982c). However, the address was first published in October, several months after the London statement was issued. Both the occasion of the address and the provenance of its

publication have been confused in the scholarship. It is for this reason, perhaps, that its proper place until now has been almost unrecognized in the scholarship on Du Bois (Chandler 2022b, 145–220).

16 Yet I should note that part II of *"Beyond This Narrow Now"* (Chandler 2022b, 145–220) elaborates the textual emergence of this conceptualization of "the problem of the color line" in Du Bois thought from 1897 to 1900. It is a study that I first prepared in 2006 in tandem with my production of the present text on the relation of the thought of Du Bois and Weber.

17 Two works from the discussion of the 1970s and 1980s examine Russia and Prussia, respectively, in a comparative manner with the United States, the latter invoking Weber's studies from the 1890s (see Bowman 1993; Kolchin 1987). Others are more directly and fully comparative in a theoretical sense (see Gispen 1990; Hahn 1990; Winson 1982). Also, Robert J. Steinfeld reopened the problematic of rethinking the whole development of "free labor" (see Steinfeld 1991, 2001).

18 Similar groups were founded elsewhere by students of Schmoller, Wagner, Kapp, and Brentano with the Verein in mind as an explicit model—for example, the American Economic Association in the United States (Rueschemeyer and Van Rossem 1996) and the Nihon Shakai Seisaku Gakkai (Japan Social Policy Association) (Grimmer-Solem 2005, 204–14, esp. 208).

19 The editor of these texts in their published form, Kenneth Barkin, proposes in his introductory notes that they issue from the time that Du Bois was a student in Berlin. The evidence for this judgment is tenuous. For example, the key textual reference that Barkin uses to adduce this attribution is that the text, which is focused on the question of "socialism" in Germany, especially the SPD, is signed "William Edward Burghardt Du Bois, Ph.D." (Du Bois 1998b, 196). Barkin supposes that Du Bois may have signed the text in this manner at a moment during early 1894 while he was still in Berlin, when (according to Barkin's hypothesis) he may briefly have imagined that he would receive a doctoral degree from the university there (Barkin 1998). Yet this seems improbable and would be uncharacteristic of Du Bois at this time. Indeed, statements can be found within these texts that indicate otherwise. In the text on the question of "socialism" in imperial Germany, for example, Du Bois specifically refers to *the time of his residence* in Berlin, as well as to a stay in the Rheinpfalz region of Germany, as *a past experience* at the moment of his writing (or oral presentation) of this text. He does not present his residence in Germany as an ongoing one at the time of composition or presentation. Also, the text's reference to the circumstances of its presentation—specifically, the character of the author's address to his immediate audience, as if he is giving a lecture or teaching—and his use of the self-referential pronoun "our" suggest otherwise than Barkin's attribution. Du Bois speaks as if he is addressing an audience that might be somewhat familiar with Germany and its contemporary history but would still expect from him a kind of comment and insight based on direct and recent personal experience that would be beyond their own background. That is to say, he is addressing neither a German academic audience nor a German public. Most likely, Du Bois is addressing an American audience. The preparation of these

texts may well have been connected to an enthusiastic "German Club" that Du Bois organized at Wilberforce University during his time there, as he notes in his *Autobiography* (Du Bois 1968).

These "essays" also have the character of other written texts that served as the basis for semipublic lectures that Du Bois presented during this time, offering judgments and comparative examples that find resonance there—for example, the lecture "The Art and Art Galleries of Europe" (Du Bois 1985), which most likely dates from the spring of 1896. And finally, another text that was only recently reclaimed from the archive and published, "The Afro-American" (Du Bois 1980a, 2010, 2015a), is signed "W. E. B. Du Bois, A.M.," the fact of which—along with an internal reference to his German experience as of his immediate past and his proclamation in the same breath of the new approach to the so-called race question by a young and rising "Afro-American" intelligentsia, of which the writer imagines himself an example—suggest that it dates from his time at Wilberforce, perhaps from the late autumn of 1894 to the early spring of 1895.

Thus, it is most plausible to adjudge that the texts on Germany in the 1890s were prepared by Du Bois sometime after June 1895, when he received the doctorate from Harvard, perhaps during the period from the autumn of 1895 to the early spring of 1896, his second and last year at Wilberforce. In any case, since the essays continually refer to "the last" or most recent Reichstag elections, given at several points as having taken place in 1893, they can be understood to have been composed before the elections of 1898. From the time that Du Bois arrived in Philadelphia during the late summer of 1896, his texts and preoccupations exhibited a character that was somewhat different from that presented in these two essays.

20 Thus it should almost go without saying that, as this history is rewritten in our current moment, Du Bois's inhabitation in it must be reassessed. It remains, however, that the attempts so far to name this relation almost always presume exactly the terms that must be rendered available for critical consideration by way of a predetermined theoretical concept of "influence." Among other possible references, some quite recent, see, for example, Barkin 2000.

21 It is well known that, despite support from Schmoller and Wagner, Du Bois was unable to receive the degree. Du Bois recounts his understanding at the time of the decision by the Berlin faculty in the 29 March 1894 report to the Slater Fund. In the three reports by Du Bois to the Slater Fund (March 1893, December 1893, and March 1894), the title of this project is given as "Der Gross- und Klein Betrieb des Ackerbaus, in der Südstaaten der Vereinigten Staaten, 1840–1890" (The large- and small-scale management of agriculture in the Southern United States, 1840–1890), in the report of 10 March 1893; "Der landwirtschaftliche Gross- und Kleinbetrieb in den Vereinigten Staaten" (A comparison of large- and small-scale agriculture in the United States), in the report of 6 December 1893; and "Die landwirtschaftliche Entwickelung in den Südstaaten der Vereinigten Staaten" (Agricultural development in the Southern States of the United States), in the report of 29 March 1894 (see Du Bois 1973c, 23, 26, 27).

22 And a few sentences later, he writes: "I began to unite my economics and my politics; but I still assumed that in these groups of activities and forces, the political realm was dominant" (Du Bois 1975b, 47).

23 In my judgment, Du Bois's call for the "closing of ranks" to support the entry of the United States into World War I does not compromise this disposition, for that support was predicated less on the establishment of the supremacy of a state interest of the United States than on the articulation of a limit to a certain new global militaristic imperialism, exemplified especially in the new industrial Germany, on the one hand, and the possibility of the extension of democratic rights within the United States, on the other. A debate concerning this matter took place in the *Journal of American History* in the 1990s (see Ellis 1992, 1995; Jordan 1995).

24 It is on this order that Du Bois comes parallel to Weber. Thus, Du Bois would defend Japan's military accomplishment in the 1904–1905 war with Russia (which, in contradistinction to Weber, he would follow much more closely than the unfolding revolutions in Russia). Yet again, however, the ultimate horizon of his judgment was not Japan's state sovereignty but, rather, an idea of the whole historical epoch. For him, Japan's emergence, even as an imperial entity, preempted a nearly total domination of the world under European and Euro-American imperialism. Du Bois's ambivalent affirmation of Japan's imperial announcement through the mid-twentieth century remains open for critical consideration precisely on these terms. The profound limit that can be recognized—according to Du Bois's own protocols—to configure the imperial ambition of Japan, especially, but also the ambition of Russia on the Korean peninsula, is displaced by Du Bois's disposition toward a finality of the truth that he claims to discern by way of the problem of the color line. While I would hesitate and disavow such finality, such problematization remains afoot in our own time in the form of the status of so-called national state sovereignty as a practical issue, especially in its military form. I outline aspects of Du Bois's relation to Japan, along with some of the relevant literature, adjacent to several previously unpublished writings by him on that country (Chandler 2012a, 2012b; Du Bois 2012a, 2012b, 2012c).

25 Several essays from the 1940s by Paul Honigsheim, a student of Weber's in the broadest and deepest sense of the term, had already remarked the theme but in a manner that seems limited from the standpoint of our contemporary questions (see, for example, Honigsheim 1946, 1948, 1949). One may yet note his itinerary in the United States following World War II (Honigsheim 2000).

26 Yet Lutz Kaelber has also noted how Weber's inaugural dissertation remains relatively unremarked in the scholarship on Weber, after a sustained engagement with the other studies from the 1890s through the turn of the twenty-first century (Kaelber 2003; Weber 2003).

27 Mommsen hesitated to explicitly adduce the implication of the concept of race in Weber's political thought for Weber's theoretical projection, even as he outlined his persisting engagement with the "eastern question" or the "Polish question" and relentlessly tracked his nationalism (Mommsen 1984, 35–67; see also Ringer 2004, 47–49; Tribe 1989, 111). It can be shown that the problematic that goes under the heading of

race is inextricable from those questions in Weber's thought. There would seem to be three main exceptions in the discourse on Weber, and they are from contributions by scholars situated otherwise than in the manifold of the mainstream of Weber scholarship. The most recent are Gary Abraham and Andrew Zimmerman, respectively (see Abraham 1992; Zimmerman 2006). Abraham seems to have been unconcerned or unable to make thematic just how his discussion of Weber's engagement with a so-called minority problematic—specifically, the status of Jews in Germany—might be interwoven with the so-called Negro question in the United States or a global-level problematic concerning the concept of race. Zimmerman is so strident in his condemnation of Weber (understandable, perhaps, in the face of the recalcitrant disposition of the scholarship for some eight decades) that the compelling subtleties of the matter are rendered almost unapproachable: We (whoever that is) are perhaps not as free as we might wish to be of the difficulties that attend to Weber's thought in this domain. The character of Weber's engagement with the so-called race question (as Du Bois formulates the matter in the ninth paragraph of the opening chapter of *The Souls of Black Folk* (Du Bois 1903f, 8, chap. 1, para 9) along with a passing reference from Weber to the so-called Negro question in America in his itinerary, is submitted to a judgment. The value of this notwithstanding, such an approach offers little help in recognizing and orienting us in a project that would break up the sedimented epistemic premises— both internal and external to Weber's texts—that organized his disposition and gave his perspective such a fundamental position in his thought. Thus, Manasse's survey of 1947 remains the most sustained consideration. Its citation and critical engagement by the literature on Weber is hardly commensurate. And in the end, Manasse's effort remains a fundamentally recuperative project (see Manasse 1947). This question can be addressed only in an illustrative manner in my study. A patient and exacting contemporary reengagement with this terrain in Weber's thought remains necessary. Yet, as we can see in our time, the matter that goes under the heading of race or racism is only an instance of the larger problematic that is at hand by way of Du Bois's thought of "the problem of the color line."

28   The delimitation that I pursue here is circumstantial. Yet while it is partial, I believe not only that the problematic of "interest" that I adduce later is essential in this domain of Weber's thought, but also that it is the decisive connection between his work before and after his personal hiatus of 1897–1903. First, while this whole problematic could be outlined within the frame of Weber's infamous inaugural lecture at Freiburg in 1895, which can rightly be understood as a summation and pivotal staging of the fundamentally interwoven character of his scientific and political thought (Weber 1993d, 1994), it is my interpretive judgment that the essential structure of the nationalist horizon that is rendered so starkly legible there was already firmly established by early 1893, almost from the outset of Weber's engagement with the "eastern question." Second, while in one sense Weber's lecture at the Congress of Arts and Sciences in 1904 (see Weber 1906, 1998)—which can be understood as a kind of retrospective summation and distillation of the historical interpretation of that *Soziale Frage* in Germany in a comparative context, referencing the United States above all but also including

Europe, especially England and France—can be taken as a ready scene for the elaboration of an interlocution on the track that we are following, I here leave aside sustained consideration of this text for proper consideration elsewhere. This text is especially apposite to the extent that it may be demonstrable that "Die Negerfrage" proposed an acute and almost direct engagement of the premises that organize it. Based on Weber's recollection of breakfast with Du Bois in St. Louis, it is my supposition that Du Bois heard Weber's lecture there. If so, we can plausibly suggest not only that the Congress of Arts and Sciences lecture was an occasion on which Du Bois heard Weber speak, but also that the essay Du Bois sent to Weber can be considered a direct theoretical interlocution. If so, then a full elaboration of such interlocution would need more space and an additional level of critical elaboration than is available here. Third, beyond our direct purview here (which is a commentary on Weber's relation to Du Bois) are the important texts that Weber prepared on the revolutions of 1905 in Russia (Weber 1989b, 1995), even though they are, in fact, situated on the same epistemic ground in his thought as the texts on which I remark later. Weber undertook this engagement in the weeks and months following the correspondence discussed earlier.

29 Tribe cites August Meitzen's programmatic statement on agrarian history from 1882 in this regard as a guide for Weber (Tribe 1989, 99). It should be noted that the part of Weber's *Habilitationsschrift* from 1891 on Roman agrarian history, *Die römische Agrargeschichte*, is dedicated to Meitzen. Martin Riesebrodt suggests that Weber is affirming the example not only of Theodor Mommsen, whose philological premise had guided him in that study, but also that of Gustav Schmoller, even if as a foil, in that Schmoller offered an interpretive approach in economic history (Riesebrodt 1989, 144). (Theodor Mommsen [1817–1903] was the famous nineteenth-century classical scholar and Nobel prize winner whose great-grandson, Wolfgang Mommsen, would propose a major statement at the close of the 1950s with regard to Max Weber's political thought and practice; see Mommsen 1984). It should also be noted that Weber had already alluded to the situation of agriculture in eastern Germany in that eary text (Weber 1986, 312–17).

30 Riesebrodt claims to recognize a reading of the Karl Marx of *Capital* (1977, 1981) in this analysis (Riesebrodt 1989,140).

31 I thank Joseph Fracchia for helpful guidance with the English translation presented here, although its final form is my own. It accents the telic or tendential character of Weber's statement. Some might choose otherwise (Tribe 1989, 108). The full paragraph in German reads as follows:

> Ob man die Konsequenzen dieser Situation entschlossen zieht, davon wird die Zukunft des deutschen Osten abhängen. Die Dynastie der Könige von Preußen ist nicht berufen zu herrschen über ein vaterlandsloses Landproletariat und über slawisches Wandervolk neben polnischen Parzellenbauern und entvölkerten Latifundien, wie sie die jetzige Entwickelung im Osten bei weiterem Gehenlassen zu zeitigen vermag, sondern über deutsche Bauern neben einem Großgrundbesitzerstand, dessen Arbeiter das Bewußtsein in sich tragen, in der Heimat ihre Zukunft im Aufsteigen zu selbständiger Existenz finden zu können. Ob dieses Ziel erreich-

bar ist, steht dahin. Aber auch wer die Fähigkeit des Staates, die im socialen Leben wirksamen Kräfte zu leiten, niedrig veranschlagt, wird zugeben, daß seine Macht gerade auf agrarischem Gebiete eine gewaltige ist. Wie sie gebraucht werden soll, davon wird auf der bevorstehenden Versammlung des Vereins zu sprechen sein. (Weber 1984b, 928–29 [804 in the original text])

32 The title "Die ländliche Arbeitsverfassung" is not susceptible to any literal translation, because it bespeaks a whole problematic and not just a given circumstance. Thus, it seems to me that one should render an understanding of it in the direction of something like the rural organization of labor relations, but in the sense of the organization of social problem—that is, the legal, political, and economic conditions governing the organization of labor, including the articulations that determine specific sorts of people by way of such conditions of relation. We can specify further that it entails the *ordination* of groups of people.

33 Again, I thank Joseph Fracchia for his guidance in translating this paragraph (see also Tribe 1989, 112). I have given the direct English translation of the German *Stande* as "social estate" in this context. The passage in German reads:

> Ich betrachte die "ländliche Arbeiterfrage" hier ganz ausschließlich unter dem Gesichtspunkt der Staatsraison; sie ist fur mich keine Frage der Landarbeiter, also nicht die Frage: geht es ihnen schlecht oder gut, wie ist ihnen zu helfen? Diese Fragen können wir aufgrund der Enquete nur sehr bedingt beantworten, und jedenfalls ist es nicht derjenige Gesichtspunkt, unter dem ich die Sache betrachtet habe; aber freilich: noch viel weniger ist sie die Frage: wie sind den östlichen Großgrundbesitzern Arbeitskräfte zu verschaffen? Das Interesse des Staates und einer Nation kann differieren von dem Interesse jedes einzelnen Standes, nicht nur von dem des Großgrundbesitzes, was gelegentlich vergessen wird, sondern auch von dem des Proletariats, was neuerdings mindestens ebenso oft vergessen wird. Das Interesse des Staates an der ländlichen Arbeiterfrage im Osten is lediglich begriffen in der Frage, wie es um die Fundamente der socialen Organisation bestellt ist, ob der Staat sich darauf stützen kann, auf die Dauer, zum Zweck der Lösung derjenigen politischen Aufgaben, welche ihm im Osten demnächst bevorstehen. Diese Frage ist meines Erachtens zu verneinen. (Weber 1893, 74; 1993c, 180–81)

34 When Du Bois confronts a form of this question as posed, for example, in the speech "The Conservation of Races" (see Du Bois 1897a, 2015b) at the founding meeting of the American Negro Academy (just five years after the first of Weber's texts we have noticed above), he explicitly affirms such heterogeneity and insists on the illimitability of becoming of all those who come "late to the threshold of the historicity of the present,"' to take a turn on the thought of Aimé Césaire (2000). As I propose in a related study, there is no presumption of purity there (Chandler 2023). Yet the comparison adduced here is not simply hypothetical. Across his "autobiographical" writings, Du Bois records the event of an invitation and a first visit to Poland in the early 1890s, during the winter, following the spring 1893 meeting of the Verein at which Weber spoke:

While at Berlin, I found myself once explaining to a schoolmate, Stanislaus Ritter von Estreicher, the race problem in America. He was not as impressed as I
thought he should be. He said: 'I understand only too well; but you should see the
race antagonism in my home. Come to Krakow and see the clash of German and
Pole!' I promised that I would visit when near. . . . Finally, I came to Krakow and
my friend. It was an interesting visit and an old tale. Tyranny in school and work;
insult in home and on the street. Of course, here, in contrast to America, there
were privileged Poles who escaped personal insult; there was the aristocracy who
had some recognized rights. The whole mass of the oppressed were not reduced
to one level; nevertheless the degradation was only too familiar. . . . I never saw my
schoolmate again, but I heard later that in the Second World War, the Germans
tried to make him a Quisling for them. In 1940 von Estreicher died in a German
concentration camp, after he had refused to be one of Germany's puppet rulers of
Poland. (Du Bois 1968, 174–75)

While Du Bois first mentioned this visit to Poland, somewhat obliquely, in *Darkwater* ("I looked on the boundaries of Russia" [Du Bois 1920, 16; 1975a, 16]), in his
1940 reflection *Dusk of Dawn*, he elaborates just ever so briefly ("From this friend,
Stanislaus von Estreicher, I learned of the race problems of the Poles" [Du Bois 1975b,
48]). However, it was after the war and a visit to Warsaw in 1949 that Du Bois was led
to fully elaborate his sense of the stakes of the so-called Polish question, certainly to
underscore retrospectively the contemporaneous implication of his winter 1893 visit
to Poland in his own development, but more fundamentally to situate the whole problematic as the terms of a concomitant articulation of "the Jewish problem of the modern world." This reflection appeared three years later in the essay "The Negro and the
Warsaw Ghetto" (Du Bois 1982g). Although only the most indicative quotation can
be given here, the entire text must be indexed as part of this annotation. Du Bois then
wrote in signal fashion of his sense of the "problem of the color line" in 1952:

> In the first place, the problem of slavery, emancipation, and caste in the United
> States was no longer in my mind a separate and unique thing as I had so long con-
> ceived it. It was not even solely a matter of color and physical and racial character-
> istics, which was particularly a hard thing for me to learn, since for a lifetime the
> color line had been a real and efficient cause of misery. It was not merely a matter of
> religion. . . . No, the race problem the problem in which I was interested cut across
> lines of color and physique and belief and status. (Du Bois 1982g, 175)

While Du Bois himself emphasizes the revelatory impact of his visit to the Warsaw Ghetto, and while this has been productively recalled in a generous meditation
by the scholar Michael Rothberg (2001), it remains that the global and comparative
lineaments of this conception were directly thematized by Du Bois from the very first
enunciations of his theoretical claim that "the problem of the twentieth century is the
problem of the color line" in late 1899 (Du Bois 1900b). In addition to the outline provided earlier in this volume, I have elsewhere elaborated this thought in a
consideration of the turn-of-the-century moment of Du Bois's discourse in general

(Chandler 2022b). In addition, across another passage of this theme in his autobiographical considerations, Du Bois, at twenty-six, wrote in the diary of his return to "America" in June 1894 by way of steerage about his sense of the "Prussian Poles" who were also aboard the ship. The account of the trip seems to make its first sustained appearance in print only in the autobiographical text on which he was working at the end of his life, and that was published posthumously as *The Autobiography of W. E. B. Du Bois: A Soliloquy on Viewing My Life from the Last Decade of Its First Century* (Du Bois 1968, 178–79). Yet the account that is published in the *Autobiography* does not reproduce all that is in the manuscript of the diary, which covers some twenty-two pages of hand script. In particular, concerning my order of attention here, it should be noted that Du Bois offers in the manuscript text characterizations of several different social "types" of people traveling with him in steerage on the ship, which he closes with descriptions of "The Jew," "The Negro," and, finally, "The Prussian Pole." He produces key negative stereotypes of people of supposed Jewish background and, likewise, of those of supposed Polish background, despite his affirmative characterization of each group as a whole; his characterization of the Negro by stereotype, by contrast, appears more benign. Du Bois's social emplacement, if not direct inscription, within anti-Semitic premises at this time in his life course and of this time and place—Germany of the 1890s—also should be remarked here. Its legible presence is registered in two other texts of the 1890s, perhaps dating from 1895–96 (see Du Bois 1998a, 1998b). Du Bois then writes about "the Prussian Pole": "Yet they seem to me to have the making of a nation in them. It will take of course long years—they have evidently been trained to dirt and wallowing, yet they have not been physically debauched and they have the openheartedness of [*sic*] willingness of the learner" (Du Bois 1894[circa]b). The scale and destination of the migration of Poles, especially laborers from Prussia, remains of considerable historical bearing for thinking through the problematic that Du Bois described as the problem of the color line, and it suggests the character of its relation to the so-called Negro question in the United States and throughout the Americas and the Caribbean region (Zubrzycki 1953). In the context of the discussion at hand, there is now the striking projection of a new form of the "problem of the color line" within post-1989 Poland as it becomes part of the European Union in which new or renewed articulations of anti-Semitism and racism have become normative (Marciniak 2006).

35 This would also connect to such a question in the Baltic states and the western regions of the Russian empire. Also, I reference the history of the *Judenfrage* in Germany only in relation to Weber (Abraham 1992, 42–52, 91–105, 115), which is profoundly apposite to any consideration of Weber's discourse, despite the absence of citation of this discussion in the mainstream literature and leaving aside the other propositions given there. This whole stratum of our question solicits is own engagement and elaboration according to the problematic I have adduced in this study. On this problematic, I note the historiography of William W. Hagen (see Hagen 1980, 2002, 2012, 2018).

36 Their respective relation to the status of the symbolic and the problem of understanding or interpretation in the human sciences in terms of the epistemic horizon of their generational configuration, which might include not only Émile Durkheim but also

Franz Boas, Sigmund Freud, and Edmund Husserl (along with Georg Simmel, Wilhelm Dilthey, and Friedrich Nietzsche of an earlier moment), is notwithstanding here. It is another line of comparison between these two figures, but it remains common to their whole moment and to the configuration just mentioned.

37 "Of the Culture of White Folk" was collected in *Darkwater* (Du Bois 1975a, 28–52) conjoined with an earlier essay, "The Souls of White Folk" (Du Bois 1910).

REFERENCES

....

Abraham, Gary A. 1992. *Max Weber and the Jewish Question: A Study of the Social Outlook of His Sociology*. Urbana: University of Illinois Press.

Adelson, Leslie. 2005. *The Turkish Turn in Contemporary German Literature: Toward a New Critical Grammar of Migration*. New York: Palgrave Macmillan.

American Negro Academy. 1969. *The American Negro: His History and Literature*. American Negro Academy Occasional Papers, 1–22. New York: Arno.

Ando, Tadao. 2005. "The Chichu Art Museum." In *The Chichu Art Museum: Tadao Ando Builds for Claude Monet, Walter De Maria and James Turrell*, edited by J. R. Yuji Akimoto and Hiroyuki Suzuki, 88. Berlin: Hatje Cantz.

Appiah, Kwame Anthony. 2014. *Lines of Descent: W. E. B. Du Bois and the Emergence of Identity*. Cambridge, MA: Harvard University Press.

Aptheker, Herbert. 1971. "The Souls of Black Folk: A Comparison of the 1903 and 1952 [*sic*] Editions." *Negro History Bulletin* 34 (January): 15–17.

Aptheker, Herbert. 1973. *Annotated Bibliography of the Published Writings of W. E. B. Du Bois*. Millwood, NY: Kraus-Thomson.

Aptheker, Herbert. 1989. *The Literary Legacy of W. E. B. Du Bois*. White Plains, NY: Kraus International.

Ay, Karl-Ludwig. 1993. "Max Weber und der Begriff der Rasse." *Aschkenas* 3, no. 1: 189–218.

Backhaus, Jürgen G., ed. 1996. *Werner Sombart (1863–1941): Social Scientist*. 3 vols. Marburg: Metropolis.

Baehr, Peter R., and Gordon C. Wells. 2002. "The Protestant Ethic and the 'Spirit' of Capitalism: Editor's Introduction." In *The Protestant Ethic and the "Spirit" of Capitalism and Other Writings*, edited and translated by Peter R. Baehr and Gordon C. Wells, ix–lxviii. New York: Penguin.

Baker, Keith M., ed. 1987. *The French Revolution and the Creation of Modern Political Culture*. 4 vols. Oxford: Pergamon.

Balibar, Étienne. 2004. *We, the People of Europe? Reflections on Transnational Citizenship*. Princeton, NJ: Princeton University Press.

Bancroft, George. 1844–75. *History of the United States*. 10 vols. Boston: Little, Brown.

Barkin, Kenneth D. 1970. *The Controversy over German Industrialization, 1890–1902*. Chicago: University of Chicago Press.

Barkin, Kenneth D. 1998. "Introduction." *Central European History* 31, no. 3: 155–69.

Barkin, Kenneth D. 2000. "'Berlin Days,' 1892–1894: W. E. B. Du Bois and German Political Economy." *Boundary 2* 27, no. 3 (Fall): 79–101.

Bendix, Reinhard. 1960. *Max Weber: An Intellectual Portrait*. Garden City, NY: Doubleday.

Bessone, Magali, and Matthieu Renault. 2021. "La ligne de partage des couleurs." In *W. E. B. Du Bois: Double conscience et condition raciale*, 21–41. Paris: Éditions Amsterdam.

Blanke, Richard. 1981. *Prussian Poland in the German Empire (1871–1900)*. Boulder, CO: East European Monographs.

Bowman, Shearer Davis. 1993. *Masters and Lords: Mid-19th Century U.S. Planters and Prussian Junkers*. New York: Oxford University Press.

Carlyle, Thomas. 1888. *The French Revolution: A History*. 3 vols. London: Chapman and Hall.

Césaire, Aimé. 2000. *Cahier d'un retour au pays natal*. Edited by Abiola Irele. Columbus: Ohio State University Press.

Chalcraft, David J., and Austin Harrington, eds. 2001. *The Protestant Ethic Debate: Max Weber's Replies to His Critics, 1907–1910*. Translated by Austin Harrington and Mary Shields. Liverpool: Liverpool University Press.

Chamberlain, Houston Stewart. 1911. *The Foundations of the Nineteenth Century*. Translated by John Lees. London: J. Lane.

Chandler, Nahum Dimitri. 1996. "The Figure of the X: An Elaboration of the Du Boisian Autobiographical Example." In *Displacement, Diaspora, and Geographies of Identity*, edited by Smadar Lavie and Ted Swedenburg, 235–72. Durham, NC: Duke University Press.

Chandler, Nahum Dimitri. 2006. "The Possible Form of an Interlocution: W. E. B. Du Bois and Max Weber in Correspondence, 1904–1905, Part I: The Letters and the Essay." *CR: The New Centennial Review* 6, no. 3 (Winter): 193–239.

Chandler, Nahum Dimitri. 2007. "The Possible Form of an Interlocution: W. E. B. Du Bois and Max Weber in Correspondence, 1904–1905, Part II: The Terms of Discussion." *CR: The New Centennial Review* 7, no. 1 (Spring): 213–72.

Chandler, Nahum Dimitri. 2008. "Of Exorbitance: The Problem of the Negro as a Problem for Thought." *Criticism* 50, no. 3: 345–410.

Chandler, Nahum Dimitri. 2012a. "Introduction: On the Virtues of Seeing—at Least, but Never Only—Double." *CR: The New Centennial Review* 12, no. 1 (Spring): 1–39.

Chandler, Nahum Dimitri. 2012b. "A Persistent Parallax: On W. E. B. Du Bois's Writings on Japan and China, 1936–1937." *CR: The New Centennial Review* 12, no. 1 (Spring): 291–316.

Chandler, Nahum Dimitri. 2014. "Of Exorbitance: The Problem of the Negro as a Problem for Thought." In *X: The Problem of the Negro as a Problem for Thought*, 11–67. New York: Fordham University Press.

Chandler, Nahum Dimitri. 2021. *Toward an African Future—Of the Limit of World*. Albany: State University of New York Press.

Chandler, Nahum Dimitri. 2022a. "'Beyond This Narrow Now': Elaborations of the Example in the Thought of W. E. B. Du Bois—at the Limit of World." In *"Beyond This Narrow Now": Or, Delimitations, of W. E. B. Du Bois*, 25–142. Durham, NC: Duke University Press.

Chandler, Nahum Dimitri. 2022b. "The Problem of the Centuries: A Contemporary Elaboration of 'The Present Outlook for the Dark Races of Mankind,' Circa the 27th of December, 1899—Or, at the Turn to the Twentieth Century." In *"Beyond This Narrow Now" Or, Delimitations, of W. E. B. Du Bois*, 145–220. Durham, NC: Duke University Press.

Chandler, Nahum Dimitri. 2023. *Annotations on the Early Thought of W. E. B. Du Bois*. Durham, NC: Duke University Press.

Chesnutt, Charles W. 1901. *The Marrow of Tradition*. Boston: Houghton Mifflin.

Cohn, Bernard S. 1984. "The Census, Social Structure, and Objectification in South Asia." *Folk* 26: 25–49.

Collins, Winfield H. 1904. *The Domestic Slave Trade of the Southern States*. New York: Broadway.

Conference for the Study of the Negro Problems. 1896. *Mortality Among Negroes in Cities: Proceedings of the Conference for the Investigation of City Problems, Held at Atlanta University, May 26–26, 1896*. Atlanta: Atlanta University Press.

Conference for the Study of the Negro Problems. 1897. *Social and Physical Condition of Negroes in Cities: Report of an Investigation Under the Direction of Atlanta University; and Proceedings of the Second Conference for the Study of Problems Concerning Negro City Life, Held at Atlanta University, May 25–26, 1897*. Atlanta: Atlanta University Press.

Cox, Oliver C. 1948. *Caste, Class, and Race: A Study in Social Dynamics*. Garden City, NY: Doubleday.

Denzel, Markus A. 2010. *Handbook of World Exchange Rates, 1590–1914*. Farnham, UK: Ashgate.

Dirks, Nicholas B. 2001. *Castes of Mind: Colonialism and the Making of Modern India*. Princeton, NJ: Princeton University Press.

Douglass, Frederick. 1979. *The Frederick Douglass Papers: Series One, Speeches, Debates and Interviews*. 5 vols. Edited by J. W. Blassingame. New Haven, CT: Yale University Press.

Douglass, Frederick. 1994. *Autobiographies: Library of America*. New York: Library of America.

Du Bois, W. E. B. 1894[circa]a. "The Afro-American." Typescript unpublished essay. Series 3, Subseries C. MS 312. Papers of W. E. B. Du Bois. Special Collections and University Archives, W. E. B. Du Bois Memorial Library, University of Massachusetts, Amherst.

Du Bois, W. E. B. 1894[circa]b. "'Diary of My Steerage Trip Across the Atlantic.'" Series 3, Subseries C. MS 312. Papers of W. E. B. Du Bois. Special Collections and University Archives, W. E. B. Du Bois Memorial Library, University of Massachusetts, Amherst.

Du Bois, W. E. B. 1896. *The Suppression of the African Slave-Trade to the United States of America, 1638–1870*. New York: Longmans, Green.

Du Bois, W. E. B. 1897a. *The Conservation of Races*. American Negro Academy Occasional Papers, no. 2. Washington, DC: American Negro Academy.

Du Bois, W. E. B. 1897b. "Philadelphia, Pa., June 14, 1897: W. E. B. Du Bois Presents Plans for the Proposed Study of the Negro Question." Handwritten letter. Department of Labor Records, National Archives, Washington, DC.

Du Bois, W. E. B. 1897c. "Philadelphia, Pa., May 5, 1897. W. E. B. Du Bois. Presents Plan for the Proposed Study of the Negro Question." Handwritten letter. Department of Labor Records, National Archives, Washington, DC.

Du Bois, W. E. B. 1898a. "The Negroes of Farmville, Virginia: A Social Study." *Bulletin of the Department of Labor* 3, no. 14 (January): 1–38.

Du Bois, W. E. B. 1898b. *Some Efforts of American Negroes for Their Own Social Betterment: Report of an Investigation Under the Direction of Atlanta University; Together with the Proceedings of the Third Conference for the Study of the Negro Problems, Held at Atlanta University, May 25–26, 1898.* Atlanta: Atlanta University Press.

Du Bois, W. E. B., ed. 1898c. "The Study of the Negro Problems." *Annals of the American Academy of Political and Social Science* 11, no. 1 (January): 1–23.

Du Bois, W. E. B. 1899a. "The Negro and Crime." *Independent* 51 (18 May): 1355–57.

Du Bois, W. E. B. 1899b. "The Negro in the Black Belt: Some Social Sketches." *Bulletin of the [US] Department of Labor* 4, no. 22 (May): 401–17.

Du Bois, W. E. B., ed. 1899c. *The Negro in Business: Report of a Social Study Made Under the Direction of Atlanta University; Together with the Proceedings of the Fourth Conference for the Study of the Negro Problems, Held at Atlanta University, May 30–31, 1899.* Atlanta: Atlanta University Press.

Du Bois, W. E. B., ed. 1900a. *The College-Bred Negro: Report of a Social Study Made Under the Direction of Atlanta University; Together with the Proceedings of the Fifth Conference for the Study of the Negro Problems, Held at Atlanta University, May 29–30, 1900.* Atlanta: Atlanta University Press.

Du Bois, W. E. B. 1900b. "The Present Outlook for the Dark Races of Mankind." *A.M.E. Church Review* 17, no. 2 (whole number 66): 95–110.

Du Bois, W. E. B. 1901a. "The Freedmen's Bureau." *Atlantic Monthly* 87, no. 59 (March): 354–65.

Du Bois, W. E. B. 1901b. "The Negro as He Really Is." *World's Work* 2, no. 2 (June): 848–66.

Du Bois, W. E. B., ed. 1901c. *The Negro Common School: Report of a Social Study Made Under the Direction of Atlanta University; Together with the Proceedings of the Sixth Conference for the Study of the Negro Problems, Held at Atlanta University, on May 28th, 1901.* Atlanta: Atlanta University Press.

Du Bois, W. E. B. 1901d. "The Negro Landholder of Georgia." *Bulletin of the [US] Department of Labor* 6, no. 35 (July): 647–777.

Du Bois, W. E. B. 1901e. "The Relation of the Negroes to the Whites in the South." *Annals of the American Academy of Political and Social Science* 18, no. 1 (July): 121–40.

Du Bois, W. E. B. 1901f. "The Spawn of Slavery: The Convict-Lease System in the South." *Missionary Review of the World* 14, no. 10 (October): 737–45.

Du Bois, W. E. B., ed. 1902. *The Negro Artisan: Report of a Social Study Made Under the Direction of Atlanta University; Together with the Proceedings of the Seventh Conference for the Study of the Negro Problems, Held at Atlanta University, on May 27th, 1902.* Atlanta.: Atlanta University Press.

Du Bois, W. E. B., ed. 1903a. *The Negro Church: Report of a Social Study Made Under the Direction of Atlanta University; Together with the Proceedings of the Eighth Conference for the Study of the Negro Problems, Held at Atlanta University, May 26th, 1903.* Atlanta: Atlanta University Press.

Du Bois, W. E. B. 1903b. "Of the Black Belt." In *The Souls of Black Folk: Essays and Sketches*, 110–34. Chicago: A. C. McClurg.

Du Bois, W. E. B. 1903c. "Of the Quest of the Golden Fleece." In *The Souls of Black Folk: Essays and Sketches*, 135–62. Chicago: A. C. McClurg.

Du Bois, W. E. B. 1903d. "Of the Sons of Master and Man." In *The Souls of Black Folk: Essays and Sketches*, 163–88. Chicago: A. C. McClurg.

Du Bois, W. E. B. 1903e. "The Sorrow Songs." In *The Souls of Black Folk: Essays and Sketches*, 250–64. Chicago: A. C. McClurg.

Du Bois, W. E. B. 1903f. *The Souls of Black Folk: Essays and Sketches*. Chicago: A. C. McClurg.

Du Bois, W. E. B. 1903g. *The Souls of Black Folk: Essays and Sketches*. 2d ed. [Chicago: A. C. McClurg.] *Documenting the American South*, University Library, University of North Carolina at Chapel Hill. https://docsouth.unc.edu/church/duboissouls /dubois.html.

Du Bois, W. E. B. 1904a. "The Negro Farmer." *Bulletin 8:Negroes in the United States.* US Bureau of the Census. (Washington, DC: Government Printing Office, 1904).

Du Bois, W. E. B., ed. 1904b. *Some Notes on Negro Crime, Particularly in Georgia: Report of a Social Study Made Under the Direction of Atlanta University; Together with the Proceedings of the Ninth Conference for the Study of the Negro Problems, Held at Atlanta University, May 24, 1904.* Atlanta: Atlanta University Press.

Du Bois, W. E. B, ed. 1905. *A Select Bibliography of the Negro American: A Compilation Made Under the Direction of Atlanta University; Together with the Proceedings of the Tenth Conference for the Study of the Negro Problems, Held at Atlanta University, on May 30, 1905.* Atlanta: Atlanta University Press.

Du Bois, W. E. B. 1906a. "Die Negerfrage in den Vereinigten Staaten." *Archiv für Sozialwissenschaft und Sozialpolitik* 22 (January): 31–79.

Du Bois, W. E. B. 1906b. "The Negro Farmer." In *Supplementary Analysis and Derivative Tables: Twelfth Census of the United States, 1900*, 511–79. Washington, DC: Government Printing Office.

Du Bois, W. E. B. 1906c. "L'ouvrier nègre." *Révue Économique Internationale* 4: 298–348.

Du Bois, W. E. B. 1909. *John Brown*. Philadelphia: G. W. Jacobs.

Du Bois, W. E. B. 1910. "The Souls of White Folk." *Independent* 69: 339–42.

Du Bois, W. E. B. 1911. *The Quest of the Silver Fleece: A Novel*. Chicago: A. C. McClurg.

Du Bois, W. E. B. 1915. "The African Roots of War." *Atlantic Monthly* 115, no. 5 (May): 707–14.

Du Bois, W. E. B. 1917. "Of the Culture of White Folk." *Journal of Race Development* 7: 434–47.

Du Bois, W. E. B. 1920. *Darkwater: Voices from Within the Veil*. New York: Harcourt, Brace and Howe.

Du Bois, W. E. B. 1928. *Dark Princess: A Romance*. New York: Harcourt, Brace.

Du Bois, W. E. B. 1935. *Black Reconstruction: An Essay Toward a History of the Part Which Black Folk Played in the Attempt to Reconstruct Democracy in America, 1860–1880*. New York: Harcourt, Brace.

Du Bois, W. E. B. 1945. *Color and Democracy: Colonies and Peace*. New York: Harcourt, Brace.

Du Bois, W. E. B. 1947. *The World and Africa: An Inquiry into the Part Which Africa Has Played in World History*. New York: Viking.

Du Bois, W. E. B. 1953. *The Souls of Black Folk: Essays and Sketches*. New York: Blue Heron.

Du Bois, W. E. B. 1957–61. *The Black Flame: A Trilogy*. New York: Mainstream.

Du Bois, W. E. B. 1959[1903]a. *Ames noires: Essais et nouvelles [The Souls of Black Folk]*. Translated by Jean-Jacques Fol. Paris: Présence Africaine.

Du Bois, W. E. B. 1959[1903]b. *Hei Ren de Ling Hun [The Souls of Black Folk]*. Translated by Wéi Qún Yì. Beijing: Rénmín Chūbǎn Shè.

Du Bois, W. E. B. 1965 [1903]. *Kokujin no Tamashii [The Souls of Black Folk]*. Translated by Hajime Kijima, Shigetoshi Iijima, and Torahiko Ko. Tokyo: Miraisha.

Du Bois, W. E. B. 1968. *The Autobiography of W. E. B. Du Bois: A Soliloquy on Viewing My Life from the Last Decade of Its First Century*. Edited by Herbert Aptheker. New York: International.

Du Bois, W. E. B. 1973a. *The Correspondence of W. E. B. Du Bois*. Compiled and edited by Herbert Aptheker. Amherst: University of Massachusetts Press.

Du Bois, W. E. B. 1973b. *John Brown*. Edited by Herbert Aptheker. Millwood, NY: Kraus-Thomson.

Du Bois, W. E. B. 1973c. *Selections, 1877–1934*. Vol. 1 of *The Correspondence of W. E. B. DuBois*. Compiled and edited by Herbert Aptheker. Amherst: University of Massachusetts Press.

Du Bois, W. E. B. 1973d. *Selections, 1945–1963*. Vol. 3 of *The Correspondence of W. E. B. Du Bois*. Compiled and edited by Herbert Aptheker. Amherst: University of Massachusetts Press.

Du Bois, W. E. B. 1973e. *The Souls of Black Folk: Essays and Sketches*. Edited by Herbert Aptheker. Millwood, NY: Kraus-Thomson.

Du Bois, W. E. B. 1975a. *Darkwater: Voices from Within the Veil*. Edited by Herbert Aptheker. Millwood, NY: Kraus-Thomson.

Du Bois, W. E. B. 1975b. *Dusk of Dawn: An Essay Toward an Autobiography of a Race Concept*. Edited by Herbert Aptheker. Millwood, NY: Kraus-Thomson.

Du Bois, W. E. B. 1976. *Black Reconstruction: An Essay Toward a History of the Part Which Black Folk Played in the Attempt to Reconstruct Democracy in America, 1860–1880*. Edited by Herbert Aptheker. Millwood, NY: Kraus-Thomson.

Du Bois, W. E. B. 1977. *Book Reviews*. Compiled and edited by Herbert Aptheker. Millwood, NY: Kraus-Thomson.

Du Bois, W. E. B. 1980a. "The Afro-American." Typescript. Unpublished essay in *The Papers of W. E. B. Du Bois, 1803 (1877–1963) 1979*, compiled and edited by Herbert Aptheker. Microfilm, reel 82, frames 1232–42. Sanford, NC: Microfilming Corporation of America.

Du Bois, W. E. B. 1980b. "Caste in America." Typescript in *The Papers of W. E. B. Du Bois, 1803 (1877–1963) 1965*, compiled and edited by Herbert Aptheker. Microfilm, reel 80, frames 121–25. Sanford, NC: Microfilming Corporation of America.

Du Bois, W. E. B. 1980c. "The Negro Farmer." In *Contributions by W. E. B. Du Bois in Government Publications and Proceedings*, edited by Herbert Aptheker, 231–95. Millwood, NY: Kraus-Thomson.

Du Bois, W. E. B. 1980d. "The Negro Landholder of Georgia." In *Contributions by W. E. B. Du Bois in Government Publications and Proceedings*, edited by Herbert Aptheker, 95–228. Millwood, NY: Kraus-Thomson.

Du Bois, W. E. B. 1980e. "The Negroes of Farmville, Virginia: A Social Study." In *Contributions by W. E. B. Du Bois in Government Publications and Proceedings*, edited by Herbert Aptheker, 5–44. Millwood, NY: Kraus-Thomson.

Du Bois, W. E. B. 1980f. *The Papers of W. E. B. Du Bois, 1803 (1877–1963) 1979*. Microfilm ed. Compiled and edited by Herbert Aptheker and Robert C. McDonnell. Sanford, NC: Microfilming Corporation of America.

Du Bois, W. E. B. 1980g. "Sociology Hesitant." Typescript in *The Papers of W. E. B. Du Bois, 1803 (1877–1963) 1965*, compiled and edited by Herbert Aptheker. Microfilm, reel 82, frames 1307–12. Sanford, NC: Microfilming Corporation of America.

Du Bois, W. E. B. 1980h. "Testimony Before the United States Industrial Commission." In *Contributions by W. E. B. Du Bois in Government Publications and Proceedings*, edited by Herbert Aptheker, 65–94. Millwood, NY: Kraus-Thomson.

Du Bois, W. E. B. 1982a. "The Beginning of Emancipation." In *Writings by W. E. B. Du Bois in Periodicals Edited by Others*. Vol. 1, *1891–1909*, compiled and edited by Herbert Aptheker, 242–45. Millwood, NY: Kraus-Thomson.

Du Bois, W. E. B. 1982b. "The Beginning of Slavery." In *Writings by W. E. B. Du Bois in Periodicals Edited by Others*. Vol. 1, *1891–1909*, compiled and edited by Herbert Aptheker, 235–37. Millwood, NY: Kraus-Thomson.

Du Bois, W. E. B. 1982c. "Caste: That Is the Root of the Trouble." In *Writings by W. E. B. Du Bois in Periodicals Edited by Others*. Vol. 1, *1891–1909*, compiled and edited by Herbert Aptheker, 231–34. Millwood, NY: Kraus-Thomson.

Du Bois, W. E. B. 1982d. "The Development of a People." In *Writings by W. E. B. Du Bois in Periodicals Edited by Others*. Vol. 1, *1891–1909*, compiled and edited by Herbert Aptheker, 203–15. Millwood, NY: Kraus-Thomson.

Du Bois, W. E. B. 1982e. "My Evolving Program for Negro Freedom." In *Writings by W. E. B. Du Bois in Non-Periodical Literature Edited by Others*, compiled and edited by Herbert Aptheker, 216–41. Millwood, NY: Kraus-Thomson.

Du Bois, W. E. B. 1982g. "The Negro and the Warsaw Ghetto." In *Writings by W. E. B. Du Bois in Periodicals Edited by Others*. Vol. 4, *1945–1961*, compiled and edited by Herbert Aptheker, 173–76. Millwood, NY: Kraus-Thomson Organization.

Du Bois, W. E. B. 1982h. "Serfdom." In *Writings by W. E. B. Du Bois in Periodicals Edited by Others*. Vol. 1, *1891–1909*, compiled and edited by Herbert Aptheker, 246–49. Millwood, NY: Kraus-Thomson.

Du Bois, W. E. B. 1982i. "Slavery in Greece and Rome." In *Writings by W. E. B. Du Bois in Periodicals Edited by Others*. Vol. 1, *1891–1909*, compiled and edited by Herbert Aptheker, 238–41. Millwood, NY: Kraus-Thomson.

Du Bois, W. E. B. 1985. "The Art and Art Galleries of Modern Europe." In *Against Racism: Unpublished Essays, Papers, Addresses, 1887–1961*, edited by Herbert Aptheker, 33–43. Amherst: University of Massachusetts Press.

Du Bois, W. E. B. 1986a. "A Pageant in Seven Decades, 1878–1938." In *Pamphlets and Leaflets*, compiled and edited by Herbert Aptheker, 244–74. White Plains, NY: Kraus-Thomson.

Du Bois, W. E. B. 1986b. *Pamphlets and Leaflets*. Compiled and edited by Herbert Aptheker. White Plains, NY: Kraus-Thomson.

Du Bois, W. E. B. 1997. *The Correspondence of W. E. B. Du Bois*. 3 vols. Compiled and edited by Herbert Aptheker. Amherst: University of Massachusetts Press.

Du Bois, W. E. B. 1998a. "The Present Condition of German Politics (1893)." *Central European History* 31, no. 3: 170–87.

Du Bois, W. E. B. 1998b. "The Socialism of German Socialists." *Central European History* 31, no. 3: 189–96.

Du Bois, W. E. B. 2001. *Las Almas del Pueblo Negro* [*The Souls of Black Folk*]. Translated by Rubén Casado and Francisco Cabrera. Havana: Fundación Fernando Ortiz.

Du Bois, W. E. B. 2003. *Die Seelen der Schwarzen: The Souls of Black Folk*. Translated by Jürgen Meyer-Wendt and Barbara Meyer-Wendt. Freiburg: Orange.

Du Bois, W. E. B. 2006. "Die Negerfrage in den Vereinigten Staaten (The Negro Question in the United States)." Translated by Joseph Fracchia. *CR: The New Centennial Review* 6, no. 3 (Winter): 241–90.

Du Bois, W. E. B. 2010. "The Afro-American." *Journal of Transnational American Studies* 2, no. 1. http://escholarship.org/uc/item/2pm9g4q2.

Du Bois, W. E. B. 2012a. "'Chapter 16—Jones in Japan' from *A World Search for Democracy* (1937)." *CR: The New Centennial Review* 12, no. 1 (Spring): 257–74.

Du Bois, W. E. B. 2012b. "'Chapter 17—Jones Looks Back on China' from *A World Search for Democracy* (1937)." *CR: The New Centennial Review* 12, no. 1 (Spring): 275–90.

Du Bois, W. E. B. 2012c. "The Meaning of Japan (1937)." *CR: The New Centennial Review* 12, no. 1 (Spring).

Du Bois, W. E. B. 2015a. "The Afro-American." In *The Problem of the Color Line at the Turn of the Twentieth Century: The Essential Early Essays*, compiled and edited by Nahum D. Chandler, 33–50. New York: Fordham University Press

Du Bois, W. E. B. 2015b. "The Conservation of Races." In *The Problem of the Color Line at the Turn of the Twentieth Century: The Essential Early Essays*, compiled and edited by Nahum D. Chandler, 51–65. New York: Fordham University Press.

Du Bois, W. E. B. 2015c. "The Development of a People." In *The Problem of the Color Line at the Turn of the Twentieth Century: The Essential Early Essays*, compiled and edited by Nahum D. Chandler, 243–70. New York: Fordham University Press.

Du Bois, W. E. B. 2015d. "Die Negerfrage in den Vereinigten Staaten (The Negro Question in the United States)." In *The Problem of the Color Line at the Turn of the Twentieth Century: The Essential Early Essays*, compiled and edited by Nahum D. Chandler, 285–338. New York: Fordham University Press.

Du Bois, W. E. B. 2015e. "The Present Outlook for the Dark Races of Mankind." In *The Problem of the Color Line at the Turn of the Twentieth Century: The Essential Early Essays*, compiled and edited by Nahum D. Chandler, 111–38. New York: Fordham University Press.

Du Bois, W. E. B. 2015f. *The Problem of the Color Line at the Turn of the Twentieth Century: The Essential Early Essays*. Compiled and edited by Nahum D. Chandler. New York: Fordham University Press.

Du Bois, W. E. B. 2015g. "Sociology Hesitant." In *The Problem of the Color Line at the Turn of the Twentieth Century: The Essential Early Essays*, compiled and edited by Nahum D. Chandler, 271–84. New York: Fordham University Press.

Du Bois, W. E. B. 2015h. "The Study of the Negro Problems." In *The Problem of the Color Line at the Turn of the Twentieth Century: The Essential Early Essays*, edited by Nahum D. Chandler, 71–88 and 99–109. New York: Fordham University Press.

Du Bois, W. E. B., and Isabel Eaton. 1899. *The Philadelphia Negro: A Social Study, by W. E. B. Du Bois; Together with a Special Report on Domestic Service by Isabel Eaton*. Philadelphia: University of Pennsylvania.

Du Bois, W. E. B., and Isabel Eaton. 1973. *The Philadelphia Negro: A Social Study*. Edited by Herbert Aptheker. Millwood, NY: Kraus-Thomson.

Dunbar, Paul L. 1905. *Lyrics of Sunshine and Shadow*. New York: Dodd, Mead.

Durkheim, Émile. 1995. *The Elementary Forms of Religious Life*. Translated by Karen E. Fields. New York: Free Press.

Edgerton, Charles E., and E. Dana Durand. 1901. *Reports of the Industrial Commission on Labor Organizations, Labor Disputes, and Arbitration*. Reports of the US Industrial Commission, vol. 17. Washington, DC: Government Printing Office.

Ellis, Mark. 1992. "'Closing Ranks' and 'Seeking Honors': W. E. B. Du Bois in World War I." *Journal of American History* 79, no. 1 (June): 96–124.

Ellis, Mark. 1995. "W. E. B. Du Bois and the Formation of Black Opinion in World War I: A Commentary on 'The Damnable Dilemma.'" *Journal of American History* 81, no. 4 (March): 1584–90.

Ely, R. T. 1890. *The Labor Movement in America*. New York: Crowell.

Factor, Regis A. 1988. *Guide to the Archiv für Sozialwissenschaft und Sozialpolitik Group, 1904–1933: A History and Comprehensive Bibliography*. New York: Greenwood.

Fairbairn, Brett. 1997. *Democracy in the Undemocratic State: The German Reichstag Elections of 1898 and 1903*. Toronto: University of Toronto Press.

Fields, Barbara Jeanne. 1985. "The Advent of Capitalist Agriculture: The New South in a Bourgeois World." In *Essays on the Postbellum Southern Economy*, edited by

Thavolia Glymph and John JKushma, 73–94. College Station: Texas A&M University Press.

Fields, Karen. 2002. "Individuality and the Intellectuals: An Imaginary Conversation Between W. E. B. Du Bois and Émile Durkheim." *Theory and Society* 31, no. 4 (August): 435–62.

Fisher, Rebecka Rutledge. 2005. "Cultural Artifacts and the Narrative of History W. E. B. Du Bois and the Exhibiting of Culture at the 1900 Paris Exposition Universelle." *Modern Fiction Studies* 51, no. 4 (Winter): 741–74.

Fracchia, Joseph G. 2022. *Bodies and Artefacts: Historical Materialism as Corporeal Semiotics.* 2 vols. Leiden: Brill.

Ghosh, Pater. 2014. *Max Weber and The Protestant Ethic: Twin Histories.* Oxford: Oxford University Press.

Gispen, Kees, ed. 1990. *What Made the South Different? Essays and Comments.* Jackson: University Press of Mississippi.

Grimmer-Solem, Erik. 2003. *The Rise of Historical Economics and Social Reform in Germany, 1864–1894.* Oxford: Clarendon.

Grimmer-Solem, Erik. 2005. "German Social Science, Meiji Conservatism, and the Peculiarities of Japanese History." *Journal of World History* 16, no. 2 (June): 187–222.

Grimmer-Solem, Erik, and Roberto Romani. 1998. "The Historical School, 1870–1900: A Crossnational Reassessment." *History of European Ideas* 24, nos. 4–5 (July): 267–99.

Green, Martin Burgess. 1988. *The von Richthofen Sisters: The Triumphant and the Tragic Modes of Love; Else and Frieda von Richthofen, Otto Gross, Max Weber, and D. H. Lawrence, in the Years 1870–1970.* Albuquerque: University of New Mexico Press.

Green, Martin Burgess. 1999. *Otto Gross, Freudian Psychoanalyst, 1877–1920.* Lewiston, NY: E. Mellen.

Hagemann, Harald. 2001. "The Verein für Sozialpolitik from Its Foundation (1872) Until World War I." In *The Spread of Political Economy and the Professionalisation of Economists: Economic Societies in Europe, America and Japan in the Nineteenth Century,* edited by Massimo M. Augello and Marco E. L. Guidi, 152–75. London: Routledge.

Hagen, William W. 1980. *Germans, Poles, and Jews: The Nationality Conflict in the Prussian East, 1772–1914.* Chicago: University of Chicago Press.

Hagen, William W. 2002. *Ordinary Prussians: Brandenburg Junkers and Villagers, 1500–1840.* New York: Cambridge University Press.

Hagen, William W. 2012. "'German Citizens of Jewish Faith' (Deutsche Staatsbürger Jüdischen Glaubens): Jews, Germans, German Jews, 1789–1914." In *German History in Modern Times: Four Lives of the Nation,* 205–24. New York: Cambridge University Press.

Hagen, William W. 2018. *Anti-Jewish Violence in Poland, 1914–1920.* New York: Cambridge University Press.

Hahn, Steven. 1990. "Emancipation and the Development of Capitalist Agriculture: The South in Comparative Perspective." In *What Made the South Different? Essays and Comments,* edited by Kees Gispen, 71–88. Jackson: University Press of Mississippi.

Harnack, Adolf von. 1898–1912. *History of Dogma*. Edited by A. B. Bruce. Translated by Neil Buchanan, James Millar, Ebenezer Brown Speirs, William M'Gilchrist, and Alexander Balmain Bruce. London: Williams and Norgate.

Hennis, W. 1988. *Max Weber: Essays in Reconstruction*. London: Allen and Unwin.

Herbert, Ulrich. 1990a. *A History of Foreign Labor in Germany, 1880–1980: Seasonal Workers, Forced Laborers, Guest Workers*. Translated by William Templer. Ann Arbor: University of Michigan Press.

Herbert, Ulrich. 1990b. "The Manpower Shortage and *Überfremdung*: The Danger of Foreign Infiltration, 1880–1914." In *A History of Foreign Labor in Germany, 1880–1980: Seasonal Workers, Forced Laborers, Guest Workers*, translated by William Templer, 1–86. Ann Arbor: University of Michigan Press.

Herbst, Jurgen. 1965. *The German Historical School in American Scholarship: A Study in the Transfer of Culture*. Ithaca, NY: Cornell University Press.

Honigsheim, Paul. 1946. "Max Weber as Rural Sociologist." *Rural Sociology* 11: 207–18.

Honigsheim, Paul. 1948. "Max Weber as Applied Anthropologist." *Applied Anthropology* 7, no. 4: 27–35.

Honigsheim, Paul. 1949. "Max Weber as Historian of Agriculture and Rural Life." *Agricultural History* 23: 170–213.

Honigsheim, Paul. 2000. *The Unknown Max Weber*. Edited by Alan Sica. New Brunswick, NJ: Transaction.

Ito, Toyo. 2016. "Tomorrow's Architecture." Kenzo Tange lecture delivered to the Harvard Graduate School of Design, Cambridge, MA, March 7. https://www.gsd.harvard.edu/event/toyo-ito-tomorrows-architecture.

Johnson, Edward A. 1904. *Light Ahead for the Negro*. New York: Grafton.

Jordan, William. 1995. "'The Damnable Dilemma': African-American Accommodation and Protest During World War I." *Journal of American History* 81, no. 4 (March): 1562–83.

Judy, Ronald A. T. 2000. "Introduction: On W. E. B. Du Bois and Hyperbolic Thinking." *Boundary 2* 27, no. 3 (Fall): 1–35.

Kaelber, Lutz. 2003. "Max Weber's Dissertation." *History of the Human Sciences* 16, no. 2: 27–56.

Kahn, Nathaniel, dir. 2003. *My Architect: A Son's Journey*. Documentary film. Louis Kahn Project/Mediaworks/New Yorker Films.

Käsler, Dirk. 1988. "Social Change in German Society." In *Max Weber: An Introduction to His Life and Work*, translated by Philippa Hurd, 51–73. Chicago: University of Chicago Press.

Keeter, Larry G. 1981. "Max Weber's Visit to North Carolina." *Journal of the History of Sociology* 3, no. 2 (Spring): 108–14.

Kolchin, Peter. 1987. *Unfree Labor: American Slavery and Russian Serfdom*. Cambridge, MA: Harvard University Press.

Koslowski, Peter, ed. 1997. *Methodology of the Social Sciences, Ethics, and Economics in the Newer Historical School: From Max Weber and Rickert to Sombart and Rothacker*. Berlin: Springer.

Krüger, Dieter. 1987. "Max Weber and the Younger Generation in the Verein für Sozial-politik." In *Max Weber and His Contemporaries*, edited by Wolfgang J. Mommsen and Jürgen Osterhammel, 71–87. London: Allen and Unwin.

Lehmann, Hartmut, and Guenther Roth, eds. 1993. *Weber's "Protestant Ethic": Origins, Evidence, Contexts*. Washington, DC: German Historical Institute.

Lenin, Vladimir Ilich. 1962. "The Agrarian Programme of Social-Democracy in the First Russian Revolution." In *Lenin Collected Works*. Vol. 13, *June 1907–April 1908*, edited by Clemens Dutt, translated by Bernard Isaacs, 217–431. Moscow: Foreign Languages.

Lenin, Vladimir Ilich. 1974. *The Development of Capitalism in Russia*. 2nd rev. ed. Moscow: Progress.

Lewis, David Levering. 1993a. "From Philadelphia to Atlanta." In *W. E. B. Du Bois: Biography of a Race, 1868–1919*, 179–210. New York: Henry Holt.

Lewis, David Levering. 1993b. *W. E. B. Du Bois: Biography of a Race, 1868–1919*. New York: Henry Holt.

Lidtke, Vernon L. 1966. *The Outlawed Party: Social Democracy in Germany, 1878–1890*. Princeton, NJ: Princeton University Press.

Lindenlaub, Dieter. 1967. *Richtungskämpfe im Verein für Sozialpolitik Wissenschaft und Socialpolitik im Kaiserreich Vornehmlich vom Beginn des "Neuen Kurses" bis zum Ausbruch des 1. Weltkrieges (1890–1914)*. Wiesbaden: F. Steiner.

Love, John. L. 1899. *The Disfranchisement of the Negro*. American Negro Academy Occasional Papers, no. 6. Washington, DC: American Negro Academy.

Lunn, Eugene. 1973. *Prophet of Community: The Romantic Socialism of Gustav Landauer*. Berkeley: University of California Press.

Lunn, Eugene. 1982. *Marxism and Modernism: An Historical Study of Lukács, Brecht, Benjamin, and Adorno*. Berkeley: University of California Press.

Manasse, Ernst Moritz. 1937. *Platons Sophistes und Politikos: Das Problem der Wahrheit*. Berlin-Schöneberg: Siegfried Scholem.

Manasse, Ernst Moritz. 1947. "Max Weber on Race." *Social Research* 14, no. 1: 191–221.

Marciniak, Katarzyna. 2006. "New Europe: Eyes Wide Shut." *Social Identities* 12, no. 5: 615–33.

Marcuse, Herbert. 1971. "Industrialization and Capitalism." In *Max Weber and Sociology Today*. Edited by Otto Stammer. Translated by Kathleen Morris. Oxford: Blackwell.

Marx, Karl. 1977. *Capital: A Critique of Political Economy, Volume 1*. Translated by Ben Fowkes. New York: Random House.

Marx, Karl. 1981. *Capital, Volume 2*. Translated by David Fernbach. New York: Random House.

McAuley, Christopher A. 2019. *The Spirit Versus the Souls: Max Weber, W. E. B. Du Bois, and the Politics of Scholarship*. Notre Dame, IN: University of Notre Dame Press.

McCarter, Robert M. 2005. *Louis I. Kahn*. London: Phaidon.

McNeill, George E., ed. 1887. *The Labor Movement: The Problem of To-day*. Boston: A. M. Bridgman.

Mezzadra, Sandro. 2010. "Introduzione." In *W. E. B. Du Bois: Sulla linea del colore; Razza e democrazia negli Stati Uniti e nel mondo*. Edited by Sandro Mezzadra. Bologna: Società Editrice il Mulino.

Mitzman, Arthur. 1970. *The Iron Cage: An Historical Interpretation of Max Weber*. New York: Knopf.

Mommsen, Wolfgang J. 1984. *Max Weber and German Politics, 1890–1920*. Translated by Michael S. Steinberg. Chicago: University of Chicago Press.

Mommsen, Wolfgang J. 2005. "From Agrarian Capitalism to the 'Spirit' of Modern Capitalism: Max Weber's Approaches to the Protestant Ethic." *Max Weber Studies* 5, no. 2: 185–203.

Morris, Aldon D. 2015. *The Scholar Denied: W. E. B. Du Bois and the Birth of Modern Sociology*. Oakland: University of California Press.

Moss, Alfred A., Jr. 1981. *The American Negro Academy: Voice of the Talented Tenth*. Baton Rouge: Louisiana State University Press.

Myrdal, Gunnar. 1944. *An American Dilemma: The Negro Problem and Modern Democracy*. New York: Harper and Brothers.

Newman, Richard. 1984. *Black Access: A Bibliography of Afro-American Bibliographies*. Westport, CT: Greenwood.

Page, Thomas Nelson. 1904. *The Negro: The Southerner's Problem*. New York: C. Scribner's Sons.

Partington, Paul G. 1977. *W. E. B. Du Bois: A Bibliography of His Published Writings*. Whittier, CA: Penn-Lithographics.

Peukert, Helge. 2001. "The Schmoller Renaissance." *History of Political Economy* 33, no. 1: 71–116.

Powderly, Terence V. 1889. *Thirty Years of Labor*. Columbus, OH: Excelsior.

Radkau, Joachim. 2005. *Max Weber: Die Leidenschaft des Denkens*. Munich: Hanser.

Radkau, Joachim. 2009. *Max Weber: A Biography*. Translated by Patrick Camiller. Cambridge: Polity.

Ransom, Roger L., and Richard Sutch. 1977. *One Kind of Freedom: The Economic Consequences of Emancipation*. Cambridge: Cambridge University Press.

Rickert, Heinrich. 1902. *Die Grenzen der naturwissenschaftlichen Begriffsbildung: Eine logische Einleitung in die historischen Wissenschaften*. Tübingen: J. C. B. Mohr.

Rickert, Heinrich. 1986. *The Limits of Concept Formation in Natural Science: A Logical Introduction to the Historical Sciences*. Edited and translated by Guy Oakes. Cambridge: Cambridge University Press.

Ringer, Fritz K. 2004. *Max Weber: An Intellectual Biography*. Chicago: University of Chicago Press.

Riesebrodt, Martin. 1989. "From Patriarchalism to Capitalism: The Theoretical Context of Max Weber's Agrarian Studies (1892–3)." In *Reading Weber*, edited by Keith Tribe, 131–57. London: Routledge.

Rogers, Howard J., ed. 1905–7. *Congress of Arts and Science, Universal Exposition, St. Louis, 1904*. 8 vols. Boston: Houghton Mifflin.

Rollmann, Hans. 1993. "'Meet Me in St. Louis': Troeltsch and Weber in America." In *Weber's "Protestant Ethic": Origins, Evidence, Contexts*, edited by Hartmut Lehmann and Guenther Roth, 357–83. Washington, DC: German Historical Institute.

Roth, Guenther. 2001. *Max Webers Deutsch-Englische Familiengeschichte, 1800–1950: Mit Briefen und Dokumenten*. Tübingen: Mohr Siebeck.

Roth, Guenther. 2002. "Max Weber: Family History, Economic Policy, Exchange Reform." *International Journal of Politics, Culture and Society* 15, no. 3 (Spring): 509–20.

Roth, Guenther. 2005. "Transatlantic Connections: A Cosmopolitan Context for Max and Marianne Weber's New York Visit 1904." *Max Weber Studies* 5, no. 1: 81–112.

Rothberg, Michael. 2001. "W. E. B. Du Bois in Warsaw: Holocaust Memory and the Color Line, 1949–1952." *Yale Journal of Criticism* 14, no. 1: 169–89.

Rueschemeyer, Dietrich, and Ronan Van Rossem. 1996. "The Verein für Sozialpolitik and the Fabian Society: A Study in the Sociology of Policy-Relevant Knowledge." In *States, Social Knowledge, and the Origins of Modern Social Policies*, edited by Dietrich Rueschemeyer and Theda Skocpol, 117–62. Princeton, NJ: Princeton University Press.

Scaff, Lawrence A. 1998a. "The 'Cool Objectivity of Sociation': Max Weber and Marianne Weber in America." *History of the Human Sciences* 11, no. 2: 61–82.

Scaff, Lawrence A. 1998b. "Weber's Amerikabild and the African American Experience." In *Crosscurrents: African Americans, Africa, and Germany in the Modern World*, edited by David McBride, Leroy Hopkins, and Carol Blackshire-Belay, 82–95. Columbia, SC: Camden House.

Scaff, Lawrence A. 2005. "Remnants of Romanticism: Max Weber in Oklahoma and Indian Territory." In *The Protestant Ethic Turns 100: Essays on the Centenary of the Weber Thesis*, edited by William H. Swatos and Lutz Kaelber, 77–110. Boulder, CO: Paradigm.

Scaff, Lawrence A. 2011a. "The Color Line." In *Max Weber in America*, 98–116. Princeton, NJ: Princeton University Press.

Scaff, Lawrence A. 2011b. *Max Weber in America*. Princeton, NJ: Princeton University Press.

Schluchter, Wolfgang. 1981. *The Rise of Western Rationalism: Max Weber's Developmental History*. Translated by Guenther Roth. Berkeley: University of California Press.

Schweitzer, Christoph E. 1996. "Ernst Moritz Manasse: A Black College Welcomes a Refugee." In *They Fled Hitler's Germany and Found Refuge in North Carolina*, edited by Henry A. Landsberger, Christoph E. Schweitzer, and Frances B. Schultzberg, 41–49. Chapel Hill, NC: Center for the Study of the American South.

Schwenker, Wolfgang. 1987. "Passion as a Mode of Life: Max Weber, the Otto Gross Circle and Eroticism." In *Max Weber and His Contemporaries*, edited by Wolfgang J. Mommsen and Jürgen Osterhammel, 483–98. London: Allen and Unwin.

Seyfarth, Constans, and Walter M. Sprondel, eds. 1973. *Seminar: Religion und gesellschaftliche Entwicklung: Studien zur Protestantismus–Kapitalismus–These Max Webers*. Frankfurt am Main: Suhrkamp.

Shionoya, Yuichi, ed. 2001. *The German Historical School: The Historical and Ethical Approach to Economics*. London: Routledge.

Sinclair, William A. 1905. *The Aftermath of Slavery: A Study of the Condition and Environment of the American Negro*. Boston: Small, Maynard.

Sombart, Werner. 1905. "Quellen und Literatur zum Studium der Arbeiterfrage und des Sozialismus in den Vereinigten Staaten von Amerika (1902–1904)." *Archiv für Sozialwissenschaft und Sozialpolitik* 20: 634–703.

Sombart, Werner. 1924. *Der moderne Kapitalismus: Historisch-systematische Darstellung des gesamteuropäischen Wirtschaftslebens von seinen Anfängen bis zur Gegenwart*. Munich: Duncker and Humblot.

Stammer, Otto, ed. 1971. *Max Weber and Sociology Today*. Translated by Kathleen Morris. Oxford: Blackwell.

Steinfeld, Robert J. 1991. *The Invention of Free Labor: The Employment Relation in English and American Law and Culture, 1350–1870*. Chapel Hill: University of North Carolina Press.

Steinfeld, Robert J. 2001. *Coercion, Contract, and Free Labor in the Nineteenth Century*. Cambridge: Cambridge University Press.

Swatos, William H., and Lutz Kaelber, eds. 2005. *The Protestant Ethic Turns 100: Essays on the Centenary of the Weber Thesis*. Boulder, CO: Paradigm.

Tribe, Keith. 1989. "Prussian Agriculture—German Politics: Max Weber 1892–7." In *Reading Weber*, edited by Keith Tribe, 85–130. London: Routledge.

Verein für Socialpolitik. 1893. *Verhandlungen der am 20. und 21. Marz in Berlin abgehaltenen Generalversammlung des Vereins für Socialpolitik über die ländiche Arbeiterfrage und über die Bodenbesitzverteilung und die Sicherung des Kleingrundbesitzes*. Vol. 59. Leipzig: Duncker and Humblot.

Viereck, Louis. 1903. *Leitfaden für Deutsche Einwanderer nach den Vereinigten Staaten von Amerika*. New York: L. Boeker.

Walker, David 1829. *Walker's Appeal, in Four Articles: Together with a Preamble, to the Colored Citizens of the World, but in Particular, and Very Expressly to Those of the United States of America*. Boston: David Walker.

Washington, Booker T. 1901. *Up from Slavery: An Autobiography*. New York: Doubleday, Page.

Washington, Booker T. 1902. *Vom Sklaven Empor: Eine Selbstbiographie*. Translated by Estell Du Bois-Reymond. Berlin: Dietrich Reimer (Ernst Vohsen).

Washington, Booker T. 1904. *Working with the Hands: Being a Sequel to "Up from Slavery," Covering the Author's Experiences in Industrial Training at Tuskegee*. New York: Doubleday, Page.

Weber, Marianne. 1919. *Frauenfragen und Frauengedanken: Gesammelte Aufsatze*. Tübingen: J. C. B. Mohr.

Weber, Marianne. 1988. *Max Weber: A Biography*. Edited and translated by Harry Zohn. New Brunswick, NJ: Transaction.

Weber, Max. 1893. "Die ländliche Arbeitsverfassung." In Verein für Socialpolitik, *Verhandlungen der am 20. und 21. Marz in Berlin Abgehaltenen Gernalversammlung des Vereins für Socialpolitik über die ländiche Arbeiterfrage und über die Bodenbesitz-verteilung und die Sicherung des Kleingrundbesitzes*, 59:62–86, 129–33, 216. Leipzig: Duncker and Humblot.

Weber, Max. 1905a. "Die Protestantische Ethik und der 'Geist' des Kapitalismus I." *Archiv für Sozialwissenschaft und Sozialpolitik* 20: 1–54.

Weber, Max. 1905b. "Die Protestantische Ethik und der 'Geist' des Kapitalismus II." *Archiv für Sozialwissenschaft und Sozialpolitik* 21: 1–110.

Weber, Max. 1906. "The Relations of the Rural Community to Other Branches of Social Science." Translated by Charles W. Seidenadel. In *Congress of Arts and Science Universal Exposition, St. Louis, 1904*. Vol. 7, *Economics, Politics, Jurisprudence, Social Science*, edited by Howard J. Rogers, 725–46. Boston: Houghton Mifflin.

Weber, Max. 1911. "Diskussionsbeiträge in der Debatte über Alfred Plötz, die Begriff Rasse und Gesellschaft und einige damit und zusammenhängende Probleme." In *Verhandlungen des ersten Deutschen Soziologentages vom 19.–22. Oktober 1910 in Frankfurt a. M.*, edited by Georg Simmel, Ferdinand Tönnies, Max Weber, et al., 151–65. Tübingen: J. C. B. Mohr.

Weber, Max. 1946. *From Max Weber: Essays in Sociology*. Edited and translated by H. H. Gerth and C. Wright Mills. New York: Oxford University Press.

Weber, Max. 1949. *Max Weber on the Methodology of the Social Sciences*. Edited and translated by Edward Shils and Henry A. Finch. Glencoe, IL: Free Press.

Weber, Max. 1951. *The Religion of China: Confucianism and Taoism*. Edited and translated by Hans H. Gerth. New York: Free Press.

Weber, Max. 1952. *Ancient Judaism*. Edited and translated by Hans H. Gerth and Don Martindale. New York: Free Press.

Weber, Max. 1958a. *The Protestant Ethic and the Spirit of Capitalism*. Translated by Talcott Parsons. New York: Scribner's.

Weber, Max. 1958b. *The Religion of India: The Sociology of Hinduism and Buddhism*. Edited and translated by Hans H. Gerth and Don Martindale. New York: Free Press.

Weber, Max. 1971. "Max Weber on Race and Society." Translated by Jerome Gittleman. *Social Research* 38, no. 1 (Spring): 30–41.

Weber, Max. 1973. "Max Weber, Dr. Alfred Plötz, and W. E. B. Du Bois." Translated by Benjamin Nelson and Jerome Gittleman. *Sociological Analysis* 34, no. 4 (Winter): 308–12.

Weber, Max. 1984a. *Max Weber–Gesamtausgabe*. Compiled and edited by Horst Baier, Jürgen Deininger, and Martin Riesebrodt, et al. Tübingen: J. C. B. Mohr (Paul Siebeck).

Weber, Max. 1984b. *Die Lage der Landarbeiter im ostelbischen Deutschland*. Edited by Martin Riesebrodt. Tübingen: J. C. B. Mohr (Paul Siebeck).

Weber, Max. 1986. *Die römische Agrargeschichte in ihrer Bedeutung für das Staats- und Privatrecht*. Edited by Jürgen Deininger. Tübingen: J. C. B. Mohr (Paul Siebeck).

Weber, Max. 1988. "The Social Causes of the Decline of Ancient Civilization." In *The Agrarian Sociology of Ancient Civilizations*, translated by R. I. Frank, 389–411. London: Verso.

Weber, Max. 1989a. "Developmental Tendencies in the Situation of East Elbian Rural Labourers." In *Reading Weber*, edited by Keith Tribe, 158–87. London: Routledge.

Weber, Max. 1989b. *Zur Russischen Revolution von 1905: Schriften und Reden 1905–1912*. Edited by Wolfgang J. Mommsen. Tübingen: J. C. B. Mohr (Paul Siebeck).

Weber, Max. 1993a. "Entwickelungstendenzen in der Lage der ostelbischen Landarbeiter 1894." In *Landarbeiterfrage, Nationalstaat und Volkswirtschaftspolitik: Schriften und Reden 1892–1899*, edited by Wolfgang J. Mommsen, 425–62. Tübingen: J. C. B. Mohr (Paul Siebeck).

Weber, Max. 1993b. *Landarbeiterfrage, Nationalstaat und Volkswirtschaftspolitik: Schriften und Reden 1892–1899*. Edited by Wolfgang J. Mommsen. Tübingen: J. C. B. Mohr (Paul Siebeck).

Weber, Max. 1993c. "Die ländliche Arbeitsverfassung: Referat und Diskussionsbeiträgeaufer Generalversammlung des Vereins für Socialpolitik am 20. und 21. März 1893." In *Landarbeiterfrage, Nationalstaat und Volkswirtschaftspolitik: Schriften und Reden 1892–1899*, edited by Wolfgang J. Mommsen, 165–207. Tübingen: J. C. B. Mohr (Paul Siebeck).

Weber, Max. 1993d. "Der Nationalstaat und die Volkswirtschaftspolitik." In *Landarbeiterfrage, Nationalstaat und Volkswirtschaftspolitik: Schriften und Reden 1892–1899*, edited by Wolfgang J. Mommsen, 542–74. Tübingen: J. C. B. Mohr (Paul Siebeck).

Weber, Max. 1994. "The Nation State and Economic Policy (Inaugural Lecture)." In *Weber Political Writings*, edited and translated by Peter Lassman and Ronald Speirs, 1–28. Cambridge: Cambridge University Press.

Weber, Max. 1995. *The Russian Revolutions*. Edited and translated by Gordon C. Wells and P. R. Baehr. Ithaca, NY: Cornell University Press.

Weber, Max. 1998. "The Relations of the Rural Community to the Other Branches of Social Science." In *Wirtschaft, Staat und Sozialpolitik: Schriften und Reden 1900–1912*, edited by Wolfgang Schluchter, 212–43. Tübingen: J. C. B. Mohr (Paul Siebeck).

Weber, Max. 2002a. "Appendix: Prefatory Remarks to *Collected Essays in the Sociology of Religion*." In *The Protestant Ethic and the "Spirit" of Capitalism and Other Writings*, edited and translated by P. R. Baehr and Gordon C. Wells, 356–72. New York: Penguin.

Weber, Max. 2002b. "'Churches' and 'Sects' in North America: An Ecclesiastical and Sociopolitical Sketch." In *The Protestant Ethic and the "Spirit" of Capitalism and Other Writings*, edited and translated by Peter R. Baehr and Gordon C. Wells, 203–20. New York: Penguin.

Weber, Max. 2002c. *The Protestant Ethic and the Spirit of Capitalism*. Translated by Stephen Kalberg. Oxford: Blackwell Roxbury.

Weber, Max. 2002d. *The Protestant Ethic and the "Spirit" of Capitalism and Other Writings*. Edited and translated by Peter R. Baehr and Gordon C. Wells. New York: Penguin.

Weber, Max. 2003. *The History of Commercial Partnerships in the Middle Ages*. Translated by Lutz Kaelber. Lanham, MD: Rowman and Littlefield.

Weber, Max. 2015. *Briefe 1903–1905*. Edited by Gangolf Hübinger. Tübingen: J. C. B. Mohr (Paul Siebeck).

Weber, Max. 2021. *Die Protestantische Ethik und der Geist des Kapitalismus/Die Protestantischen Sekten und der Geist des Kapitalismus: Schriften 1904–1920*. Edited by Wolfgang Schluchter. Tübingen: J. C. B. Mohr (Paul Siebeck).

Weber, Max, and Eduard Baumgarten. 1964. *Max Weber: Werk und Person*. Edited and compiled by Eduard Baumgarten. Tübingen: J. C. B. Mohr.

Whimster, Sam, and Gottfried Heuer. 1998. "Otto Gross and Else Jaffé and Max Weber." *Theory, Culture, and Society* 15, nos. 3–4: 129–60.

Wilcox, Walter F. 1904. "The Census Statistics of the Negro." *Yale Review* (May): 274–86.

Williams, George W. 1883. *History of the Negro Race in America from 1619 to 1880: Negroes as Slaves, as Soldiers, and as Citizens; Together with a Preliminary Consideration of the Unity of the Human Family, an Historical Sketch of Africa, and an Account of the Negro Governments of Sierra Leone and Liberia*. 2 vols. New York: G. P. Putnam's Sons.

Winson, Anthony. 1982. "The 'Prussian Road' of Agrarian Development: A Reconsideration." *Economy and Society* 11, no. 4: 381–408.

Wise, Michael. 2006. "Max Weber Visits America: A Review of the Video." *Sociation Today* 4, no. 2 (Fall). http://www.ncsociology.org/sociationtoday/v21/outline3.htm.

Witte, Ron, ed. 2002. *Toyo Ito: Sendai Mediathèque*. Munich: Prestel.

Young, Arthur. 1792. *Travels, During the Years 1787, 1788, and 1789: Undertaken More Particularly with a View of Ascertaining the Cultivation, Wealth, Resources, and National Prosperity, of the Kingdom of France*. 2 vols. London: Bury St. Edmund's.

Zimmerman, Andrew. 2006. "Decolonizing Weber." *Postcolonial Studies* 9, no. 1: 53–79.

Zubrzycki, J. 1953. "Emigration from Poland in the Nineteenth and Twentieth Centuries." *Population Studies* 6, no. 3: 248–72.

INDEX

....

concept of race, 32, 71, 81. *See also* categorical distinction

Congress of Arts and Sciences (St. Louis, 1904), 73, 141nn1–2, 145n14, 153n44; Weber's 1910 reference to meeting Du Bois, 42; Weber's lecture, 35, 55, 72, 73, 149n27

"Conservation of Races, The" (Du Bois), 45, 83

Constitution of the United States. *See* Fifteenth Amendment; Fourteenth Amendment; Thirteenth Amendment, 117

contemporary thought, 74

contracts, 95; contract laborers, 91, 94; freedmen refused to work under, 91; and sharecropping, 92; by workers, 56

convict labor, 89, 97, 101. *See also* convict lease

convict lease, 98, 100, 131n6; effects on convictions for Negroes and whites, 101; as slavery, 98

cotton, 88, 90, 93, 94; cotton culture, 95

cotton market, 90

cotton prices, 96, 134n16

Cox, Oliver, 152n41

CR: The New Centennial Review, xix, 130, 141

Cravath, Erastus Milo, 109, 136n29

credit, 92, 93

criminal justice: 70 percent of all Southern prisoners were black partially explained by this system, 101; bands of convicts became schools for criminals, thus habitual black criminal, 101; Negroes lost faith in the integrity of, 101; only exceptional cases could slave be seen as a criminal, 98; postwar regular courts sought to make freedman a bondsman: Freedmen's Bureau, 100; prewar system was destroyed in a single blow by the war and emancipation, 99; real black criminal: agitated the South, 102; tailored for whites before Civil War, 98; for whites concepts of crime and slavery inseparably linked, 101

criminals, 98, 107–108

Crisis: A Record of the Darker Races, The (magazine), 11. *See also* NAACP

Cromwell, John W., 145n14

croppers, 94, 132n8, 134n13. *See also* sharecropper; sharecropping

Crummell, Alexander, 145n14

cultivation [*Bildung*] of America, 88

culture, 73

Debs, Eugene V., 126, 139n58

debt, 93

Declaration of Independence, 117

Delaware, 107

democratic ideas, 88

Department of Labor Archives, 25

desedimentation: theoretical breaking up the epistemic bedrock, 44

Des Moines, Iowa, 142n5

Deutsche Gesellschaft der Stadt New York (German Society of the City of New York), 146n15

Deutsche Gesellschaft für Soziologie (German Sociological Society), 41, 148nn23–24; October 1910 meeting, 141n1

Dial, The (magazine), 145

"Die Negerfrage in den Vereinigten Staaten" (Du Bois) xviii, 14, 17–27; 1894 dissertation title and, 59; the third, final, section, 49–50, 51; parallel with early work of Max Weber, 67;

difference among groups of humans: categorical difference, 10; delicate differences in race psychology, 50; differences of appearance of diverse groups of humans, 72; fundamental difference, 10; matters of the apparition of historical difference, 81; a new form of the question of, 54; scientific status in situation or horizon that is in common, 65; status in national or state level context, 65; Weber on classes and national, cultural, racial differences, 65

Dilthey, Wilhelm, 166n36

District of Columbia, 107

doormen and vergers, 105

Dougherty County, Georgia, 24, 95, 151

Douglass, Frederick, 108, 135; autobiography of, 108

drivers, 104

Du Bois, W. E. B.: on the absence of common "interest" in post-Reconstruction South, 67; on Africa, 77; on the antebellum planter class, like Weber's criticism of the Junkers, 64; art and science of the "dago" mediterranean shore, 77; Asia, 77; at Atlanta University, 13; audition at the Congress in St. Louis, 153n44; colonial laborer in African Diaspora and in Africa as part of laboring class, 64; commentators on the work of, 79; common horizon for interlocution with Weber, 41; comparative horizon with Weber for social organization of American South, 67; comparative view of Prussian and American agriculture, 55; diary of his return to America in June 1894: ethnic stereotypes, 165n34; diary of his trip to northern Germany (*Harzreise*) in March 1893, 41; did not make distinction of kind between himself and group he studied, 67; differences with Weber's views, 67; dissertation on laws and statutes on the suppression of slavery, 75; doctoral dissertation, 131n2; doctoral thesis title in report to

Du Bois (*cont.*)

the Slater Fund, 59; Du Bois's thought useful for understanding Europe today, 73–74, 82; first visit to Poland in the early 1890s, 163n34; Harvard dissertation on efforts to suppress the slave trade, 61; "heard . . . Max Weber," 39; heard Weber's lecture at the Congress of Arts and Sciences, 162n28; "I began to see the race problem in America," 60; intellectual habitation with "Nationalökonomie" seminar and the Verein, 60; invitation for Weber and his wife, 29; "I wrote on American agriculture for Schmoller," 60; laboring class as the guide understanding modern historicity, 64; letter to Manasse, 38; meeting Weber, 40; member of the "Nationalökonomie" seminar at Berlin and the Verein, 41, 60; *Papers of W. E. B. Du Bois*, 141n1, 157n13; project of African American studies, 23; "the problem of the color line" in Du Bois's thought and practice, 82; "the problem of the color line" as a question in common with Weber, 52; question of labor most decisive issue in aftermath of the Civil War, 61; race problem in America and problems of peoples of Africa and Asia, Europe, 60; on the reasons for the triumph of European civilization, 77; reasons of state do not preempt the historical truth of the question of *labor,* 63; relation to German thought and culture, 79; reports to John F. Slater Fund on thesis for "Nationalökonomie" seminar, 133n9; research in economic history at Harvard, 61; respective thoughts about the dominant classes and the laboring class, 64; rural sociology, 67; rural studies, 64; same movement of epistemic problematization as Weber, 53; on size of farm holdings among African Americans after the Civil War, 59; strata of Negro agricultural workers, 67; study of Reconstruction, 64; "the talented tenth," 136; testimony to the US Industrial Commission of 1901, 134n12; undertook the empirical work directly, 67; and the Verein für Sozialpolitik (Association for Social Policy), 41, 58; view of the problems of different human groups as one, 60; views of the changing status of labor and state policy, 60; Weber not a decisive figure in his pedagogical formation, 40

—*Works*: "The African Roots of War," 84; "The Afro-American," 55, 159n19; "The Art and Art Galleries of Europe," 159n19; *Autobiography of W. E. B. Du Bois: A Soliloquy . . . ,* 39, 45, 159n19, 165n34; bibliography attached to

"Die Negerfrage," 146n14; *The Black Flame: A Trilogy*, 84; *Black Reconstruction: An Essay Toward a History*, 56, 84; "Caste in America," 50, 142n5; *Color and Democracy: Colonies and Peace*, 39, 84; "The Conservation of Races," 83, 145n14, 163n34; *Dark Princess: A Romance*, 84; *Darkwater: Voices from Within the Veil*, 39, 45, 76, 84, 164n34, 166n37; "Development of a People," 26; *Dusk of Dawn: An Essay Toward an Autobiography of a Race Concept*, 39, 60, 156, 164n34; essay on the twelfth census, 145n14; "Final Word" of *The Philadelphia Negro*, 49; "The Freedmen's Bureau," 135n23; *John Brown*, 84; kind of stump speech, 21, 136n27; "A Litany of Atlanta," 155n6; "My Evolving Program for Negro Freedom", 39; "The Negro and the Warsaw Ghetto," 164n34; *The Negro Artisan*, report of the seventh Atlanta University study, 136n27, 137–38, 139; "The Negro as He Really Is," 24, 132n8, 134n12, 134nn15–16 135nn20–21; "The Negro Farmer," 132, 133, 145; "The Negro Landholder of Georgia," 132n7, n12133; "Of the Culture of White Folk," 77, 166n37; pamphlets for proposed meetings of Niagara movement group, 148n25; *The Philadelphia Negro: A Social Study*, 46, 48, 49, 83; "The Present Condition of German Politics (1893)," 158–59n19; "The Present Outlook for the Dark Races of Mankind," 47, 48, 49, 84; *The Quest of the Silver Fleece*, 25; "The Relation of the Negroes to the Whites in the South," 49–50, 137n31, 137n34, 151n40; "The Socialism of German Socialists," 158–59n19; "Sociology Hesitant," 26, 153n44; "The Souls of White Folk," 166n37; "The Spawn of Slavery: The Convict-Lease System in the South," 132n6, 135n22; "The Study of the Negro Problems," 46; thesis for "Nationalökonomie" seminar, University of Berlin, 133n9; two essays, one on Germany in the 1890s and one comparing German and US history, 57–58; *The World and Africa: An Inquiry*, 84. *See also* "Die Negerfrage in den Vereinigten Staaten" (Du Bois); *Souls of Black Folk: Essays and Sketches, The* (Du Bois); other individual works

Dunbar, Paul Laurence, 135n24

Durkheim, Émile, 12, 149n28, 165n36

duty, 111

eastern provinces: Prussia, Pomerania, Posen, Mecklenburg, Brandenburg, Silesia, Lauenberg, 63. *See also* German Reich

eastern question, 70, 72, 133n9; workers from German, Russian, and Austrian Polish territories,
69. *See also* Weber, Max

economic classes: laboring class, middle class, and
"noble" class, 72

economic classes, four: agricultural wage laborer,
cropper, renter [*Pächter*], and sharecropper
[*Halbpächter*], 94

economic development of the South, 111

economic system in the South and black workers: class of black landowners and artisans,
despite racial prejudice and legacy of slavery,
112; lack of protection from usury and fraud,
112; like England in the earliest years of the
nineteenth century, 111; long working hours,
low wages, child labor, 112; Negro economic
struggles like political and civil rights struggle, 117; no protective laws, written, unwritten
modes of experience, 111; not comparable to
US North, England or France, 111; situation
aggravated for black workers, 112. *See also*
Arbeitsverfassung

economic system in the South and white workers, 112,
113, 114, 117

education of the modern independent democratic
worker., 111

education of the voters, 120

elaboration, 83

emancipation, 92; South's resistance to it weakened
its moral feeling, respect for law and order,
99

Emancipation Proclamation, 113; seen only as a stipu-
lation about the slave trade, 99. *See also* Thirteenth Amendment

emigration, 98

employers of the black belt, 96

England, 132, 162

English East Indian, 49. *See also* problem of the
color line

enslavement: modern systems and practices of, 83

epistemic: epistemic capacity and sovereign legal authority, 71; epistemic capacity to stand beyond
any given interest, 71; epistemic presumption
of an ultimate historical vision, 70–71. *See also*
problematization

epistemic horizon, 54, 61, 165n36

epistemological, 43, 83, 86; and the political, 70

epistemological order, 29, 31; and epistemic horizon,
36

epistemological problematization, 33

erroneous approach: interlocution of Du Bois and
Weber, 34

Estreicher, Stanislaus Ritter von, 164n34

Europe, 82; the color line a major question on the
continent, 73; old idea of, 19; question of the
"union" of the "European" states, 74. *See also*
problem of the color line

European civilization, 76

Europeans, 102

Evans brothers (abolitionist reformers), 112

existential, 71; struggle for existence *(Kampf ums
Dasein)*, 72

Exposition Universelle (Universal Exposition, Paris,
1900), 24

extra-economic mechanisms, 56. *See also* relations of
landowners and laborers

F. C. B. Mohr Verlag, 9, 14, 147–48n22. *See also*
Siebeck, Paul

farmers, planters, overseers, 104

farms, cultivated by Negroes, 103; animal products
like meat, milk, butter, eggs and poultry, 106;
buildings, 106; funds spent on Negro farms
for labor and for fertilizer, 106; machines and
implements, 106; new cultivation, 106; percent
of Negro farmers who had become property
owners, 106; total a little smaller than half of
Prussia, 103; value of livestock, 106; value of
the land and of the improvements, 106. *See also*
"Negro Farmer, The" (Du Bois)

farms in the South, average area, 92

farm workers, 97

feudal forms of exploitation and political domination, 53

Fields, Barbara Jeanne: "The Advent of Capitalist
Agriculture," 56; Du Bois's contribution on
advent of capitalist agriculture, 56

Fields, Karen E., 149n28

Fifteenth Amendment, 117. *See also* Fourteenth
Amendment; Thirteenth Amendment

Fisher, Rebecka Rutledge: translated "L'ouvrier
négre" (Du Bois) into English, 151n39

fishermen and oystermen, 105

Fisk University, 136

Florida, 107

foreign slave trade, 90

Fourteenth Amendment, 117. *See also* Fifteenth
Amendment; Thirteenth Amendment

Fracchia, Joseph, xiv, xix, 130, 150n30, 162n31,
163n33

France, 132n8, 162n28

freedmen: after the liberation freedmen in competitive struggle with the best modern workers,
111

ideals, 48

ideology [*Ideenkreis*] of the American people, 124–25; axioms of, 127; and the color line, 125–26; inequality noticed, 126; rise of imperialism and, 126. *See also* public opinion

immigration, 62. *See also* labor

imperial horizon: global and eastern frontier of Prussia, 70

imperialism: European and Euro-American, 160n24; global, 160n23; rise in United States, 124–25

imperial Rome, 66

Indian Ocean (or Oceanus Ethiopicus), 83

Indian Territory, 107

inhabitation, 86

insurrections of the enslaved: attempted by Cato, Gabriel, Vesey, Turner, and Toussaint, 98

intellectual and spiritual life: no commonality of, 123

intellectuals of African reference and Du Bois, 82

intellectuals of colonial and postcolonial context and Du Bois, 82

interests (of community), 67, 68, 69. *See also Gemeinschaft*

interlocution: new forms of, 83; in Weber's work and itinerary, 83

interstate slave trade, 90

Ireland: peasants of, 112

iron and steelworkers, 105

iron founders, 113

ironworkers, 113

irony: Weber's use of in October 1910, 42

Italy, 132n8

Ito, Toyo: Sendai Mediatheque, Japan, 85

Jackson, Andrew, 88; War of 1812, 131n3; war against the Creek and British (1814), 131n3

Jaffé, Edgar, xviii, 5, 13, 14, 130, 141n2, 144n12, 150n31

Jaffé-von Richthofen, Elisabeth (Else) (aka Else von Richthofen; Else Jaffé), xviii, 5, 7, 12–14, 15, 17, 130, 144n12, 150–51n38

Jaffé, Elisabeth (Else). *See* Jaffé-von Richtofen, Elisabeth (Else)

Japan: 1904–1905 war with Russia, 160n24; Naoshima island in the Seto Inland Sea, 85; Sendai (Miyagi prefecture), 85

Jaspers, Gertrud, 150n29

Jaspers, Karl, 150n29; devoted former student and associate of Weber, 156n8

Jewish question (*Judenfrage*), 53, 73, 74, 164n34. *See also* Polish question; problem of the color line

Jews, 112: Jewish Prussians, 53; negative stereotypes, 165n34; phrase "unscrupulous Jews," 112,

137n34; Polish-speaking, 62, 69; status in Germany 161n27

John F. Slater Fund for the Education of Freedmen, 40, 41, 59, 60, 133n9, 159n21

Johns Hopkins University, 148n24

Johnson, David E., 141

Johnson, Edward A., 8, 145n14

Journal of American History, 160n23

Judenfrage. See Jewish question

Judy, Ronald A. T., 153n44

Junkers, 69, 70; large estates of, 62, 63; Junker landowner class, 63, 69; Prussian, 56, 63; Prussian military tradition and state civil service, 63; Weber's view of, 63–64, 69–70. *See also Arbetisverfassung*

Kaelber, Lutz, 160n26

Kahn, Louis: Salk Institute for Biological Sciences, 85

Kapp, Georg Friedrich: and the Verein für Sozialpolitik (Association for Social Policy), 57, 158n18

Kentucky, 90, 107, 114

Knights of Labor, 114–16, 134; leader ("Grand-Master Workman"), 138n41, 138n48

Kovacs, Danielle: curator, W. E. B. Du Bois Library, University of Massachusetts, Amherst, 143–44n8

Krakow, Poland, 15

Krell, David Farrell, 153n44

Ku Klux Klan, 99. *See also* criminal justice; rural police

L'Année Sociologique: founded by Durkheim, 12

labor: child, 99; Du Bois's views of its changing status and state policy, 60; of freed blacks, 99; as historical form of major epistemological horizon for both Du Bois and Weber, 61; immigration of workers from Prussian and Russian Poland to Junker estates, 62; importation of, 69; post-Civil War laws regarding freedmen, 99; relation of the laborer to land in the African American situation, 61; rural labor studied by Weber and the Verein für Sozialpolitik (Association for Social Policy), 70; self-initiative of "free labor": including labor unions, 61; South believed in slave labor, 99; Southern laws about apprenticeships and vagrancy to force Blacks to work at near no wage, 99; study of the organization and conditions of, 62; suppressing the slave trade as part of the history of labor relations, 61; two labor systems in the South: mortgaging the harvest: renting convicts, 98; unmarried workers from Russian Poland and Galicia in German Prussia, 62; unpaid labor, 111. *See also* convict labor

sharecropping, 19; chronic bankruptcy of the tenant, 95; system [*Halbpachtsystem*], 91, 132n8; system in the South, 92; system of mortgaging the harvest, 95; villeinage, 98. *See also* labor; sharecropper; tenant [*Pächter*] (farmer)

Siebeck, Paul, 9, 147–48n22. *See also* F. C. B. Mohr Verlag

silver-currency man. *See* Bryan, William Jennings

Simmel, Georg, 12, 150n29, 166n36

Sinclair, William, 8

singularity, 72; idea of, 72; of the German state, 76; of the West in the figure of "Europe," 76

Slater Fund. *See* John F. Slater Fund for the Education of Freedmen

slave foremen [*Obersklaven*]: called "drivers," 89

slave revolts. *See* insurrections of the enslaved

slave trade, 61, 87, 89, 90; cessation of, 99; convict labor as new form of, 100; suppression of in 1807, 131n2

slavery (American), 88; slaves: regular, domestic servants, artisans, and field workers, 89–90; sharecropping and convict labor as direct descendants of slavery, 98. *See also* labor

Slavic: "Slavic invasion" (*slavische Überflutung*), 73; Slavic immigrant workers, 68

smiths (workers), 105

social conflict: between blacks and whites, 109, 124, 127; curse of narrowness, blindness, 129; racial antipathy and, 128, 129; ways of viewing, 109; political relations, 117–20; public opinion and, 120–21; state or nation vs. "individual social estate" [*einzelnen Standes*], 70, 163n33. *See also* common life of blacks and whites; social cooperation; *Staatsraison*

social cooperation (living together): between blacks and whites, 109; economic cooperation, 127; organizations for mutual benefit, 109; political relations, 109, 117–20, 127; social freedom, 128

social organization: in the post–Civil War South, 19; discussed in Du Bois's work, 27, 67; discussed in Weber's work, 67, 70; in the eastern provinces of German Reich, 70. *See also Arbeitsverfassung*; *Staatsraison*

Social Research: journal of the New School for Social Research, New York, 156n9

socialist thought, 58

Society for Ethical Culture, New York, 155n6

sociology, xx, 16, 17, 26, 36, 154n44; Lowndes County, Alabama, project (Du Bois), 24; rural and agrarian, 24–25, 67, 156n10; "Sociology Hesitant" (Du Bois), 26–27, 153n44; Weber's projections of, 81

sociology of religion, 149n27. *See also Protestant Ethic and the Spirit of Capitalism, The* (Weber)

Sombart, Werner, xviii, 2, 12, 13, 130, 141n2, 145n14, 150n29

sons of poor whites, 112

sorrow-songs, 108

Souls of Black Folk: Essays and Sketches, The (Du Bois), xx, 5, 6, 8, 12–13, 15, 17, 29, 36, 45, 49, 52, 83–84, 132n8; chapter 1, 74, 161n27; chapter 2, 33; chapter 7, 135n21; chapter 8, 134nn15–17; chapters 7 and 8, 24, 55–56, 64, 134n12, 153; chapter 9, 20, 50, 136n25, 136n27, 137n31, 137n43; 151n40; "black belt" in, 153n42; German translation of, 13, 150n35; introduction by Aptheker, 143n6, 154n3; read by Weber?, 146n17; reception of, 142n5; on spirituals, 136n25

South America: workers of, 112

South Carolina, 90, 91, 107, 118, 119; South Carolina Constitutional Convention, 139n56

Southern plantation owner, 89

Sozialdemokratische Partei Deutschlands (German Social Democratic Party [SPD]), 57

Sozial Frage (social question), 53, 58, 161n28

Spanish Negroes, 49. *See also* problem of the color line

special interest lobbies, 57. *See also* Verein für Sozialpolitik (Association for Social Policy)

spiritual struggle of black freedmen, 122

Staatsraison (reasons of state interest), 69–70, 163n33. *See also* Weber, Max,

stable hands (workers), 105

Stande ("social estate"), 163. *See also* social conflict

state: claim to sovereign legal authority, 71. *See also Staatsraison*

state intervention, 70

Steinfeld, Robert J., 158n17

stock exchange, 36

study: as critical inquiry, 51

subterranean, 29, 43, 44, 83. *See also* available light

sugar, 90; from Louisiana, 90

suppression of the slave trade by UK Parliament and US Congress in 1807, 131n2

surveillance of slaves, 98. *See also* rural police

survey: of agricultural labor for the Verein für Sozialpolitik (Association for Social Policy), 62

Sutch, Richard, 132n8. *See also* Ransom, Roger L.

symbolic currency, 43; the terms of a relation of intellectual and symbolic exchange, 44

sympathies, 129

tailors, 105

Tanner, Henry O., 108

The Protestant Ethic and the Spirit of Capitalism, 157; turning point in the formulation of his interpretation of Germany's situation, 60; two originating essays of 1904–1905 on the Protestant ethic, 81; on what created the "unity of the Reich," 69; viewpoint of on the question of the Verein für Sozialpolitik's study, 70; work and legacies of, 81; work on the so-called eastern question from 1892 to 1897, 64–65; world economy generated a new playing field, 63
—*Works:* "'Churches' and 'Sects' in North America," 147n17; *Collected Essays on the Sociology of Religion,* 76; "Developmental Tendencies in the Situation of East Elbian Rural Labourers" (translation of "Entwickelungstendenzen in der Lage der ostelbischen Landarbeiter"), 66, 72; *Die Lage der Landarbeiter: im ostelbischen Deutschland,* 66; "Die ländliche Arbeitsverfassung," 66, 163n32; "Die ländliche Arbeitsverfassung": 1893 Verein für Sozialpolitik lecture, 68; dissertation on the history of medieval business organizations, prepared as an associate of the "Nationalökonomie" seminar, 59; *Habilitationsschrift* (doctoral dissertation) on Roman agrarian history (*Die römische Agrargeschichte*), 40, 59, 66, 162n29; initial two-part essay on "the Protestant ethic," 149. *See also Protestant Ethic and the Spirit of Capitalism, The* (Weber)
Weber, Max, and Marianne Weber, travels: to Tuskegee, AL, 144n14, 153n42, 155n4; to Mt. Airy, NC, 155n4; through Atlanta by train, 155n4; to relatives outside Mt. Airy, NC, 152–53n42
West Virginia, 107

Westphalia University, 153n44
Whitehall Street, Atlanta, 123
whites: poor and uneducated, 97; white masters, former, 111; white owner: almost or completely bankrupt after abolition, 93
Wilberforce University, 159n19
Wilcox, Walter F., 5; speaker at Atlanta Conference (May 1905), 145n14
Williams College, 136n30
Williams, George Washington, 108, 135n24
Work, Monroe, 24
worker uprisings in New York and Philadelphia (1829 to after the Civil War), 113; Negroes endured much from white workers and the labor movement, 113.
workers: conflicts with landlords, 98
working people (after the Civil War): left alone and without leadership, without capital and land, 111
Workingmen's Convention of 1830, 113
world economy: structural transformations, 54
world literature, 108. *See also* sorrow-songs
World War I, 76, 144n12, 150n29, 160n23
World War II, 160n25
Wright, Carroll D., 153n43
Wright, R. R., 24
Württemberg, 9

Yale University, 136n28
Yankees: ambitious and greedy, 112
Young, Arthur, 132n8

Zimmerman, Andrew, 161n27